# Taking Rites Seriously

*Taking Rites Seriously* is about how religious beliefs and religious believers are assessed by judges and legal scholars and are sometimes mischaracterized and misunderstood by those who are critical of the influence of religion in politics or in the formation of law. Covering three general topics – reason and motive, dignity and personhood, nature and sex – philosopher and legal theorist Francis J. Beckwith carefully addresses several contentious legal and cultural questions over which religious and nonreligious citizens often disagree: the rationality of religious belief, religiously motivated legislation, human dignity in bioethics, abortion and embryonic stem cell research, reproductive rights and religious liberty, evolutionary theory, and the nature of marriage. In the process, he responds to some well-known critics of public faith – including Brian Leiter, Steven Pinker, Suzanna Sherry, Ronald Dworkin, John Rawls, and Richard Dawkins – as well as to some religiously conservative critics of secularism such as the advocates for intelligent design.

Francis J. Beckwith is Professor of Philosophy and Church-State Studies at Baylor University, where he also serves as Associate Director of the Graduate Program on Philosophy as well as Co-Director (with Trent Dougherty) of the Program in Philosophical Studies of Religion. He has held visiting faculty appointments at Princeton and Notre Dame and has published extensively on social ethics, applied ethics, legal philosophy, and the philosophy of religion. A graduate of Fordham University (Ph.D., philosophy) and the Washington University School of Law, St. Louis (M.J.S.), his many books include *Politics for Christians: Statecraft as Soulcraft* (2010) and *Defending Life: A Moral and Legal Case Against Abortion Choice* (Cambridge University Press, 2007).

# Taking Rites Seriously

*Law, Politics, and the Reasonableness of Faith*

FRANCIS J. BECKWITH

*Baylor University*

CAMBRIDGE
UNIVERSITY PRESS

# CAMBRIDGE
UNIVERSITY PRESS

32 Avenue of the Americas, New York, NY 10013-2473, USA

Cambridge University Press is part of the University of Cambridge.

It furthers the University's mission by disseminating knowledge in the pursuit of education, learning, and research at the highest international levels of excellence.

www.cambridge.org
Information on this title: www.cambridge.org/9781107533059

First published 2015

Printed in the United States of America

*A catalog record for this publication is available from the British Library.*

*Library of Congress Cataloging in Publication Data*
Beckwith, Francis.
Taking rites seriously : law, politics, and the reasonableness of faith /
Francis J. Beckwith, Baylor University.
    pages  cm
Includes bibliographical references and index.
ISBN 978-1-107-11272-8 (hardback) – ISBN 978-1-107-53305-9 (pbk.)
1. Religion and law.   2. Religion and politics.   3. Religious ethics.
4. Faith and reason.   I. Title.
BL65.L33B43   2015
201′.72–dc23        2015018986

ISBN 978-1-107-11272-8 Hardback
ISBN 978-1-107-53305-9 Paperback

To Robert P. George

A man in whom many of us have found, what St. Thomas More's contemporaries found in him: "friendship and courage, cheerfulness and charity, diligence in duties, counsel in adversity, patience in pain – their good servant, but God's first." (from "A Lawyer's Prayer to St. Thomas More")

# Contents

# Acknowledgments

Earlier versions of portions of this book were published previously as articles (or parts of articles) in journals or as chapters in books. They have been revised, updated, and expanded, in many cases significantly, to not only ensure that this book is an integrated whole but also to respond to critics of the earlier works as well as to include new material or to restate arguments with greater precision and clarity. I would like to thank the editors and publishers for permission to republish this material, which appeared in the following publications:

"*Fides, Ratio et Juris*: How Some Courts and Some Legal Theorists Misrepresent the Rational Status of Religious Beliefs." In *Reason, Revelation, and the Civic Order: Political Philosophy and the Claims of Faith*. Edited by Paul R. DeHart and Carson Holloway. DeKalb, IL: Northern Illinois University Press, 2014. Pp. 173–202. Used with permission of Northern Illinois University Press.

"The Court of Disbelief: The Constitution's Article VI Religious Test Prohibition and the Judiciary's Religious Motive Analysis." *Hastings Constitutional Law Quarterly* 33.2 (2006): 337–360.

"Dignity Never Been Photographed: Scientific Materialism, Enlightenment Liberalism, and Steven Pinker." *Ethics & Medicine: An International Journal of Bioethics* 26.2 (Summer 2010): 93–110.

"Must Theology Sit in the Back of Secular Bus?: The Federal Courts' View of Religion and Its Status as Knowledge." *Journal of Law & Religion* 24.2 (2008–2009): 547–568.

"The Human Being, a Person of Substance: A Response to Dean Stretton." In *Persons, Moral Worth, and Embryos: A Critical Analysis of Pro-Choice Arguments from Philosophy, Law, and Science*. Edited by Stephen Napier. Dordrecht, The Netherlands: Springer, 2011. Pp. 67–83. Copyright © 2011, Springer Science+BUSINESS Media B.V.

"How to Be an Anti-Intelligent Design Advocate." *St. Thomas Journal of Law and Public Policy* 4.1 (2009–2010): 35–65.

"Justificatory Liberalism and Same-Sex Marriage." *Ratio Juris: A International Journal of Jurisprudence and Philosophy of Law* 26.4 (December 2013): 487–509. © 2013 The Author. Ratio Juris © 2013 John Wiley & Sons Ltd.

"Interracial Marriage and Same-Sex Marriage: Why the Analogy Fails." *Public Discourse: Ethics, Law, and the Common Good.* Online Publication of the Witherspoon Institute (21 May 2010), available at http://www .thepublicdiscourse.com/2010/05/1324/.

Some of the ideas and arguments that I include in this book were initially presented in columns I published in the online magazine *The Catholic Thing* (http://catholicthing.org), for which I have been writing a regular column every two weeks since October 2010. I would like to thank both its editor-in-chief, Robert Royal, and senior editor, Brad Miner, for providing me with such a wonderful platform.

With the exception of Chapter 3, I began the initial work on this book while serving as the 2008–2009 Mary Ann Remick Senior Visiting Fellow in the Notre Dame Center for Ethics & Culture at the University of Notre Dame. I would like to thank the center's director, W. David Solomon, as well as its associate directors, Elizabeth Kirk and Daniel McInerny, for providing me with the opportunity to have a productive year in an idyllic environment with outstanding colleagues that included Alasdair MacIntyre and Sarah Borden (a philosopher from Wheaton College who was the other visiting fellow for 2008–2009). I would like to also thank two of my Baylor colleagues: the chair of Baylor's philosophy department, Michael Beaty, for supporting my application for research leave at Notre Dame; and Byron Johnson, Director of Baylor's Institute for Studies of Religion (ISR), where I serve as a Resident Scholar, and which awarded me a grant to supplement my Notre Dame fellowship. In the summer of 2012, with the financial assistance of Baylor's generous summer sabbatical program, I was able to work on many of the final details of the initial manuscript I submitted to Cambridge University Press for its consideration.

Over the years I have had the opportunity, while working through the ideas in this book, to publicly present some of them either as prepared papers at academic conferences or as invited distinguished or endowed lectures: The 2015 John Cardinal Glennon Lecture (Kenrick-Glennon Seminary, St. Louis, Missouri, 31 January 2015); The 2014 President's Distinguished Scholar Lecture (Palm Beach Atlantic University, West Palm Beach, Florida, 20 October 2014); Science, Faith, and Culture Lecture Series (Azusa Pacific University, Azusa, California, 26 February 2013); Evangelical Philosophical Society (San Francisco, California, 16–18 November 2011); The Archbishop's Lecture Series (Archdiocese of Denver, Colorado, 29 September 2011); Fall Bioethics Conference (Franciscan University, Steubenville, Ohio, 23–25 October 2009);

Global Bioethics: Emerging Challenges Facing Human Dignity (Center for Bioethics & Human Dignity, Deerfield, Illinois, 16–18 July 2009); The Church and the Biomedical Revolution: A Lecture Series (University of St. Thomas, St. Paul, Minnesota, 13 November 2008); Law and Religion Symposium and Award Luncheon: *Journal of Law and Religion* 25th Anniversary Conference (Hamline University School of Law, St. Paul, Minnesota, 23–25 October 2008); American Political Science Association (Boston, Massachusetts, 28–31 August 2008); The 2008 John Woolman Lectures (Malone University, Akron, Ohio, 25–26 February 2008); American Political Science Association (Washington, DC, 1–5 September 2005); American Enterprise Institute (Washington, DC, 1 September 2005).

I have also been invited to give less formal presentations of this material at a number of law schools and meetings of legal associations, usually under the auspices of the Federal Society for Law and Public Policy (though sometimes sponsored or cosponsored by the American Constitution Society, the Christian Legal Society, and/or the Thomas More Society): University of Miami School of Law (5 March 2014); University of Texas School of Law (5 February 2014): University of Pennsylvania Law School (25 September 2013); Birmingham Federalist Society (18 April 2013); University of Colorado Law School (13 March 2013); Trinity Law School (25 February 2013); Baylor University Law School (4 September 2012); James E. Rogers College of Law, University of Arizona (19 March 2012); University of St. Thomas School of Law (5 March 2012); Orange County Federalist Society (21 September 2011); William H. Bowen School of Law, University of Arkansas, Little Rock (10 March 2011); University of Nebraska College of Law (7 March 2011); University of Mississippi School of Law (18 October 2010); Notre Dame Law School (6 April 2009); Regent University School of Law (6 February 2009); Southern University Law Center (4 February 2009); Paul M. Hebert Law Center, Louisiana State University (3 February 2009); Sandra Day O'Connor College of Law, Arizona State University (17 March 2008); University of Houston Law Center (16 October 2006); UCLA Law School (20 September 2006); Washburn University School of Law (9 February 2006); Notre Dame Law School (9 November 2005); University of Denver School of Law (3 February 2005)

I mention all these presentations so that I can express my deepest gratitude to the numerous attending faculty, students, colleagues, and guests, some of whom offered me valuable feedback and critique. I cannot imagine successfully completing this book without first having to wrestle with the many insightful and candid comments I have received at these venues over the years.

Special thanks to Baylor philosophy doctoral student, Hilary Yancey, who served as my research and teaching assistant in Fall 2014. She did outstanding work in proofreading the final version of the manuscript. At every stage of writing, I received from several colleagues important feedback on different portions of the manuscript: Christopher Tollefsen (University of South Carolina), Trent

Dougherty (Baylor University), Paul DeHart (Texas State University), Carson Holloway (University of Nebraska, Omaha), J. Budziszewski (University of Texas, Austin), Logan Gage (Franciscan University), Ross Parker (Charleston Southern University), George Mavrodes (University of Michigan), J. P. Moreland (Biola University), Casey Luskin (Discovery Institute), Barry Hankins (Baylor University), Jack Wade Nowlin (University of Mississippi School of Law), and several anonymous referees, some of whom read the initial manuscript I submitted to Cambridge while others read individual chapters in their more primitive versions. I was also given valuable suggestions by Lewis Bateman, the Cambridge University Press editor with whom I have worked for several years. Without the assistance and insights of all these individuals, any success I may achieve with this book would be significantly diminished. Nevertheless, any shortcomings of the final product are entirely mine. It should, of course, go without saying that one should not infer from my acknowledgment of the named individuals that any of them agrees with all or even some of the views I defend in this book.

But no one deserves more praise and acknowledgment than my wife, Frankie. She is not only beautiful and smart, she keeps my life in order. From the managing of my speaking engagements to reminding me, by word and deed, that the life of the mind leads to a diminished existence if it is untethered from the rhythms of ordinary life, I dare not imagine what I would have become without her.

The title of this book, *Taking Rites Seriously*, is taken from the title of an article by Paul Weithman, "Taking Rites Seriously," *Pacific Philosophical Quarterly* 75 (1994): 272–294. It is such a clever title that I wish I had thought of it myself. Fortunately, for me, titles cannot be copyrighted. Thus, no one can accuse me of not taking *copyrights* seriously.

This book is the first I have published since the death of my father, Harold Joseph Beckwith (1930–2015). It is because of his support and love, in tandem with the same from my mother, Elizabeth, that I chose to pursue the life of a college professor. *Risposa in pace, mio padre.*

# Introduction: Faith Seeking Understanding

I do not endeavor, O Lord, to penetrate your sublimity, for in no wise do I compare my understanding with that; but I long to understand in some degree your truth, which my heart believes and loves. For I do not seek to understand that I may believe, but I believe in order to understand. For this also I believe, – that unless I believed, I should not understand

St. Anselm of Canterbury (1033–1109)[1]

I want atheism to be true and am made uneasy by the fact that some of the most intelligent and well-informed people I know are religious believers. It isn't just that I don't believe in God and, naturally, hope that I'm right in my belief. It's that I hope there is no God! I don't want there to be a God; I don't want the universe to be like that.

Thomas Nagel (1937–)[2]

In February 2004 I was invited to give an address at the Texas Tech University School of Law. The title of my talk, "Law, Darwinism, and Public Education," was based largely on my book of the same name.[3] News of the event had apparently reached the university's biology department, and several of its members had shown up, accompanied by a local attorney from the American Civil Liberties Union (ACLU). My lecture focused on whether the controversial theory of "Intelligent Design" (ID), a view embraced almost exclusively by religious scholars,[4] could pass constitutional muster if a school board either

---

[1] St. Anselm of Canterbury, *Proslogium*, trans. Sidney Norton Deane (1903) (Internet Medieval Source Book), ch. 1, available at http://www.fordham.edu/halsall/basis/anselm-proslogium.asp.

[2] Thomas Nagel, *The Last Word* (New York: Oxford University Press, 1977), 130.

[3] Francis J. Beckwith, *Law, Darwinism, and Public Education: The Establishment Clause and the Challenge of Intelligent Design* (Lanham, MD: Rowman & Littlefield, 2003).

[4] What I mean by "religious scholars" is not "scholars of religion." Rather, what I mean are scholars, from a variety of disciplines, who happen to be personally religious.

required or permitted it to be taught in its science classes. Although I had nagging doubts about ID as a theory, and I did not think that as a matter of policy it was a good idea for the government to require the teaching of it, the focus of my talk, as with the book, was to answer a question of constitutional jurisprudence. On that question I concluded that I could not find a persuasive reason to believe that the Constitution forbids the teaching of ID in public schools. (As un-luck would have it, the following year [2005] a Federal District Court in Pennsylvania thought otherwise,[5] a point that I address in Chapter 6 of this present volume).

Nevertheless, the biology professors in the audience seemed to miss these subtle distinctions. During the question and answer session, one of them issued this public judgment, "Your talk consists of cleverly disguised religious arguments." I promptly replied, "I'm relieved. I was afraid you were going to accuse me of making *bad* arguments." The audience laughed.

Another professor, in private conversation with me and other audience members after the talk, accused me of being a "creationist." It was an odd charge, because I had for years never hidden the fact that I believed that evolution and God's existence were perfectly compatible[6] and that I was sympathetic to St. Pope John Paul II's anti-creationist understanding of the relationship between Darwinism and Christian theology.[7]

That lecture and the encounters that followed occurred over eleven years ago. (I am writing in July 2015). Since that time my nagging doubts about ID have developed into full-blown criticisms, and much of what I wrote in my 2003 book about the relationship between science and theology I would write much differently today (as I explain in Chapter 6). Nevertheless, the queries raised by the two professors point to deeper questions that are of enormous importance to how those of us who live in liberal democracies ought to conduct our public disagreements that touch on religious beliefs and their attendant notions. In my reply to the first professor, my caustic quip was implying that however one wants to assess the quality of my arguments, applying the adjective "religious" to those arguments contributes nothing to making that assessment or advancing a respectful conversation about it. Arguments, depending on their level of formality, are either sound or unsound, valid or invalid, strong or weak. Pope Emeritus Benedict, for example, is religious, and he is known to make arguments, even religious ones. But when it comes to the quality of his arguments, religious or otherwise, they stand or fall based on the

---

[5] Kitzmiller v. Dover, 400 F. Supp. 2d 707 (2005).

[6] Francis J. Beckwith, "Are Creationists Philosophically and Scientifically Justified in Postulating God?: A Critical Analysis of Naturalistic Evolution," *Interchange* 46 (1989). In this article I distinguish between "naturalistic evolution" and "theistic evolution," maintaining that evolution as a scientific theory – uncoupled from the philosophical position of naturalism – is perfectly compatible with the existence of God.

[7] John Paul II, "Truth Cannot Contradict Truth," Address to the Pontifical Academy of Sciences (22 October 1996), available at http://www.newadvent.org/library/docs_jp02tc.htm.

rules by which we assess all arguments, religious or otherwise. The professor, for some reason, thought that labeling my arguments "religious" was equivalent to showing that they were "bad."

The other professor, rather than focusing on my arguments, focused on what he mistakenly thought were my religious motivations and convictions. By suggesting that I was a champion for a scientifically disreputable point of view, creationism, he was relieved of the burden of assessing the content of the legal case I was making and the subtle philosophical issues that percolated beneath that case. He seemed unwilling to entertain the possibility that a view, such as ID, pregnant with positive implications for one sort of theism, may in fact rest on arguments, untouched by Scripture or personal piety, that in an earlier and more learned age would have been labeled as *natural theology* or *metaphysics*. For this reason, he did not seem to appreciate, or even remotely understand, the numerous and contentious debates among theologians, philosophers of religion, philosophers of science, and biblical scholars over the relationship between natural theology, biblical interpretation, science, and the philosophy of nature. (I touch on this in Chapter 6). The range of views and the sophistication of the ongoing conversation in which these views are assessed, considered, and critiqued were outside this professor's ken. From where I stood, it seemed that for him anyone who takes theology seriously – or, God forbid, may believe in God – is a "creationist."

Unfortunately, this diminished understanding of religious belief exhibited by these professors is ubiquitous in the way in which the most educated and respected citizens in our liberal democracies conduct their public disagreements. The point of this book is to address this problem. This is a book about how religious beliefs and religious believers are assessed by powerful actors in our public life,[8] and how those beliefs and believers are sometimes mischaracterized and seemingly misunderstood by mostly (although not exclusively) those who are critical of the influence of religion and religious citizens in politics or the formation of law.

As should be evident by the story that opened this introduction, what I mean by religious beliefs is not merely those doctrines that we associate with the world's great faiths such as Christianity – that is, that God exists, that Jesus of Nazareth was his Son, or that the Torah is the inspired Word of God – but also those moral and philosophical beliefs that are tightly tethered to a variety of religious traditions, and that are in most cases thought defensible by their adherents apart from the religious tradition from which these beliefs and believers herald.

---

[8] What I mean by "powerful actors" includes not only those who have real legal and political power – for example, judges, political office holders – but also highly respected and influential academics, writers, and media figures, some of whom – like Steven Pinker, Ronald Dworkin, and Martha Nussbaum – fit in two or three categories.

Among these moral and philosophical beliefs are beliefs about what counts as knowledge, whether the physical world is all that exists, the nature of the human being and when does he become a moral subject, whether natural objects include formal and final causes, and whether our sexual powers have a proper function and are ordered toward a particular good end. Beliefs about these questions are at the heart of the political and legal disputes that dominate what sociologist James Davison Hunter calls "the culture wars."[9] Take, for example, the contentious question over the morality of abortion, an issue that I address in several places in this book. Those who oppose abortion (or prolife advocates) typically ground their conviction in the belief that each human being begins his existence at the moment of conception (or at least very early in pregnancy),[10] and each human being is a person with immeasurable worth and intrinsic dignity. Although typically not disagreeing with the abortion opponent's *biological* claim that an individual human being begins his existence at the moment of conception (or at least very early in pregnancy), supporters of abortion rights (or prochoice advocates) *dispute* the prolifer's *moral* claim that all human beings are persons with immeasurable worth and intrinsic dignity. Most prochoice advocates make a distinction between being a *human being* and being a *person*. What makes one a moral subject is not one's humanity but, rather, one's personhood. The latter, according to its champions, arises either gradually or at some decisive moment in fetal development or after birth. As I point out in Chapter 2, prochoice advocates disagree among themselves as to when personhood arises and what sorts of characteristics a being must possess for us to attribute personhood to it. But a dominant view in the literature – one embraced by several distinguished philosophers including Michael Tooley[11] and Peter Singer[12] – is that human beings are not persons until they are "able to make aims and appreciate their own life."[13] So, even though a vast majority of prolife advocates would agree that their position is informed by their theological traditions, the conflict between their view and those that oppose it is not a conflict between "religion" and "nonreligion." It is a dispute over two contested philosophical understandings of the nature of the human person, one of which finds its more natural home in certain theological traditions.

[9] James Davison Hunter, *Culture Wars: The Struggle To Control The Family, Art, Education, Law, And Politics In America* (New York: Basic Books, 1991).

[10] I say "at least very early in pregnancy" to take into consideration (1) the fact that twinning may occur after conception, and thus one (or two) human being(s) begin(s) his (or their) existence after conception (depending on whether one thinks that the original conceptus survives twinning or two new ones arise from it), and (2) those opponents of abortion who, because of the phenomenon of twinning (and recombination), do not believe that an individual human being exists until twinning (and recombination) is (are) no longer possible.

[11] Michael Tooley, *Abortion and Infanticide* (New York: Oxford University Press, 1983).

[12] Peter Singer, *Practical Ethics*, 2nd ed. (New York: Cambridge University Press, 1993), 169–174, 181–191.

[13] Alberton Giubilini and Francesca Minerva, "After Birth Abortion: Why Should The Baby Live?," *Journal of Medical Ethics* 39.5 (May 2013): 262.

Yet, with few exceptions, this is not the way in which the abortion debate – or virtually any other bioethical issue – is approached in the public square, or even in the enclaves that our more sophisticated and cerebral analysts inhabit. Take, for example, comments made by Cornell law professor Sherry F. Colb on the debate over federal funding of embryonic stem cell research during the first year of the second Bush administration (2001). Rather than presenting the differing views of the embryo's personhood as contrary philosophical accounts of the nature of the human person, she writes: "The particular pro-life position to which [President George W.] Bush referred – the idea that full-fledged human life begins at conception – is a religious notion, and it is one to which some, but not all, religions subscribe. The idea of 'ensoulment' is, of course, a purely religious concept. The notion that life begins at conception is counterintuitive if understood in secular terms."[14]

Colb reframes the philosophical dispute as a conflict between "religion" and "secularism." By arguing that the "religious" view is counterintuitive to the secular understanding, Colb need not go any deeper in assessing the prolife case. For "secular" is presented as virtually equivalent to "deliverance of reason." The implication is clear: the differing views of the nature of the embryo are not two contrary accounts of the same subject – each the result of rational argument – but rather, each view is about a different subject, one religious and the other rational. (This will come up again in Chapter 5.)

The inadequacy of this and similar approaches to controversial cultural issues that touch on religious beliefs is the focus of this book. Aside from its introductory and concluding chapters (1 and 8, respectively), this book consists of three main sections: (I) Reason and Motives; (II) Dignity and Personhood, and (III) Nature and Sex. Each section, representing a general category in which these contested cultural issues dwell, addresses two of these issues in each of its two chapters. Part I concerns beliefs: the rationality of religious beliefs and those beliefs we call motives. Part II engages the good of life: the reality of human dignity and the nature of personhood. And Part III addresses the end of life (as in "its purpose" or "that to which it is ordered") : the nature of nature and the nature of human sexuality.

Part I (Reasons and Motives) begins with Chapter 2 ("*Juris, Fides, et Ratio*: What Judges and Some Legal Scholars Miss About Reason and Religious Beliefs"). In this chapter I present and critique the claim made by certain jurists and a growing number of legal scholars that religious belief is irrational. This understanding of religion has implications for how we think about the public participation of religious citizens as well as how courts may assess policies and laws that are tightly tethered to religious traditions. If religious beliefs are irrational, not only do these beliefs have no intellectual content, it does not seem

---

[14] Sherry F. Colb, "A Creeping Theocracy: How The U.S. Government Uses Its Power To Enforce Religious Principles," *FindLaw* (21 November 2001), available at http://writ.news.findlaw.com/colb/20011121.html.

far fetched to suggest that those who embrace and are motived by those beliefs, religious citizens, could be justly excluded from the public square in order to ensure the primacy of reason in our political life.

In Chapter 3 ("Theological Exclusionary Rule: The Judicial Misuse of Religious Motives") I critically assess what I believe is a modest application of this sort of exclusion. Over the years several courts have declared certain statutes and policies in violation of the Establishment Clause of the First Amendment because these laws have a religious purpose. These courts, however, do not find the law's purpose in its text, but rather, in the motives of its supporters in either the government or the general public. This, I argue, is, ironically, a violation of the spirit of the U.S. Constitution's article VI prohibition of religious tests for office (when it comes to the law's advocates in the government).[15] Moreover, because motives are types of beliefs, the courts cannot appeal to a citizen's motives in order to deprive her of her political right to participate in deliberative democracy. This conclusion, as I argue in the chapter, is based on the Supreme Court's own interpretation that the Constitution forbids the government (including the judiciary) from depriving citizens of their fundamental rights simply based on their religious beliefs.

Part II (Dignity and Personhood) focuses on issues in bioethics, an area of study and research in which one finds many questions over which citizens of good will strongly disagree (e.g., abortion, embryonic stem cell research, euthanasia, distribution of health care resources). In Chapter 4 ("Dignity Never Been Photographed: Bioethics, Policy, and Steven Pinker's Materialism"), I address an argument offered by renowned Harvard psychologist, Steven Pinker.[16] He maintains that the concept of human dignity contributes nothing to the field of bioethics that cannot be achieved by the principle of autonomy. As is well known, the idea of human dignity is often associated with religious worldviews, such as Christianity and Judaism, in which the concept of the *imago dei* (the image of God) is central to the equal dignity that many of us believe our fellow human beings possess by nature. Pinker, like many of his colleagues in the academy, embraces an understanding of metaphysics (Philosophical Materialism) and political institutions (Political Liberalism) that grounds his rejection of human dignity as ultimately irrational and inconsistent with government neutrality on religious belief. I do not argue for the falsity of Pinker's position. But rather, I make the case that his account of dignity and autonomy is not the only deliverance of reason on these matters, and thus, the religious

---

[15] I say "a violation of the spirit" because, as I point in chapter 3, Article VI applies only to the federal government, and it was only after the U.S. Supreme Court began applying the First Amendment's free exercise and establishment clauses to the states that religious tests for office were forbidden in all governments in the United States, federal, state, and local. These nonfederal prohibitions of religious tests are not literally an application of Article VI, but "in its spirit."

[16] Steven Pinker, "The Stupidity of Dignity," *The New Republic* Vol. 238 Issue 9 (28 May 2008): 28–31.

worldview that grounds human dignity, which he enthusiastically rejects, cannot be so easily dismissed.

Chapter 5 ("Personhood, Prenatal Life, and Religious Belief") concerns the type of argument raised by both Professor Colb (which I briefly mentioned earlier) as well as by Supreme Court Justice John Paul Stevens.[17] It is an argument that maintains that because the prolife view on prenatal life is tightly tethered to a religious worldview, the separation of church and state is violated if it is employed to guide the protection of prenatal life by our legal and political institutions. In reply, I argue that every position on prenatal life, including the prolife position, is philosophical, and thus the prolife view is no more or less "religious" than its rivals. The bulk of my case is devoted to explaining the intricacies and sophistication of the prolife position by interacting with the works of philosophers Dean Stretton[18] and Jeff McMahan,[19] both of whom reject the prolife understanding of prenatal life. I conclude with a discussion of the 2014 U.S. Supreme Court case, *Burwell v. Hobby Lobby*,[20] in which the Court held that a Health and Human Services Department regulation, allowed by the 2010 Affordable Care Act,[21] violated the 1993 Religious Freedom Restoration Act (RFRA).[22] The regulation required that all businesses that employ over fifty people, and are not exempted from the regulation for other reasons (e.g., they are houses of worship), must provide in their employee health plans a menu of birth control options including some that may result in the death of an embryo soon after fertilization. Hobby Lobby, along with the other defendant, Conestoga Wood Specialties, are family-owned closely held companies whose ownerships consist exclusively of devout Christians who believe that to offer such birth control options to their employees puts them in the position of cooperating with the destruction of nascent human life.

Part III (Nature and Sex) deals with the issues of intelligent design (ID) and same-sex marriage (SSM). In Chapter 6 ("How to Be An Anti–Intelligent Design Advocate: Science, Religion, and the Problem of Intelligent Design") I offer an analysis of the dispute over ID. Although, as I noted earlier, I was once cautiously sympathetic to ID – although never actually espousing it – I have over the years grown overtly critical of the view.[23] Nevertheless, I argue in this chapter that both sides in the dispute – despite the usual hostility that each has for the other – embrace a common understanding of nature as mechanistic. It is

---

[17] Webster v. Reproductive Health Services, 492 U.S. 490, 560–72 (1989) (Stevens, J., dissenting).

[18] Dean Stretton, "Critical Notice" – *Defending Life: A Moral and Legal Against Abortion Choice*," *Journal of Medical Ethics* 34 (2008): 793–797.

[19] Jeff McMahan, *The Ethics of Killing: Problems at the Margins of Life* (New York: Oxford University Press, 2002).

[20] Burwell v. Hobby Lobby Stores, Inc., 134 S. Ct. 2751 (2014).

[21] Patient Protection and Affordable Care Act (2010), Public Law, 111–148.

[22] Religious Freedom Restoration Act (1993), Public Law 103–141.

[23] See Francis J. Beckwith, "Or We Can Be Philosophers: A Response to Barbara Forrest," *Synthese*. Published Online First: 05 March 2011. doi 10.1007/s11229-011-9891-y.

an understanding that I argue does not do justice to the theism to which most ID advocates claim they subscribe. For this reason, some of the atheistic critics of ID – such as Richard Dawkins – think that their good reasons to reject ID may also serve as good reasons to reject theism or other ways of thinking about design in nature. I not only argue that such an inference is mistaken, but that the key assumption they make in the process of critiquing ID and its advocates requires a belief in intrinsic purposes in nature, which seems far more congenial to a theistic universe than a materialist one. This chapter also includes a brief critique of a portion of the U.S. District Court opinion in *Kitzmiller v. Dover* (2005),[24] the case that overturned a Pennsylvania school district policy that required its ninth-grade biology teachers to read in class a disclaimer that said that Darwinian evolution was not a fact and that the students should have an open mind and consider the alternative of ID. Because both sides of the ID question – whether in the courts or the public square – think of their dispute as a zero-sum game (i.e., you must choose God or Darwin but not both) they mistakenly think of the deliverances of "science" as a confirmation of either theism or philosophical naturalism (or materialism). But once one abandons this false dilemma and sees that it is practically impossible to forsake intrinsic purpose in nature without undercutting confidence in the normative judgments about proper ends and functions that even hard line materialists do not hesitate in issuing, it seems, as I conclude, that the only way that one can be an anti-ID advocate is to believe in design. (But not the design of the ID advocates!)

In Chapter 7 ("Same-Sex Marriage and Justificatory Liberalism: Religious Liberty, Comprehensive Doctrines, and Public Life") I deal with what is arguably the most contentious issue that tends to divide along religious lines, SSM. Virtually all supporters of SSM, including Ronald Dworkin,[25] Frank I. Michelman,[26] Martha Nussbaum,[27] and Linda McClain[28] appeal to some version of Justificatory Liberalism (JL) as the most fundamental reason why laws that limit marriage to one man and one woman are unjust. JL maintains that the state may not coerce its citizens on matters of constitutional essentials unless it can provide public justification that the coerced citizens would be irrational in rejecting. Because the right to marry is a constitutional essential, and because same-sex couples are not irrational in rejecting marriage as limited to one man and one woman, SSM ought to be legally recognized.

---

[24] *Kitzmiller*, 400 F. Supp. 2d.

[25] Ronald Dworkin, *Is Democracy Possible Here?: Principle for a New Political Debate* (Princeton, NJ: Princeton University Press, 2006). 1–24, 86–89.

[26] Martha Nussbaum, "A Right to Marry?: Same Sex Marriage and Constitutional Law," *Dissent* (Summer 2009): 43–55.

[27] Frank I. Michelman, "Rawls on Constitutionalism and Constitutional Law," in *The Cambridge Companion to Rawls*, ed. Samuel Freeman (New York: Cambridge University Press, 2003), 410–414.

[28] Linda C. McClain, "Deliberative Democracy, Overlapping Consensus, and Same-Sex Marriage," *Fordham Law Review* 66 (1997–98): 1241–1252.

However, because the issue under scrutiny – the nature of marriage – is deeply embedded in, and in most cases integral to, many of the reasonable worldviews (including religious ones) of citizens who reject SSM, the effects and consequences of legal recognition of SSM will likely include coercion, punishment, and marginalization of these dissenters in a variety of public enterprises and venues found in the plethora of institutions that inhabit the worlds of business, education, government, and law. For this reason, I argue in this chapter that because these dissenters almost certainly will suffer these consequences because of their unwillingness to honor and affirm in their actions a view of marriage that they are not unreasonable in rejecting, legal recognition of SSM will likely require violations of JL as well.

This book's eighth and concluding chapter ("Conclusion: Taking Rites Seriously") includes two parting examples, one fictional and the other concerning what some jurists have called "ceremonial deism."[29] With both examples I hope to reinforce the underlying theme of this book: when it comes to the understanding of religious belief among powerful figures in public life, "a small error at the outset can lead to great errors in the final conclusions."[30]

Not only does it not look as if the hostilities that are endemic to the culture wars will soon abate, it is probably safe to say that they will continue to increase. One reason for this is that one side sees itself and its advocates as the guardians of rationality while it views its adversaries as embracing nonrational delusions that deserve no greater constitutional protections or civil respect than other fanciful beliefs and private self-regarding hobbies.[31] That account of our present cultural conflicts, although popular and unchallenged in some insular circles, is seriously mistaken. It is the burden of this book to show why that is so.

---

[29] According to Justice William Brennan, "such practices as the designation of 'In God We Trust' as our national motto, or the references to God contained in the Pledge of Allegiance to the flag can best be understood, in Dean Rostow's apt phrase, as a form a 'ceremonial deism,' protected from Establishment Clause scrutiny chiefly because they have lost through rote repetition any significant religious content." (Lynch v. Donnelly 465 U. S. 688, 716 [1984] [Brennan, J., dissenting]).

[30] St. Thomas Aquinas, *On Being and Essence*, trans. Robert T. Miller (Internet Medievel Sourcebook, 1997), prologue, citing Aristotle, *De Caelo et Mundo* cap. 5 (271b8–13), available at http://www.fordham.edu/halsall/basis/aquinas-esse.asp.

[31] See Richard Dawkins, *The God Delusion* (New York: Houghton Mifflin, 2006); and Brian Leiter, *Why Tolerate Religion?* (Princeton, NJ: Princeton University Press, 2013).

PART I

# REASON AND MOTIVE

**2**

## *Juris, Fides, et Ratio*: What Judges and Some Legal Scholars Miss About Reason and Religious Beliefs

> Secular theorists often assume that they know what a religious argument is like: they present it as a crude prescription from God, backed up with threat of hellfire, derived from general or particular revelation, and they contrast it with the elegant complexity of a philosophical argument by Rawls (say) or Dworkin. With this image in mind, they think it obvious that religious argument should be excluded from public life.... But those who have bothered to make themselves familiar with existing religious-based arguments in modern political theory know that this is mostly a travesty ...
>
> Jeremy Waldron (1953–)[1]

Religious citizens, like their nonreligious compatriots, attempt to shape public policy in order to advance what they believe is the common good. Critics have suggested that there is something untoward with such activism, for the positions these citizens advocate are informed by their religious beliefs. Some of these critics ground this judgment in the claim that most (if not all) religious beliefs are by their very nature not amendable to rational assessment, and are thus irrational.

This view should not be confused with what is sometimes called Political Liberalism and often associated with the work of John Rawls and his numerous disciples.[2] According to that view, policies informed by religious or secular comprehensive doctrines that limit the fundamental liberties of citizens who do not share those comprehensive doctrines are justified if and only if the coerced citizens would be irrational in rejecting the coercion. Rawls himself concedes that many of these comprehensive doctrines, including the religious ones, are

---

[1] Jeremy Waldron, *God, Locke, and Equality: Christian Foundations of John Locke's Political Thought* (New York: Cambridge University Press, 2002), 20.

[2] John Rawls, *Political Liberalism*, rev. ed. (New York: Columbia University Press, 1996).

*reasonable.*[3] This is why Rawls distinguishes between reasonable comprehensive doctrines and the grounds by which the government may be justified in coercing its citizens.[4] (In Chapter 7 I critically assess a Rawlsian approach to the debate over same-sex marriage.)

The focus of this chapter is on those who eschew Rawls's modest approach and argue that *all* religious worldviews are at their core unreasonable because they are dependent on beliefs not amendable to reason. The implication of this view – that some, albeit not all, proponents of it explicitly acknowledge – is that religiously informed policy proposals have no place in a secular liberal democracy that requires the primacy of reason.

Although this view of religion's rational status is found or implied in several U.S. Supreme Court opinions as well as among some legal and political theorists, it is far more controversial than its advocates contend, as I show in this chapter.

## 2.1. FAITH, REASON, AND LAW

### 2.1.A. The Courts

Historian James Hitchcock has carefully documented how modern U.S. courts treat the rational status of theological beliefs,[5] concluding that "the incoherence of the modern jurisprudence of the Religious Clauses is the inescapable result of the [United States Supreme] Court's positing of religion as essentially irrational."[6] In what follows are some comments found in some of the cases

---

[3] According to Rawls, *reasonable comprehensive doctrines* have three main features:

> One is that a reasonable doctrine is an exercise of theoretical reason: it covers the major religious, philosophical, and moral aspects of human life in a more or less consistent and coherent manner. It organizes and characterizes recognized values so that they are compatible with one another and express an intelligible view of the world. Each doctrine will do this in ways that distinguish it from other doctrines, for example, by giving certain values a particular primacy and weight. In singling out which values to count as especially significant and how to balance them when they conflict, a reasonable comprehensive doctrine is also an exercise of practical reason. Both theoretical and practical reason (including as appropriate the rational) are used together in its formulation. Finally, a third feature is that while a reasonable comprehensive view is not necessarily fixed and unchanging, it normally belongs to, or draws upon, a tradition of thought and doctrine. Although stable over time, and not subject to sudden and unexplained changes, it tends to evolve slowly in the light of what, from its point of view, it sees as good and sufficient reasons (Rawls, 59).

[4] "[S]ince the political conception is shared by everyone while the reasonable doctrines are not, we must distinguish between a public basis of justification generally acceptable to citizens on fundamental political questions and the many nonpublic bases of justification belonging to the many comprehensive doctrines and acceptable only to those who affirm them" (Ibid., xix).

[5] James Hitchcock, *The Supreme Court and Religion in American Life, Volume II: From "Higher Law" to "Sectarian Scruples"* (Princeton, NJ: Princeton University Press, 2004), 67–76, 120–132.

[6] Ibid., 128.

Hitchcock cites, although there are many other judicial opinions that, because of space constraints, cannot be presented in this chapter. What is important here is not so much whether the cases involve free exercise or establishment clause questions, but how the justices who author these opinions think of the rational status of religious beliefs.

Some jurists seem to believe that the sin qua non of a rational belief is something akin to the type of empirical proof found in the natural sciences.[7] In *U.S. v. Ballard* (1944),[8] for example, Justice William O. Douglas writes:

Men may believe what they cannot prove. They may not be put to the proof of their religious doctrines or beliefs. Religious experiences which are as real as life to some may be incomprehensible to others. Yet the fact that they may be beyond the ken of mortals does not mean that they can be made suspect before the law. Many take their gospel from the New Testament. But it would hardly be supposed that they could be tried before a jury charged with the duty of determining whether those teachings contained false representations. The miracles of the New Testament, the Divinity of Christ, life after death, the power of prayer are deep in the religious convictions of many. If one could be sent to jail because a jury in a hostile environment found those teachings false, little indeed would be left of religious freedom.[9]

Justice William Brennan asserts in a 1976 opinion that "it is the essence of religious faith that ecclesiastical decisions are to be reached and are to be accepted as matters of faith, whether or not rational or measurable by objective criteria."[10] He further argues that "constitutional concepts of due process, involving secular notions of 'fundamental fairness' ... are therefore hardly relevant to such matters of ecclesiastical cognizance,"[11] which would come as quite a shock to Moses.[12]

Relying on the "insights" of that great jurist, Clarence Darrow, best known for his role of defense attorney in the famous 1925 Scopes "Monkey Trial," Justice John Paul Stevens writes in a concurring opinion in *Wolman v. Walter* (1977)[13]

---

[7] Of course, it is widely accepted by most philosophers of science that the natural sciences, for example, physics, chemistry, biology, astronomy, etc., involve more than empirical proof, requiring a host of philosophical and conceptual assumptions to even get off the ground. (This is something I address later in this chapter.) For more on this issue, see Larry Laudan and Jarrett Leplin, "Empirical Equivalence and Underdetermination," *Journal of Philosophy* 88.9 (September 1991): 449–472; and Thomas Kuhn, *The Structures of Scientific Revolutions*, 3rd ed. (Chicago: University of Chicago Press, 1996).

[8] 322 U.S. 78 (1944).

[9] Ibid., 87–88.

[10] Serbian Orthodox Diocese v. Milivojevich 426 U.S. 696, 715–716 (1976) (footnote omitted).

[11] Ibid., 716.

[12] "These things shall be a statute and ordinance for you throughout your generations wherever you live. If anyone kills another, the murderer shall be put to death on the evidence of witnesses; but no one shall be put to death on the testimony of a single witness. Moreover you shall accept no ransom for the life of a murderer who is subject to the death penalty; a murderer must be put to death" (Numbers 35: 29–31[NRSV]).

[13] 433 U.S. 229 (1977).

that "the distinction between the religious and the secular is a fundamental one. To quote from ... Darrow's argument in the Scopes case: 'The realm of religion ... is where knowledge leaves off, and where faith begins, and it never has needed the arm of the State for support, and wherever it has received it, it has harmed both the public and the religion that it would pretend to serve.' " [14] It seems that for Justice Stevens a religious belief cannot ever be an item of knowledge, for if it were, it would no longer be a religious belief.

The implication of this view is that religious beliefs ought to be of no concern to the state, unless their champions pretend that these beliefs are items of knowledge and mistakenly try to insert those beliefs into the public square. Thus, it is not surprising that Justice Stevens, in a dissenting opinion in *Webster v. Reproductive Health Services* (1989), calls the prolife position on fetal personhood a "religious tenet" that cannot in principle have a "secular purpose." (This sort of reasoning will be assessed more fully in Chapter 5.) In his analysis of a Missouri statute that placed restrictions on abortion and included a preamble that asserted that human life begins at conception, Justice Stevens writes:

Indeed, I am persuaded that the absence of any secular purpose for the legislative declarations that life begins at conception and that conception occurs at fertilization makes the relevant portion of the preamble invalid under the Establishment Clause of the First Amendment to the Federal Constitution. This conclusion does not, and could not, rest on the fact that the statement happens to coincide with the tenets of certain religions ... or on the fact that the legislators who voted to enact it may have been motivated by religious considerations.... Rather, it rests on the fact that the preamble, an unequivocal endorsement of a religious tenet of some, but by no means all, Christian faiths, serves no identifiable secular purpose. That fact alone compels a conclusion that the statute violates the Establishment Clause.... As a secular matter, there is an obvious difference between the state interest in protecting the freshly fertilized egg and the state interest in protecting a 9-month-gestated, fully sentient fetus on the eve of birth. There can be no interest in protecting the newly fertilized egg from physical pain or mental anguish, because the capacity for such suffering does not yet exist; respecting a developed fetus, however, that interest is valid. [15]

Of course, as a matter of simple logic, Justice Stevens's judgment begs the question, because one cannot justify the killing of a presentient human being *merely* on the grounds that it lacks sentience. That is, Justice Stevens's conclusion follows from his premises only if he assumes – rather than argues for – the truth of the belief that sentience is a power a human being must possess in order for the law to be justified in protecting it from homicide and thus for the law to

---

[14] Ibid., 265 (Stevens, J., concurring), quoting from Tr. of Oral Arg. 7, Scopes v. State, 154 Tenn. 105, 289 S. W. 363 (1927) (on file with Clarence Darrow Papers, Library of Congress) (punctuation corrected).

[15] Webster v. Reproductive Health Services 492 U.S. 490, 566–567, 569 (1989) (Stevens, J., dissenting) (notes and citations omitted).

have a secular purpose. But, as I note in Chapter 5, there are good reasons to reject this assumption. Thus, Justice Stevens begs the question.

In *Engle v. Vitale* (1962),[16] Justice Hugo Black explains why the First Amendment forbids the state from requiring its public school students to open each day with the public recitation of a government-authored prayer: "The Establishment Clause thus stands as an expression of principle on the part of the Founders of our Constitution that religion is too personal, too sacred, too holy, to permit its 'unhallowed perversion' by a civil magistrate."[17] Thirty years later, in the case of *Lee v. Weisman* (1992),[18] Justice Anthony Kennedy reinforces Black's understanding of religion when he writes that "[t]he design of the Constitution is that preservation and transmission of religious beliefs and worship is a responsibility and a choice committed to the private sphere, which itself is promised freedom to pursue that mission."[19] In his dissent, Justice Antonin Scalia wryly replies: "Church and state would not be such a difficult subject if religion were, as the Court apparently thinks it to be, some purely personal avocation that can be indulged entirely in secret, like pornography, in the privacy of one's room. For most believers it is *not* that, and has never been."[20]

The common thread in these opinions (Justice Scalia's excepted) is that religious beliefs and their attendant notions, such as moral and metaphysical beliefs, are epistemically akin to self-regarding private and personal matters of taste and thus not proper subjects of rational assessment. This is not to say that there are not justices, like Scalia, who disagree with this understanding. Rather, what I am suggesting is that the general tenor of the Court's opinions that touch on the epistemic nature of religious beliefs and their attendant notions is that these beliefs are not amenable to reason.

There is, however, a sense in which the justices' comments (including Scalia's) are consistent with the freedom of belief as the American Founders envisioned it: an *ultima facie* right that is a matter of conscience. This seems to be what Thomas Jefferson had in mind when he told the Danbury Baptists in his famous letter to them "that the legitimate powers of government reach actions only, and not opinions[.]"[21] But that is not where the real action is in contemporary church-state jurisprudence. Rather, as I argue in Section 2.2.C, the real action is in cases in which religious citizens try to shape policy while their critics claim that if these citizens were to be successful it would violate the Establishment Clause and/or the principles of liberal democracy. It is in those

---

[16] 370 U.S. 421.

[17] Ibid., 432.

[18] 505 U.S. 577.

[19] Ibid., 589.

[20] Ibid., 645 (J. Scalia, dissenting).

[21] Letter from Thomas Jefferson to the Danbury Baptists (1 January 1802), in 57 The Library of Congress Information Bulletin 6 (June 1998) (available at http://www.loc.gov/ loc/lcib/9806/ danpre.html).

instances in which the Supreme Court's assumption of religion's nonrationality has been subtly smuggled. However, in recent years, several legal theorists, rather than just assuming this position, have offered the philosophical scaffolding that had been missing from the judicial opinions. We now turn to those theorists.

## 2.1.B. The Legal Theorists

The late Stephen Gey, for instance, writes that the separationist view of the Establishment Clause that he and others embrace is grounded on two primary assumptions about the nature of politics and religion.[22] Concerning politics, "in a proper democracy, religion should be primarily a private phenomenon because religion and politics are simply incompatible."[23] This is because, writes Gey, "religion is particularly ill-suited to the sorts of pressures and influences that define the political process. Combining the typical political phenomena of personal greed, self-aggrandizement, duplicity, log-rolling, dealmaking, and unprincipled compromise, with the typical religious phenomena of theological certainty, absolute moral dictates, and the threat of eternal damnation, creates an especially dangerous cocktail."[24] As for religion, writes Gey, the separationist assumes that "it is no longer possible in the modern world to decide collectively matters that are by their nature nonrational, metaphysical, and impervious to both empirical analysis and logical proof or disproof."[25] Given the large number of such irrational and unprovable religious perspectives embraced by citizens in our pluralistic society, "the separationist perspective is that it is best for society if everyone is permitted to follow their own faith where it leads, without having to worry about their safety in the company of others who are devoted to contradictory moral and theological absolutes."[26]

Offering an account similar to Gey's, Suzanna Sherry suggests that the relationship between church and state – as embodied in the Constitution's Free Exercise and Establishment Clauses – should be viewed as analogous to what she describes as the different and contrary epistemic commitments of faith and reason.[27] Although she concedes that "while it may be possible to envision a religion based wholly or partly on reason, most of the major religions in America are based on faith as the underlying epistemology."[28] According to Sherry, "for the faithful, the ultimate authority and source of truth is extrahuman and evidence can – and in some religious traditions, must – be entirely personal to the individual." By contrast, "for the reasonable," that is, those

---

[22] Steven G. Gey, "Life After the Establishment Clause," *West Virginia Law Review* 110 (2007): 11.
[23] Ibid.
[24] Ibid.
[25] Ibid.
[26] Ibid.
[27] Suzanna Sherry, "Enlightening the Religion Clauses," *Journal of Contemporary Legal Issues* 7.1 (1996): 473–495.
[28] Ibid., 478.

who follow reason, "both the source and evidence for the truth lie in common human observation, experience, and reasoning."[29]

A person operating under the epistemology of faith, according to Sherry, is "able to ignore contradictions, contrary evidence, and logical implications. Indeed, one test of faith is its capacity to resist the blandishments of rationality; the stronger the rational arguments against a belief, the more faith is needed to adhere to it."[30] However, "secular science and liberal politics, both committed to the primacy of reason, necessarily deny that any truth is incontestable."[31]

Following along the same lines as Gey and Sherry, although in a clearly more philosophically sophisticated fashion, Brian Leiter maintains that:

[f]or all religions, there are at least some beliefs central to the religion that

(1) issue in *categorical* demands on action – that is, demands that must be satisfied no matter what an individual's antecedent desires and no matter what incentives or disincentives the world offers up; and

(2) do not answer ultimately (or at the limit) to *evidence* and *reasons*, as these are understood in other domains concerned with knowledge of the world. Religious beliefs, in virtue of being based on "faith," are insulated from ordinary standards of evidence and rational justification, the ones we employ in both common sense and in science.[32]

It should be noted that Leiter's project, unlike the ones advanced by Gey and Sherry, is not primarily about the rational status of religious belief, although it plays an important part in his work, which is to make the case that religious belief is not special and thus should not be accorded any more respect or deference in our legal institutions than nonreligious claims of conscience or other personal subjective beliefs that are not subject to the standards of science or what he calls "common sense."[33] In addition, Leiter, like Sherry, uses the term "faith" in an idiosyncratic way. Each, in their own way, asserts that faith is by its very nature incompatible with reason, even though that is not the way religious believers understand faith. In the Christian tradition, for example, although "faith"

---

[29] Ibid.

[30] Ibid., 482.

[31] Ibid., 479.

[32] Brian Leiter, *Why Tolerate Religion?* (Princeton, NJ: Princeton University Press, 2013), 33–34. Although Leiter is claiming that "[f]or all religions, there are *at least some* beliefs," but apparently not to *all* beliefs, "central to the religion" that satisfy (1) and (2), it is not clear what Leiter believes those other religious beliefs that do not satisfy (1) and (2) would be (emphasis added). For this reason, I will assume – given the religious beliefs he maintains are outside the ken of reason, and given his commitment to the epistemic norm that one ought to adjust one's beliefs in light of new evidence – that he is commendably cautious in his formulation, just in case it turns out that there happens to be a religious belief central to a particular religion that may be rationally supported.

[33] As he writes in his book's introduction: "The central puzzle in this book is why the state should have to tolerate exemptions from generally applicable laws when they conflict with *religious* obligations but not with other equally serious obligations of conscience" (Ibid., 3).

is one of the three infused theological virtues,[34] that same tradition for nearly two millennia has produced numerous sophisticated and careful works, by its most important philosophers, theologians, and scholars, on the complementarity of faith and reason. Not only does Leiter show no evidence of having consulted such treatises, he completely ignores what is perhaps the most widely read and influential modern Catholic encyclical on the matter, *Fides et Ratio: On Relationship Between Faith and Reason*, authored in 1998 by the late philosopher, pope, and saint St. Pope John Paul II.[35] This is not to say that Leiter (or Sherry) could not be correct in their understanding of faith, or that it is a mistake to believe that faith and reason are complementary. Rather, what I am suggesting is that if one is going to issue the judgment that a large swath of the human experience – the faiths that inspired some of the greatest philosophical, literary, scientific, charitable, religious, educational, political, artistic, and musical accomplishments the world has ever known[36] – is incompatible with the deliverances of reason, one should at the very least consult and engage those who offer a contrary account.

Concerning (1), Leiter points out that because of the categorical nature of their beliefs, some religious citizens have been in the forefront of many important movements for social justice, including the abolitionist movement, the American civil rights movement, and the cause to end apartheid in South Africa. On the other hand, the categorical nature of their beliefs has led other religious devotees to engage in all sorts of horrific mischief, such as supporting American racial segregation, bombing abortion clinics, and flying airplanes into buildings.[37] However, for the purposes of this chapter, my focus will be on (2).[38]

---

[34] "The theological virtues are the foundation of Christian moral activity; they animate it and give it its special character. They inform and give life to all the moral virtues. They are infused by God into the souls of the faithful to make them capable of acting as his children and of meriting eternal life. They are the pledge of the presence and action of the Holy Spirit in the faculties of the human being. There are three theological virtues: faith, hope, and charity." (*Catechism of the Catholic Church: Revised in Accordance With the Official Latin Text Promulgated by Pope John Paul II*, 2nd ed. [Washington, DC: United States Conference of Catholic Bishops, 2000], 1813 [note omitted]).

[35] John Paul II, *Fides Et Ratio: On the Relationship between Faith and Reason* (14 September 1998), 44–45, available at http://www.vatican.va/holy_father/john_paul_ii/encyclicals/documents/hf_jp-ii_enc_15101998_fides-et-ratio_en.html.

[36] See, e.g., Robert Royal, *The God That Did Not Fail* (San Francisco: Encounter Books, 2006); Rodney Stark, *For the Glory of God* (Princeton, NJ: Princeton University Press, 2002); and Rodney Stark, *The Victory of Reason* (New York: Random House, 2005); David Bentley Hart, *Atheist Delusions: The Christian Revolution and Its Fashionable Enemies* (New Haven, CT: Yale University Press, 2009).

[37] Leiter, *Why Tolerate Religion?*, 36–37.

[38] In addition to (1) and (2), Leiter suggests that religious beliefs may also (3) "involve, explicitly or implicitly, *a metaphysics of ultimate reality*" (ibid., 47; emphasis in original) and (4) "render intelligible and tolerable the basic existential facts about human life, such as suffering and death" (ibid., 52). Although these are certainly important considerations when assessing the nature of religion, only (3) touches on the concerns of this chapter. For this reason, I will briefly address (3) in Section 2.2.B.1.

Leiter brings up three possible counters to (2). The first is what he calls "'intellectualist' traditions of religious thought." He offers up Paley's "natural theology," neo-Thomist arguments, and Intelligent Design as examples,[39] and promptly dismisses them as "insulated from the evidence," for two reasons. First, writes Leiter, "it is dubious (to put the matter gently) that these positions are really serious about following the evidence where it leads, as opposed to manipulating it to fit preordained ends." And second, "in the case of the sciences, beliefs based on evidence are also revisable in light of the evidence; but in the intellectualist traditions in religious thought just noted, it never turns out that the fundamental beliefs are revisable in light of new evidence."[40]

The second possible counter to (2) that Leiter suggests is the believer who may offer historical evidence for miraculous events she believes support the veracity of her faith. Leiter writes: "Might not a Catholic, for example, quite reasonably appeal to testimonial evidence, as recorded in the Bible and elsewhere, in support of her belief in the resurrection of Jesus Christ?"[41] Although he concedes that a Catholic may make such an appeal, it really does not amount to much:

To be sure, testimony that Christ rose from the dead is a kind of colorable evidence from a scientific point of view; that the testimony is inconsistent with everything we have reason (evidence) to believe about what happens when human bodies expire – both from massive amounts of testimonial evidence, as well as the evidence of physiology and biology – indicates that the ancient testimonial evidence deserves no credence at all.[42]

Leiter, unfortunately, does not explain how the mere observation that there are regularities in nature that are described by scientific laws – ironically, a necessary condition for any event, especially a physical resurrection, to be labeled a miracle – indicates that there is no amount of credible evidence a Catholic (or any other Christian) may marshal to show that her belief in Christ's resurrection is rational. Without offering an explanation, Leiter's argument is almost a textbook case of circular reasoning, one anticipated in C. S. Lewis's *1947* critique of David Hume's very similar,[43] and far more sophisticated, argument: "Now of course we must agree with Hume [or Leiter] that if there is absolutely 'uniform

---

[39] Ibid., 41.
[40] Ibid., 40 (note omitted).
[41] Ibid., 40–41.
[42] Ibid., 41–42.
[43] David Hume, "Miracles," in *An Enquiry Concerning Human Understanding* (1748) and *A Letter from a Gentleman to His Friend in Edinburgh* (1745), ed. Eric Steinberg (Indianapolis: Hackett, 1977). For critiques of Hume's argument and ones similar too it, see Francis J. Beckwith, "Theism, Miracles, and the Modern Mind," in *The Rationality of Theism*, ed. Paul Mosser and Paul Copan (New York: Routledge, 2003), 221–236; Francis J. Beckwith, "Hume's Evidential/Testimonial Epistemology, Probability, and Miracles," in *Faith in Theory and Practice: Essays on the Justification of Religious Belief*, ed. Elizabeth Radcliffe and Carol White (La Salle, IL: Open Court Publishing, 1993), 117–140; and John Earman, *Hume's Abject Failure: The Argument Against Miracles* (New York: Oxford University Press, 2000).

experience' against miracles [or is 'inconsistent with everything we have reason (evidence) to believe'], if in other words they have never happened, why then they never have. Unfortunately we know the experience against them to be uniform [or 'inconsistent with everything we have reason (evidence) to believe'] only if we know that all the reports of them are false [or 'deserve no credence at all']. And we can know all the reports to be false [or 'deserve no credence at all'] only if we know already that miracles have never occurred [or is 'inconsistent with everything we have reason (evidence) to believe']. In fact, we are arguing in a circle."[44]

The third possible counter to (2) that Leiter brings up is Reformed Epistemology, but he promptly dismisses that as well. After mentioning two of its most important philosophical advocates, William Alston and Alvin Plantinga, Leiter writes that he is "going to assume – uncontroversially among most philosophers but controversially among reformed epistemologists – that 'reformed epistemology' is nothing more than an effort to insulate religious faith from ordinary standards of reasons and evidence in common sense and the sciences, and thus religious belief is a culpable form of unwarranted belief given those ordinary epistemic standards."[45]

There seems to be a common thread that connects the court opinions with the views of Gey, Sherry, and Leiter. I will call this common thread, Secular Rationalism (SR):

Religious beliefs are irrational because they are based on (1) unprovable claims (in the sense that they are the sorts of belief that can not in-principle be proven), (2) incontestable claims (in the sense that they are the sorts of beliefs that can not in-principle be falsified), and (3) claims that cannot change or develop because they are insulated from the ordinary standards of evidence and rational justification.

## 2.2. REASONABLE FAITH? A CRITIQUE OF SECULAR RATIONALISM

Anyone familiar with the literature in philosophy of religion, philosophy of science, metaphysics, and epistemology over the past fifty years would feel as if she has within her grasp an embarrassment of riches by which to critique SR. For this reason, I cannot possibly offer the comprehensive critique that SR so richly deserves. Thus, my focus will be on only three main points: (A) SR is Epistemically Suspect, (B) SR Begs Substantive Questions, and (C) SR Confuses Religion as Such With Particular Religions and the Beliefs Tethered to Them.

---

[44] C. S. Lewis, *Miracles*, rev. ed. (New York Macmillan Publishing Company, 1960), 102. The original edition was published in 1947.

[45] Leiter., *Why Tolerate Religion?*, 81.

## 2.2.A. SR Is Epistemically Suspect

Foundationalism in epistemology is the view that for a belief to count as rational it must be either properly basic or inferable or derived from beliefs that
are properly basic. Foundationalism comes in a variety of types,[46] although SR
seems to be similar to Narrow Foundationalism (NF). According to NF, we are
rationally justified in holding our beliefs if and only if they are properly basic
(i.e., foundational) or are based on those foundational beliefs. The only properly basic beliefs are those that are self-evident,[47] incorrigible,[48] and evident to
the senses,[49] and all rational nonbasic beliefs (i.e., those beliefs that are proper
to hold but are not basic) must be inferable or derived from these properly
basic beliefs.

It is, however, well known that NF has been savaged in the philosophical
literature because it is self-referentially incoherent.[50] That is, the claim that for
a belief to be rational it must be properly basic (i.e., self-evident, incorrigible,
or evident to the senses) or inferable or derived from a properly basic belief is
a belief that is not properly basic or inferable or derived from a properly basic
belief. Thus, NF, by its own standard, is not a rational belief, and is therefore
self-referentially incoherent.

SR falls prey to a similar error. Take, for example, Sherry's claim that "secular science and liberal politics, both committed to the primacy of reason, necessarily deny that any truth is incontestable."[51] We can put the epistemic core of
this claim in the form of a proposition:

*A.* Reason necessarily denies incontestable truths

Is this an incontestable truth? If reason necessarily denies incontestable truths,
and if Sherry is offering *A* as a canon of reason, then *A* is not an incontestable

---

[46] See Ted Poston, "Foundationalism" (updated 10 June 2010), in *Internet Encyclopedia of Philosophy: A Peer-Reviewed Academic Resource*, available at http://www.iep.utm.edu/found-ep/.

[47] A self-evident belief is a belief that is true by definition or a necessary truth, e.g, "All bachelors are unmarried males," "2 + 3 = 5," or "C = 2πr."

[48] An incorrigible belief is a subjective belief about which one cannot be mistaken, for example, "I feel pain." It may be that one's pain is illusory, in the sense there is no neurological or physical cause of one's pain. But the feeling of pain is undeniable. Or suppose that you are Mr. Scrooge and you seem to have been awoken by what appears to be a being who claims to be the Ghost of Christmas Past. You have the incorrigible belief that you are being appeared to by the Ghost of Christmas Past, even though it may be the case that you are hallucinating, dreaming, or a neigh-bor is dressed up as the ghost in order to guilt you into abandoning your greed. Nevertheless, it is incorrigibly the case that you are being appeared to Ghost-of-Christmas-Pastly.

[49] Beliefs that are evident to the senses are those beliefs about the world that come to us through our senses and about which we could be mistaken. When Tom sees a basketball court when he looks out into my backyard, he comes to believe that there is a basketball court in my backyard.

[50] See, e.g., Alvin Plantinga, *Warranted Christian Belief* (New York: Oxford University Press, 2000), 94–97.

[51] Sherry, "Enlightening the Religion Clauses," 479.

truth. But in that case, it is not incontestable that reason necessarily denies incontestable truths. Thus, reason may in fact affirm incontestable truths. On the other hand, if *A* is an incontestable truth, and Sherry is offering *A* as a canon of reason, then it is not the case that reason necessarily denies incontestable truths. Consequently, reason requires that we believe at least one incontestable truth, namely, that reason necessarily denies incontestable truths. In that case, reason would be downright unreasonable.

But not only can one reject *A* because it is self-referentially incoherent, one can also reject it because it is simply false. Take, for example, these claims:

*B.* All bachelors are unmarried males
*C.* 2 + 2 = 4
*D.* C = 2πr

*B, C,* and *D* are necessary truths. They are true in every possible world. But necessary truths are incontestable truths. If it is reasonable to believe in necessary truths – and it would seem to be so because they are in fact "truths" – then it is not only not true that reason necessarily denies incontestable truths, but in some cases reason necessarily *affirms* incontestable truths.[52]

Now consider these claims:

*E.* It is morally wrong everywhere and always to torture children for fun.
*F.* The proper end of the human mind is the acquisition of wisdom.
*G.* Human persons are beings of immeasurable worth and dignity.

*E, F,* and *G* seem like perfectly rational beliefs for one to hold. They are, to be sure, not incontestable like *B, C,* and *D*. But they seem far less contestable than Einstein's Second Theory of Relativity, an established scientific theory if there ever was one. Nevertheless, one can easily imagine Einstein's theory being refuted, but it's difficult to imagine how one can ever be wrong about *E, F,* and *G*. (Perhaps this is why atheist philosopher Michael Ruse has said, "The man who says that it is morally acceptable to rape little children, is just as mistaken as the man who says that 2+2=5."[53]) Moreover, these beliefs are not self-evident, incorrigible, evident to the senses, or inferable or derivative from beliefs that are self-evident, incorrigible, or evident to the senses. They seem to be properly basic beliefs, perfectly rational to hold without the assistance of an argument or evidence.[54]

---

[52] These are self-evident truths, and so in this sense, the Narrow Foundationalist would also reject the "incontestable" prong of SR.
[53] Michael Ruse, *Darwinism Defended: A Guide to the Evolution Controversies* (London: Addison-Wesley, 1982), 275.
[54] This analysis is similar to what one finds among those philosophers who are advocates of Reformed Epistemology. See, for example, Plantinga, *Warranted Christian Belief*; Alvin Plantinga, *God and Other Minds* (Ithaca, NY: Cornell University Press, 1967); Alvin Plantinga and Nicholas Wolterstorff, eds., *Faith and Rationality: Reason and Belief in God* (Notre Dame, IN: University of Notre Dame Press, 1983).

So, it seems that there are beliefs that one has no obligation to contest or prove that are nevertheless perfectly rational to hold. Although this should be enough to raise suspicions about SR's epistemic credentials, advocates of SR also completely ignore the facts on the ground, which is the focus of the next section.

## 2.2.B. SR Begs Substantive Questions

SR advocates beg substantive questions by simply ignoring substantive examples of religious beliefs and defenses of them that are inconsistent with SR's depiction of religion's epistemic status. In the writings of the legal theorists discussed earlier, one does not find a hint that any of the authors has more than a superficial acquaintance with the vast literature produced by religious (and some nonreligious) thinkers who make a case for the rationality of beliefs on which religious worldviews often depend. Nevertheless, as I have already noted, Leiter makes mention of "intellectualist traditions"[55] (neo-Thomist and William Paley-type arguments in particular) and "reformed Epistemology,"[56] and Sherry concedes that "it might be possible to envision a religion based wholly or partly on reason."[57] But neither author goes any further than mention and dismissal. And in both cases, neither author (with the exception of Leiter's one citation of Plantinga's *Warranted Christian Belief*[58] and his roughly 1,000-word assessment of an argument by John Finnis[59]) connects his or her claims with any identifiable arguments or bodies of literature.

To show how SR begs substantive questions, I will assess each of the three claims SR advocates offer as support for their conclusion that religious beliefs are irrational: (1) religious claims are unprovable, (2) religious claims are incontestable, and (3) religious claims cannot change or develop because they are insulated from the ordinary standards of evidence and rational justification.

Because of space constraints, my analysis will focus on only one religion, Christianity, the theological tradition and its claims about which the courts and political theorists seem most concerned. (This is not to say that most of what we cover later would not also apply to other religious traditions. But given that one cannot cover every angle, and the fact that virtually all interest on religion and law questions in the United States concerns the claims of Christian citizens to shape public policy and be free of government coercion, focusing on Christian theism makes the most sense.) As should be obvious, Christianity, like virtually every religious tradition, is a complex and interconnected, and oftentimes interdependent, tapestry of beliefs, practices, institutions, and ways

---

[55] Leiter, *Why Tolerate Religion?*, 39.
[56] Ibid., 81.
[57] Sherry, "Enlightening the Religion Clauses," 478.
[58] Leiter, *Why Tolerate Religion?*, 158 n. 23.
[59] Ibid., 86–90.

of life that concern a variety of doctrinal, philosophical, moral, practical, liturgical, and ecclesiastical topics. Consequently, Christian theism, as it is the case with every other secular or religious comprehensive worldview, entails and depends on certain beliefs, some of which are metaphysical, epistemological, historical, and moral. My analysis of SR will concern these types of beliefs.

### 2.2.B.1. Religious Claims Are Unprovable

There are all sorts of ways that one can try to "prove" one's point of view, depending on the sort of claim one is making. If, for example, I were to claim that I am directly aware of certain universal, immutable, and abstract truths – for example, "$2 + 2 = 4$," "$C = 2\pi r$" – it would be a fool's errand for me to try to "prove" this claim in the same way that I may try to prove that the Baylor Bears beat the SMU Mustangs last night or that my wife is preparing Texas Chili in the kitchen. So, the fact that universal, immutable, and abstract truths cannot be "proven" by reading the sport's section of the *Waco Tribune-Herald* or by sense of smell does not mean that they are not susceptible to demonstration.[60] For this reason, theist (including Christian) thinkers offer different sorts of arguments for aspects of their worldview depending on the nature of the subject under discussion.

If we look at just the literature produced over the past fifty years by serious Christian thinkers defending these metaphysical, epistemological, historical, and moral beliefs, the volume and quality of the work is impressive, even if one were to remain unconvinced by most or all of their arguments. Although it probably need not be said, but a position's rationality, religious or otherwise, does not depend on whether all, most, or even some dissenters from the position are convinced of it based on the arguments offered by its champions. For if that were the case, one could simply dismiss the arguments offered by Gey, Sherry, and Leiter as irrational because some, perhaps many, sophisticated critics find their arguments unconvincing. Moreover, if total or near unanimity were the test for rationality, then virtually every contested point of view in the academy would be "irrational."

As for the central philosophical claim of Christian theism – that there exists a self-existent personal necessary eternal being on which the universe depends for its existence – numerous arguments have been offered, including cosmological, moral, ontological, and teleological ones.[61] General defenses of the

---

[60] Years ago I heard someone refer to this as "the beer in the refrigerator fallacy." Just because the best way to answer the question, "Is there beer in the refrigerator?," is by looking, does not mean that that is the way we find other things.

[61] See, e.g., William Lane Craig and J. P. Moreland, eds., *The Blackwell Companion to Natural Theology* (Oxford, UK: Wiley-Blackwell, 2009); Richard Swinburne, *The Existence of God* (New York: Oxford University Press, 1979); William Lane Craig, *The Kalam Cosmological Argument* (New York, Macmillan, 1979); C. Stephen Evans, *Natural Signs and Knowledge of God: A New Look at Theistic Arguments* (New York: Oxford University Press, 2010); Alvin

rationality of theism are plentiful.[62] The literature is also awash with sophisticated critiques of philosophical naturalism,[63] Christian theism's chief intellectual rival. One of the most influential arguments on that topic – Alvin Plantinga's "An Evolutionary Argument Against Naturalism"[64] – has been the subject of numerous critiques and defenses,[65] including an entire academic tome dedicated to assessing it.[66] Metaphysical questions concerning moral realism,[67] the existence and nature of the soul,[68] and whether living organisms are substantial beings with real natures,[69] all of which many Christian thinkers see as deeply connected to their theological tradition, have been addressed in a plethora of works. Others have argued that Christian Mystical Practice (CMP) is a doxastic practice

Plantinga, *The Ontological Argument from St. Anselm to Contemporary Philosophers* (Garden City, NY: Doubleday, 1965).

[62] See, e.g., John Haldane, *Reasonable Faith* (New York: Routledge, 2010); Paul Mosser and Paul Copan, eds., *The Rationality of Theism* (New York: Routledge, 2003); Plantinga, *Warranted Christian Belief*; Plantinga, *God and Other Minds*; Plantinga and Wolterstorff, eds., *Faith and Rationality*; Charles Taliaferro and Jill Evans, *Image in Mind: Theism, Naturalism, and the Imagination* (New York: Continuum, 2010); Richard Swinburne, *Faith & Reason*, 2nd ed. (Oxford: Clarendon, 2005); Alvin Plantinga and Michael Tooley, *Knowledge of God* (Malden, MA: Wiley-Blackwell, 2008); and Edward Feser, *The Last Superstition: A Refutation of the New Atheists* (South Bend, IN: St. Augustine Press, 2008).

[63] Robert C. Koons and Gregory Bealer, eds., *The Waning of Materialism* (New York: Oxford University Press, 2010); William Lane Craig and J. P. Moreland, eds., *Naturalism: A Critical Analysis* (New York: Routledge, 2000); Stewart Goetz and Charles Taliaferro, *Naturalism* (Grand Rapids, MI: Eerdmans, 2008); and Michael Rae, *World Without Design: The Ontological Consequences of Naturalism* (New York: Oxford University Press, 2004).

[64] Alvin Plantinga, *Warrant and Proper Function* (New York: Oxford University Press, 1993), 216–237.

[65] See, e.g., Branden Fitelson and Elliot Sober, "Plantinga's Probability Arguments Against Evolutionary Naturalism," in *Intelligent Design Creationism and Its Critics: Philosophical, Theological, and Scientific Perspectives*, ed. Robert T. Pennock (Cambridge, MA: M.I.T. Press, 2001); J. Wesley Robbins, "Is Naturalism Irrational?" *Faith and Philosophy* 11.2 (1994): 255–259.

[66] James Beilby, ed., *Naturalism Defeated? Essays on Plantinga's Evolutionary Argument Against Naturalism* (Ithaca, NY: Cornell University Press, 2002).

[67] See, e.g., John M. Rist, *Real Ethics: Reconsidering the Foundations of Morality* (New York: Cambridge University Press, 2002); John E. Hare, *God's Call: Moral Realism, God's Commands, and Human Autonomy* (Grand Rapids, MI: Eerdmans, 2001); J. P. Moreland, "Ethics Depend on God," in *Does God Exist?: The Debate Between Theists and Atheists* by J. P. Moreland and Kai Nielsen (Amherst, NY: Prometheus Books, 1993), 111–126.

[68] See, e.g., William Hasker, *The Emergent Self* (Ithaca, NY: Cornell University Press, 1999); Richard Swinburne, *The Evolution of the Soul*, 2nd ed. (New York: Oxford University Press, 1997); J. P. Moreland, *The Recalcitrant Imago Dei: Human Persons and the Failure of Naturalism* (London: SCM Press, 2009); J. P. Moreland, *Consciousness and the Existence of God: A Theistic Argument* (New York: Routledge, 2009); Ric Machuga, *In Defense of the Soul: What It Means to Be Human* (Grand Rapids, MI: Brazos Press, 2002); Mark C. Baker and Stewart Goetz, eds., *Soul Hypothesis: Investigations into the Existence of the Soul* (New York: Continuum, 2011).

[69] See, e.g., Davis S. Oderberg, *Real Essentialism* (New York: Routledge, 2007); John Haldane, ed. *Mind, Metaphysics, and Value in the Thomistic and Analytical Traditions* (Notre Dame, IN: University of Notre Dame Press, 2002).

analogous to sense perception, and thus a reliable means by which to perceive God.[70] Most religious believers and their critics consider the Problem of Evil as a possible defeater to Christian theism,[71] and many Christian thinkers have offered a variety of responses.[72]

Christianity's central historical belief is that Jesus of Nazareth died and rose from the dead, and thus vindicated his claim to be the Son of God. Numerous Christian scholars have critically assessed this belief, marshaling a case based on historical sources,[73] and have gladly engaged those who challenge it.[74] Consequently, when Sherry compares belief that Jesus is God's Son to Holocaust denial,[75] she compounds her ignorance with irony; and when Leiter dismisses the historical evidence for Christ's resurrection by a palpably circular argument (see earlier) without any apparent awareness of the mountains of scholarly literature on the subject, one wonders who are the real champions of reason in this dispute.

Leiter, to his credit, does concede that "there is a large literature in Anglophone philosophy devoted to defending the rationality of religious belief,"[76] but rather than engaging any of it, he dismisses the entirety of it in one full swoop: "suffice it to observe that its proponents are uniformly religious believers, and that much of it has the unpleasant appearance of post hoc – sometimes desperately

---

[70] See, e.g., William Alston, "Perceiving God," *Journal of Philosophy* 83.11 (1986): 655–65; and William Alston, *Perceiving God: The Epistemology Religious Experience* (Ithaca, NY: Cornell University Press, 1991).

[71] See, e.g., William L. Rowe, ed., *God and the Problem of Evil* (Malden, MA: Blackwell, 2001).

[72] See, e.g., Brian Davies, *Reality of God and the Problem of Evil* (New York: Continuum, 2006); Richard Swinburne, *Providence and the Problem of Evil* (New York: Oxford University Press, 1998); Alvin Plantinga, *God, Freedom, and Evil* (New York: Harper & Row, 1974); Trent Dougherty and Justin P. McBrayer, *Skeptical Theism: New Essays* (New York: Oxford University Press, 2014); and Trent Dougherty, *The Problem of Animal Pain: A Theodicy for All Creatures Great and Small* (New York: Macmillan Palgrave, 2014).

[73] See, e.g., N. T. Wright, *The Resurrection of the Son of God* (Minneapolis: Fortress Press, 2003); Michael R. Licona, *The Resurrection of Jesus: A New Historiographical Approach* (Downers Grove, IL: InterVarsity Press, 2011); Richard Swinburne, *The Resurrection of God Incarnate* (Oxford: Oxford University Press, 2003); Stephen T. Davis, Daniel Kendall, and Gerald O'Collins, eds., *The Resurrection: An Interdisciplinary Symposium on the Resurrection of Jesus* (New York: Oxford University Press, 1997); C. Stephen Evans, *The Historical Christ and the Jesus of Faith: The Incarnational Narrative as History* (New York: Oxford University Press, 1996); and William Lane Craig, *Assessing the New Testament Evidence for the Historicity of the Resurrection of Jesus* (Toronto: Edwin Mellen, 1989).

[74] See, e.g., Paul Copan, ed., *Will the Real Jesus Please Stand Up?: A Debate Between William Lane Craig and Dominic Crosson* (Grand Rapids, MI: Baker, 1998); Paul Copan and R. K. Tacelli, S. J., eds., *Jesus' Resurrection: Fact or Figment?: A Debate Between William Lane Craig & Gerd Ludemann* (Downers Grove, IL: InterVarsity Press, 2000); Gary R. Habermas and Antony G. N. Flew, *Did Jesus Rise from the Dead?: The Resurrection Debate*, ed. Terry Miethe (New York: Harper & Row, 1987).

[75] "There is indeed no principled way to distinguish those who maintain that the Holocaust never occurred from those who maintain that … Jesus Christ was [God's] Son." (Sherry, "Enlightening the Religion Clauses," 491).

[76] Leiter, *Why Tolerate Religion?*, 79–80.

post hoc – rationalization."[77] Remarkably, he offers virtually nothing in support of these controversial claims. He provides no evidence for the first (probably because it is irrelevant,[78] false,[79] and misleading[80]), and as for the second,

---

[77] Ibid., 80.

[78] Would anyone take seriously a philosopher who dismissed the rationality of philosophical materialism because its proponents are uniformly philosophical materialists?

[79] There are, in fact, some nontheists who reject belief in God but nevertheless maintain that belief in God is rational. They are sometimes called "friendly atheists," a term coined by atheist philosopher William Rowe. See Rowe, "Friendly Atheism, Skeptical Theism, and the Problem of Evil," chapter 12 of *William L. Rowe on Philosophy of Religion: Selected Writings* by William Rowe, ed. Nick Trakakis (Burlington, VT: Ashgate, 2007). There are, of course, nontheist philosophers whose works have lent support to metaphysical and epistemological beliefs congenial to, and some say central to, Christian theism. See, e.g., Thomas Nagel, *Mind and Cosmos: Why the Materialist Neo-Darwinian Conception of Nature is Almost Certainly False* (New York: Oxford University Press, 2012); Karl R. Popper, *Knowledge and the Body-Mind Problem*, ed. M. A. Notturno (London: Routledge, 1994); and Bradley Monton, *Seeking God in Science: An Atheist Defends Intelligent Design* (Buffalo, NY: Broadview Press, 2009).

[80] Leiter gives the impression that only theists care about the rationality of religious belief and take the arguments for it seriously. But that is simply false. There are in fact many accomplished nontheist philosophers who take the rationality of religious belief, as well as metaphysical and epistemological issues attendant to those beliefs (e.g., existence of the soul, metaphysical realism, critiques of foundationalism), very seriously, and have made assessments of those arguments an important part of their professional work. These include Rowe, Nagel, Monton, Paul Draper, Quentin Smith, Wes Morriston, Richard Gale, and Graham Oppy, and Michael Tooley. Smith, for example, writes in a 2001 piece in the journal *Philo*:

> The secularization of mainstream academia began to quickly unravel upon the publication of Plantinga's influential book on realist theism, *God and Other Minds*, in 1967. It became apparent to the philosophical profession that this book displayed that realist theists were not outmatched by naturalists in terms of the most valued standards of analytic philosophy: conceptual precision, rigor of argumentation, technical erudition, and an in-depth defense of an original world-view. This book, followed seven years later by Plantinga's even more impressive book, *The Nature of Necessity*, made it manifest that a realist theist was writing at the highest qualitative level of analytic philosophy, on the same playing field as Carnap, Russell, Moore, Grünbaum, and other naturalists. Realist theists, whom hitherto had segregated their academic lives from their private lives, increasingly came to believe (and came to be increasingly accepted or respected for believing) that arguing for realist theism in scholarly publications could no longer be justifiably regarded as engaging in an "academically unrespectable" scholarly pursuit.
>
> Naturalists passively watched as realist versions of theism, most influenced by Plantinga's writings, began to sweep through the philosophical community, until today perhaps one-quarter or one-third of philosophy professors are theists, with most being orthodox Christians. Although many theists do not work in the area of the philosophy of religion, so many of them do work in this area that there are now over five philosophy journals devoted to theism or the philosophy of religion, such as *Faith and Philosophy*, *Religious Studies*, *International Journal of the Philosophy of Religion*, *Sophia*, *Philosophia Christi*, etc. *Philosophia Christi* began in the late 1990s and already is overflowing with submissions from leading philosophers ... [I]n philosophy, it became, almost overnight, "academically respectable" to argue for theism, making philosophy a favored field of entry for the most intelligent and talented theists entering academia today. A count would show that in Oxford University Press' 2000–2001 catalogue, there are ninety-six recently published books on the philosophy of religion (ninety-four advancing theism and two presenting "both sides"). By contrast, there are twenty-eight books

he provides no actual examples, but demurs by conscripting for his purposes a quote from a nonacademic article authored by Alex Byrne,[81] an accomplished MIT philosopher with no expertise in philosophy of religion. Thus, it is not surprising that Byrne's article gets many things wrong about contemporary philosophy and its relation to the rationality of theistic belief.[82]

This, unfortunately, will not come as a shock to those well versed in the recent history of academic philosophy. As one of my former graduate school professors, the late W. Norris Clarke, S.J., pointed out in 1970,[83] the tragic unfamiliarity among anti-theistic philosophers with just one of the most famous arguments for God's existence, the cosmological argument,[84] is truly astonishing. After surveying the rampant intellectual poverty among critics of theism, Fr. Clarke concludes that "we are here in the presence of a philosophical tradition that is truly in a self repetitive rut, a tradition that has long since ceased to look outside of itself to check with reality and see whether the adversary it so triumphantly and effortlessly demolishes really exists at all."[85] Although things are generally better in the early twenty-first century than they were in 1970, some segments of academic philosophy still have a learning curve to overcome.

Take, for example, Leiter's reference to "Neo-Thomism" as one of the two "intellectualist" schools of thought found among serious religious believers that come to his mind.[86] (The other school of thought Leiter mentions is "Paley's 'natural theology,'" which may or may not refer to the work of philosophers like Richard Swinburne or William Lane Craig who are strong proponents of non-Thomistic natural theology arguments. But we don't know, because Leiter doesn't tell us. Because there is no "Paleyan" school in contemporary philosophy of religion, we are left to wonder.) Leiter asserts that "Neo-Thomist arguments" are one of a few "intellectualist" traditions in "religious thought … according to which religious beliefs (for example, belief in a Creator or, as in

in this catalogue on the philosophy of language, twenty-three on epistemology (including religious epistemology, such as Plantinga's *Warranted Christian Belief*), fourteen on metaphysics, sixty-one books on the philosophy of mind, and fifty-one books on the philosophy of science. (Quentin Smith, "The Metaphilosophy of Naturalism," *Philo* 4.2 [2001]).

[81] "[I]t is fair to say that the arguments [for God's existence] have left the philosophical community underwhelmed. The classic contemporary work is J. L. Mackie's *The Miracle of Theism*, whose ironic title summarizes Mackie's conclusion: the persistence of belief in God is a kind of miracle because it is so unsupported by reason and evidence." (Alex Byrne, "God," *Boston Review of Books* [January/February 2009], available at http://www.bostonreview.net/BR34.1/byrne.php, as quoted in Leiter, *Why Tolerate Religion?*, 80).

[82] See William Lane Craig, "Byrne on Theistic Philosophers," EPS Blog (5 January 2009), http://blog.epsociety.org/2009/01/byrne-on-theistic-philosophers.asp.

[83] W. Norris Clarke, S.J., "A Curious Blind Spot in the Anglo-American Tradition of Antitheistic Argument," *The Monist* 54.2 (April 1970): 181–200.

[84] There are, of course, several cosmological arguments, not just one. Fr. Clarke's article focused on the style of cosmological argument associated with St. Thomas Aquinas.

[85] Clarke, "A Curious Blind Spot," 197.

[86] Leiter, *Why Tolerate Religion?*, 39.

America recently, belief in 'an intelligent designer') are, in fact, supported by the kinds of evidence adduced in the sciences, once that evidence is rightly interpreted."[87] This, as we shall see, is not how Neo-Thomists (or even Thomists in general) conceive of their philosophical project. In fact, as I note extensively in Chapter 6 when I deal with the issue of Intelligent Design (ID), Thomists (and Neo-Thomists) are at the forefront in critiquing projects like ID, *precisely because* advocates mistakenly appeal to the deliverances of the hard sciences to support theological and philosophical questions that Thomists believe are by their nature outside of the purview of those sciences.

The Thomist, of course, does not deny that the impressive successes of the hard sciences are arguably the greatest accomplishments of the modern world. However, the quantifiable and measurable insights delivered by those sciences have very little to do with answering the metaphysical questions that philosophies like Thomism are attempting to answer. Take, for example, just the Thomist distinction between potency and act. Originally offered by Aristotle to account for the metaphysical problem of the apparent reality of change raised by Parmenides and Heraclitus (each of whom offered contrary answers), it was picked up by St. Thomas and other Scholastic thinkers. According to Aquinas, all things in the universe are a combination of act and potency, meaning that there is something actual about each thing – for example, this is an actual human being and he is *actually* brown-haired – and something potential about each thing – for example, this an actual human being and he is *potentially* gray-haired – given the nature of the sort of thing it is. But there are different types of potencies. Thus, an actual human being has the *intrinsic* potential to become gray as he ages, but he does not have the intrinsic potential to develop eagle wings. He could acquire them by surgery or by some weird experiment, but because he is a human being, he is not by nature intrinsically ordered to acquire eagle wings. Thus, we say that he has an *extrinsic* potential to acquire eagle wings. But regardless of whether the potential is intrinsic or extrinsic, something actual has to be the efficient cause for whatever potential to be actualized. In the case of the gray hair, the efficient cause may be the person's genes or some combination of genes, stress, and/or physical conditions (such as sleep and nutrition). In the case of the eagle wings, the efficient cause is the scientist who performs the surgery or experiments on the patient. Thus, for the Thomist, because every particular thing in the universe moves from potency to act – regardless of whether that movement involves substantial change (e.g., when the oak tree becomes a desk or the cow becomes a meal) or accidental change (e.g., when a human being's hair goes from brown to gray or he loses it altogether) – and because there cannot be an infinite regress of *per se* efficient causes moving things from potency to act, there must exist a Being of Pure Actuality, God, a Necessary Being that requires no cause to account for His existence. There is, of course, far more to the argument than what I have briefly

---

[87] Ibid.

sketched here, as its esteemed supporters have maintained.[88] My point, however, is not to defend that argument, but merely to show that its plausibility –
as with the entirety of Thomistic philosophy – does not require support "by
the kinds of evidence adduced in the sciences,"[89] as Leiter claims. This is why
the Thomistic argument we just sketched does not depend on whether science
has proven or disproven whether the universe had a beginning or has always
existed. For the Thomist, an eternally existing universe would still require a
Creator, because it is the impossibility of a *per se* infinite regress of causes and
not a *per accidens* infinite regress of causes that is central to the argument.
As Edward Feser notes (citing Patterson Brown and John Wippel), "[E]ven if
a series of causes ordered per se could somehow be said to regress to infinity,
it would remain the case, given that they are merely instrumental causes, that
there must then be something outside the entire infinite series that imparts to
them their causal power."[90]

Thus, unlike *some* versions of the Kalam Cosmological Argument – that
require scientific evidence for the universe's beginning in time – or arguments
for ID (which we will cover in Chapter 6) – that require gaps in scientific law
and randomness to show that certain natural phenomena were the result of
an intelligent designer – the Thomistic argument sketched here does not need
the assistance of science. This, as I have already noted, is also true of the entire
Thomistic enterprise. For the central categories employed in that project – such
as act/potency, form/matter, substance/accident, genus/species, essence/exis-
tence, formal/efficient/material/final causes – are metaphysical categories.

Leiter does briefly mention the possibility that metaphysics may be central
to a religious worldview, but he completely ignores the sort of analysis that we
just briefly sketched, and refers only to what he calls "*a metaphysics of ultimate reality.*"[91] He claims that "such a metaphysics seems to be distinguished,
in part, by the relationship in which it stands to the *empirical evidence of the
sciences*: namely, that such a view about the 'essence' or 'ultimate nature' of
things neither *claims support from empirical evidence* nor *purports to be constrained by empirical evidence* (its claims 'transcend' the empirical evidence,
hence its 'metaphysical' character)."[92] For this reason, Leiter concludes that
this metaphysics of ultimate reality "seems only to be a variation on the idea
that religious belief is *insulated* from evidence – insulated not only in the sense
that it does not answer to empirical evidence but also in the sense that it does
not even aspire to answer to such evidence."[93]

---

[88] See, e.g., Barry Miller, *From Existence to God: A Contemporary Philosophical Argument*
(New York: Routledge, 1992); Feser, *The Last Superstition*, 90–119.
[89] Leiter, *Why Tolerate Religion?*, 39.
[90] Edward Feser, *Aquinas: A Beginner's Guide* (Oxford: Oneworld, 2009), 72.
[91] Leiter, *Why Tolerate Religion?*, 47 (emphasis in original).
[92] Ibid (emphasis in original).
[93] Ibid (emphasis in original).

There is, of course, a sense in which a metaphysical system such as Thomism is a metaphysics of ultimate reality, because it embraces the idea that God is "subsistent existence,"[94] that He is not merely the greatest being, but Being Itself, that on which all contingent reality depends. But it would be a mistake to claim, as Leiter does, that such a conclusion is "nonempirical" and insulated from the evidence. For, as I noted earlier in my brief presentation of Aquinas's cosmological argument, the Thomist, as a good Aristotelian, is to a fault empirical, for he starts with sense experience while drawing on metaphysical categories for which he offers separate arguments,[95] and concludes that God exists. But this is true not only of the Thomist. As I have already extensively noted earlier, theists, from differing philosophical traditions, offer many arguments for their metaphysical beliefs (including ultimate ones) that rely on premises that include a variety of empirical claims, some of which have been challenged by critics, which shows, contra Leiter, that these beliefs are hardly "insulated from the evidence."

Perhaps what Leiter means by empirical evidence is what he calls the "empirical evidence of the sciences."[96] That is, Leiter may be claiming that any evidence outside of science is not really evidence. If that is what he means, then his position is just a form of *scientism*, the view "that science alone plausibly gives us objective knowledge, and that any metaphysics worthy of consideration can only be that which is implicitly in *science*."[97] In that case, not only is Leiter begging the question (i.e., he assumes, without argument, that the methods of science are appropriate to assessing metaphysical claims that do not in fact touch on the claims of science), the standard he seems to presuppose as uncontroversially true – that "science alone plausibly gives us objective knowledge, and that any metaphysics worthy of consideration can only be that which is implicitly in science"[98] – is itself not a deliverance of science. In other words, when someone like Leiter distinguishes rational enterprises (i.e., science) from nonrational enterprises (i.e., religion), he grounds his judgment in what he believes are the necessary and sufficient conditions of what constitutes a rational enterprise. But that judgment is no more a deliverance of science than is the judgment that "hip hop is not poetry" a deliverance of either hip hop or poetry. It is an exercise in philosophical reasoning about first principles of rational thought, what was once called "first philosophy." Thus, ironically,

---

[94] St Thomas Aquinas, *On Being and Essence*, trans. Robert T. Miller (1997) (Internet Medievel Sourcebook), available at http://www.fordham.edu/halsall/basis/aquinas-esse.asp.

[95] See, e.g., Edward Feser, *Scholastic Metaphysics: A Contemporary Introduction* (Neunkirchen-Seelscheid, Germany: Editiones Scholasticae, 2014) and Oderberg, *Real Essentialism*.

[96] This is probably the case given his work calling for the naturalizing of jurisprudence. See Brian Leiter, *Naturalizing Jurisprudence: Essays on American Legal Realism and Naturalism in Legal Philosophy* (Oxford: Oxford University Press, 2007). However, he is much more explicit in defending "scientism" in his highly critical review of Nagel's *Mind and Cosmos*: Brian Leiter and Michael Weisberg, "Do You Only Have a Brain?," *The Nation* (22 October, 2012): 27–31.

[97] Feser, *Scholastic Metaphysics*, 9–10.

[98] Ibid.

Leiter's scientism insulates him from even entertaining the sorts of arguments and evidence that many philosophers have taken seriously for generations and continue to do so. This puts Leiter in precisely the same position of intellectual openness as the straw theists to which he attributes invincible ignorance.

This is why Leiter, in a very brief critique of an argument by neo-Thomist John Finnis, gets Finnis's argument wrong. In a 2009 article,[99] which had been delivered as the annual John Dewey Lecture in March of that year at the University of Minnesota Law School, Finnis briefly summarizes a cosmological argument for God's existence, an argument that he had already presented in much greater detail in three different books.[100] It is that argument that Leiter claims to critique.

One cannot do better than Mark C. Murphy's brief presentation of this argument:[101] "Finnis ... [holds] that reason suggests that we pursue adequate explanations of the obtaining of contingent states of affairs and that no such explanation could be satisfactory until we reach an uncaused causing, some-thing whose existence is self-sufficient – Finnis calls it 'D' – a being the nature of which includes its existing, so that it could not not be."[102] Like the Thomistic cosmological argument we have already sketched, Finnis's argument does not depend on the deliverances of science, but rather on the contingent nature of reality and its calling out for an ultimate explanation that is itself not con-tingent. In other words, whether the universe is made up of quarks, strings, or atoms, or some other alleged irreducible entity, makes no difference to the metaphysical judgment that whatever physics (or some other science) tells us about the fundamental material nature of the contingent universe, it is still con-tingent. (For example, the impossibility of a perpetual motion machine does not depend on the material nature of its parts – whether it is made of cheese, wood, or cookie dough, or some combination. Rather, it depends on the nature of the machine *as a machine*.)

---

[99] John Finnis, "Does Free Exercise of Religion Deserve Constitutional Mention?," *American Journal of Jurisprudence* 54 (2009): 41–66.

[100] Writes Finnis:

> This thesis is consistent with the kind of argument I develop in all chapters save the last in my *Natural Law and Natural Rights* [Oxford: Clarendon, 1980] and *Fundamentals of Ethics* [Washington, DC: Georgetown University Press, 1983] – the argument that practical reason's first principles can be understood and acknowledged, and their normative implications exten-sively unfolded into rich, substantive moral, political and legal theory, without relying upon, presupposing, or even adverting to, the existence of God or providential order. *But*: if it is true, as I argue in the final chapter of each of those books, and of my *Aquinas* book, and have out-lined again today, that the rationality norms which guide us in all our fruitful thinking also, and integrally, summon us to affirm the existence and providence of God, then we should expect that refusals to make such an affirmation will rest on arguments, or to other considerations, which do not leave reason, including practical reason, intact and undistorted. (Ibid., 56).

[101] Murphy is summarizing the chapter-long version of Finnis's cosmological argument found in *Natural Law and Natural Rights*, chapter XIII.

[102] Mark C. Murphy, "Finnis on Nature, Reason, and God," *Legal Theory* 13 (2007): 192.

In order to justify the intellectual movement from contingent reality to uncaused cause, Finnis claims to rely on the "rationality norms which guide us in all our fruitful thinking ..."[103] What does he mean by "rationality norms"? In the Thomist school from which Finnis hails, "rationality norms" is a term of art that has its contemporary origin in a book (authored by Joseph M. Boyle, Germain Grisez, and Olaf Tollefsen)[104] to which Finnis gives credit in his own two books, *Natural Law and Natural Rights* (1980)[105] and *Fundamentals of Ethics* (1982),[106] both of which he mentions explicitly in his 2009 article as the places the reader should look to find a more detailed presentation of his case.[107] According to Boyle et. al, "In rationally affirming a proposition, one assumes rationality norms, not as premises from which one might deduce conclusions about the world, but as licenses or warrants legitimating the moves one makes in taking one proposition rather than its contradictory as more likely to be true of the world."[108] That is, if one is committed to pursuing the truth, whether in science, law, theology, mathematics, logic, history, or casino gambling, one's enterprise cannot even get off the ground without principles that provide direction to one's reasoning. For instance, Finnis mentions this rationality norm: "an adequate explanatory reason why something is so rather than otherwise is to be expected, unless one has a reason not to expect such an explanatory reason."[109] So, for example, suppose someone asks you why America chose to enter, rather than not enter, World War II. The questioner, in pursuing the truth of the matter, is guided by the norm that an adequate explanatory reason is to be expected. By contrast, suppose someone asks you why the number 3 is taller than the color blue. That same norm tells you that given the natures of numbers and colors, you should not expect an explanatory reason for that question. When it comes to his cosmological argument, all that Finnis is suggesting is that this rationality norm, because we apply it without controversy to a panoply of other endeavors in which we pursue the truth, should be applied without controversy to the contingent universe as a whole.

Other rationality norms, according to Boyle et al., include the following: "A full description of the data is to be preferred to a partial description. A generalization based on meticulous observation is to be accepted. Logical principles are to be adhered to in all one's thinking, even when doing so requires one to give up beliefs based on experience. Any view which meets the criteria of simplicity, predictive success, and explanatory power ... is to be accepted.... A method of interpretation which is successful is to be relied upon

---

[103] Finnis, "Free Exercise of Religion," 56.

[104] Joseph M. Boyle, Jr., Germain Grisez, and Olaf Tollefsen, *Free Choice: A Self-Referential Argument* (Notre Dame, IN: University of Notre Dame Press, 1976).

[105] Finnis, *Natural Law and Natural Rights*, 78, citing Ibid., 144–152, 168–177.

[106] Finnis, *Fundamentals of Ethics*, 152, citing Boyle, Grisez, and Tollefsen, *Free Choice*, 144–152.

[107] See footnote 100.

[108] Boyle, Grisez, and Tollefsen, *Free Choice*, 145.

[109] Finnis, "Free Exercise of Religion," 47.

in further, similar cases."[110] Finnis's lists track the one offered by Boyle et al., with slightly different emphases. Here are some rationality norms (in addition to the one already mentioned) found in Finnis's works: "[S]elf-referentially inconsistent theses are to be abandoned ..."[111] "[T]he principles of logic, for example, the forms of deductive inference, are to be used and adhered to in all of one's thinking, even though no non-circular proof of their validity is possible (because any proof would employ them).... [P]henomenona are to be regarded as real unless there is some reason to distinguish between appearance and reality."[112]

Leiter seems to think that when Finnis mentions rationality norms he is merely writing about the "epistemic norms operative in scientific practice," and for this reason, Leiter is shocked to find that "the literature is not in evidence in Finnis's discussion."[113] Because Leiter does not seem to see the role rationality norms play in Finnis's argument, his critique not only misses its mark, it actually helps establish Finnis's point. Writes Leiter:

> To the extent we expect that phenomena have causal determinants it is because of *past experience*, because it has turned out so often (at least since the Scientific Revolution) that things that seemed inexplicable actually have causes. It is not a norm of rationality – Finnis has no account of these – that things we observe are explicable in terms of antecedent causes; it is an inductive inference based on past success. It is clearly defeasible, which belies its purported status as a "norm of rationality": no one is unreasonable should they conclude that a particular phenomenon is a product of chance (chance, itself, being an object of study since the scientific revolution, but put that to one side). *Norms* of rationality, one might have thought, have the feature that should you violate them you are, necessarily, *unreasonable*. But since it is reasonable – that is, since it answers to norms of rationality and evidence – to sometimes conclude that a particular phenomenon is purely a "product" of chance, it would follow that there is no "norm of rationality" at work here.[114]

---

[110] Boyle, Grisez, and Tollefsen, *Free Choice*, 144.

[111] John Finnis, "Historical Consciousness and Theological Foundations," in *Religion & Public Reasons, Collected Essays: Volume V* by John Finnis (New York: Oxford University Press, 2011), 151. This chapter was originally delivered in 1992 as that year's Etienne Gilson Lecture at the University of Toronto: John Finnis, "'Historical Consciousness' and Theological Foundations" (Etienne Gilson Series no. 14, Pontifical Institute of Mediaeval Studies, Toronto, 1992). Special thanks to both Christopher Tollefsen (Philosophy Department, University of South Carolina) and J. Budziszewski (Philosophy and Government Departments, University of Texas, Austin) for bringing this lecture to my attention in email correspondence during the week of 28 July 2014.

[112] Finnis, *Natural Law and Natural Rights*, 68.

[113] Leiter, *Why Tolerate Religion?*, 88.

[114] Ibid., 89. Note that Leiter seems to be walking right into the problem of induction here, unless he takes it to be a priori that the future is more likely to resemble the past than not. But in that case he would be employing a rationality norm to guide his inquiry. (Special thanks to my Baylor colleague and first-rate epistemologist, Trent Dougherty, for providing me with some valuable feedback on this discussion of rationality norms).

No doubt Leiter is correct that a scientist, while investigating some phenomenon, for example, Fiore "Jimmy" Casella being dealt a promising hand in the 1974 World Series of Poker in Las Vegas,[115] may conclude that what results is a product of chance. (Finnis, by the way, *does not deny* that the mind may reasonably believe that some phenomena are the products of chance.)[116] But for such an investigation to even get off the ground – to properly take aim at the truth, so to speak – certain methodological principles, that is, norms of rationality, must be employed to guide the scientist's reasoning and justify his moves. This is why the scientist does not conclude that what results from chance is uncaused, because, after all, even chance occurrences, such as promising poker hands, require ontological preconditions – for example, efficient and material causes and scientific laws – that make the occurrences possible. (For this reason, it is strange for Leiter to claim that chance undermines Finnis' causal principle). Thus, the mind that makes the observation that X is the result of chance must be a mind that presupposes certain rationality norms, including the specific rationality norm that is central to Finnis's argument: "an adequate explanatory reason why something is so rather than otherwise is to be expected, unless one has a reason not to expect such an explanatory reason."[117] In fact, this explanatory rationality norm, ironically, is behind Leiter's account of the nature of science. To see this, consider Leiter's claim that any confidence we may have in causal claims in science depends on "an inductive inference based on past success."[118] In order to provide license or warrant for this move (to use the language of Boyle et al.), Leiter's reasoning must be guided by certain rationality norms, not only including the one of Finnis's just mentioned, but also some of those offered by Boyle et al. as well: "A full description of the data is to be preferred to a partial description. A generalization based on meticulous observation is to be accepted. Logical principles are to be adhered to in all one's thinking, even when doing so requires one to give up beliefs based on experience. Any view which meets the criteria of simplicity, predictive success, and explanatory power ... is to be accepted....

[115] Fiore "Jimmy" Casella (1924–1976) was my uncle by marriage. He was married to my father's eldest sister, Doris Beckwith (1927–2000).

[116] Writes Finnis: "Chance, of course, there is aplenty in a world where events and processes, each of which has its own intelligible explanation(s), coincide. But science progresses constantly by treating chance as the residuum of coincidence in a domain dominated by what is explicable because it is not by chance." (Finnis, "Free Exercise of Religion," 47). That is, "chance" requires a cluster of background beliefs about the intelligibility of nature itself. Thus, the only way that I can reasonably say that phenomenon X is a product of chance is that I know that nature left to its own devices would not necessarily produce X. But those "devices," the natural order and its laws, are not "chance," but the intelligible order that makes chance possible. When, for example, I throw a pair of dice, what results is a product of chance. But not "purely" a product of chance, as Leiter supposes. For the dice and the conceptual framework by which I assess the throw must be ordered so that I can make the "chance" judgment.

[117] Finnis, "Free Exercise of Religion," 47.

[118] Leiter, *Why Tolerate Religion?*, 89.

A method of interpretation which is successful is to be relied upon in further, similar cases."[119] Without these rationality norms, or at least ones similar to them, it is difficult to imagine why anyone should think that Leiter's account of the nature of science is better than any of its rivals. After all, the critic can pose the following questions. Is Leiter's view based on the fullest description of the data? Is his generalization based on meticulous observation? Does it rely on logical principles? Is it more simple, pedictive, and explanatory than its competitors? Absent persuasive answers to these queries, it is not clear why anyone should accept Leiter's account. So, even if Leiter's claim were correct – that *any confidence we may have in causal claims in science depends on "an inductive inference based on past success"*[120] – it would seem reasonable for one to withhold acceptance of Leiter's claim until one were first satisfied that it adequately answered these queries. But the rationality norms assumed in these questions are not deliverances of science, nor can they be, for they are methodological principles that guide, and are thus *presupposed*, in all truth-seeking enterprises (such as science), including Leiter's philosophical investigation about the nature of science. Because Finnis's rationality norms cannot be cabined by scientism, despite Leiter's best efforts, he does not seem to see Finnis's point and thus cannot adequately critique Finnis's case. So, what Fr. Clarke had said about his contemporaries in 1970 can be said about Leiter and his fellow travelers today: "[W]e are here in the presence of a philosophical tradition that is truly in a self repetitive rut, a tradition that has long since ceased to look outside of itself to check with reality and see whether the adversary it so triumphantly and effortlessly demolishes really exists at all."[121]

In the other place in which Leiter appears to seriously engage an identifiable philosophical school of thought that supports the rationality of theism, Reformed Epistemology,[122] he actually does not engage it at all. Leiter, as I have already noted, merely assumes as correct a negative judgment of Reformed Epistemology that he attributes to "most philosophers," even though he does not back up that claim with any data, does not explain why the thinking of "most philosophers" (most of whom are not experts in the appropriate philosophical specialties) provides sufficient warrant to discard by assumption an entire philosophical school of thought, and does not offer evidence that "most philosophers" have such an informed understanding of Reformed Epistemology that this *argumentum ad populum* is not just a fallacious appeal to authority. Moreover, Leiter ignores the fact that there are many *theist* philosophers who

---

[119] Boyle, Grisez, and Tollefsen, *Free Choice*, 144.
[120] Leiter, *Why Tolerate Religion?*, 89.
[121] Clarke, "A Curious Blind Spot," 197.
[122] As I already noted in the text, Leiter writes: "I am going to assume – uncontroversially among most philosophers but controversially among reformed epistemologists – that 'reformed epistemology' is nothing more than an effort to insulate religious faith from ordinary standards of reasons and evidence in common sense and the sciences, and thus religious belief is a culpable form of unwarranted belief given those ordinary epistemic standards." (Ibid., 81).

are critical of Reformed Epistemology, although they argue, on other grounds, for the rationality of theism (and in most cases, Christianity in particular).[123] These theists, although they may be among Leiter's "most philosophers," are not among those philosophers like Leiter who believe that religious belief is irrational.

### 2.2.B.2. *Religious Claims Are Incontestable*

As I noted in Section 2.2.A, the idea that a belief must not be incontestable in order to be rationally held is self-referentially incoherent, and there are numerous beliefs that are rational to hold even though they are incontestable or nearly so. In addition, much of the Christian philosophical and historical arguments surveyed in the previous section (2.2.B.1) are driven by the fact that Christian beliefs are in fact contestable! Thus, the charge of incontestability is wildly off the mark.

### 2.2.B.3. *Religious Claims Cannot Change or Develop Because They Are Insulated from the Ordinary Standards of Evidence and Rational Justification*

What are the ordinary standards of evidence and rational justification? As I noted in Section 2.2.B.1, it depends. Evidence and rational justification are different for metaphysics, history, epistemology, and ethics than they are for chemistry, physics, or medical pathology. Because religious claims rely more on the deliverances of the former group than the latter, Leiter, as I have already noted, is mistaken when he faults religious claims for being insulated from the "standards of evidence and reasons in the sciences."[124] It's like saying that Baseball is not a sport because it doesn't have a twenty-four-second clock like the National Basketball Association.

Claims in literature, morality, law, and philosophy are rarely within the purview of the natural sciences, but that hardly makes them irrational. It seems perfectly rational, as I noted in Section 2.2.A, to say that it is wrong always and everywhere to torture children for fun, even though it is not a belief established by any science. In fact, the claim that it is irrational to hold a belief insulated from "standards of evidence and reasons in the sciences" is itself not a deliverance of any science. Thus, on its own grounds it is irrational.

Moreover, as we noted in our assessment of Leiter's critique of Finnis, in order for any type of truth seeking enterprise (including science) to even get off the ground it must assume or presuppose certain methodological principles (or rationality norms) that are not themselves the deliverances of that enterprise. Science,

---

[123] See, for example, Trent Dougherty and Chris Tweedt, "Religious Epistemology," *Philosophy Compass* 10/8 (2015), 547–559, 10.1111/phc3.12185; Linda Zagzebski, ed., *Rational Faith: Catholic Responses to Reformed Epistemology* (Notre Dame, IN: University of Notre Dame Press, 1993); and Swinburne, *Faith & Reason.*

[124] Leiter, *Why Tolerate Religion?*, 38.

however, given its nature and projects, requires other presuppositions. As the philosopher John Kekes notes:

Science is committed to several presuppositions: that nature exists, that it has discoverable order, that it is uniform, are existential presuppositions of science; the distinctions between space and time, cause and effect, the observer and the observed, real and apparent, orderly and chaotic, are classificatory presuppositions; while intersubjective testability, quantifiability, the public availability of data, are methodological presuppositions; some axiological presuppositions are the honest reporting of results, the worthwhileness of getting the facts right, and scrupulousness in avoiding observational or experimental error. If any one of these presuppositions were abandoned, science, as we know it, could not be done. Yet the acceptance of the presuppositions cannot be a matter of course, for each has been challenged and alternatives are readily available.[125]

Consequently, if the sciences require presuppositions that cannot themselves be deliverances of the sciences, and the sciences are rational enterprises, then we have another reason not to believe that the "standards of evidence and reasons in the sciences" are the only basis by which to assess the rationality of a belief.

There are, of course, standards of evidence and reasons that are proper to the sciences. So, perhaps what the SR advocate is claiming is that there are beliefs held by some religious believers that the believers claim are established by science, even though they champion those beliefs without proper regard to the standards of evidence and reasons of the sciences. Given the examples proffered by Sherry[126] and Leiter,[127] I suspect that's what the SR advocate means. But that's a criticism of the intellectual integrity of *the believer*, and ironically, only makes sense as a judgment of the believer's character if in fact the belief in question is *not* the sort

---

[125] John Kekes, *The Nature of Philosophy* (Totowa, NJ: Rowman & Littlefield, 1980), 156–157.

[126] Sherry, in a footnote, says that what she has "in mind [are] such beliefs as creationism, see, e.g., Edwards v. Aguillard 482 U.S. 578 (1987), faith healing; Lundman v. McKown 530 N.W. 2d 807 (Minn. Ct. App. 1995), cert. denied, 116 S. Ct. 814, 828 (1996) ..."

[127] Leiter writes (some which I have already quoted in the text):

Even here, of course, we need to be careful. There are, for example, "intellectualist" traditions in religious thought – Paley's "natural theology" or neo-Thomist arguments come to mind – according to which religious beliefs (for example, belief in a Creator or, as in America recently, belief in "an intelligent designer") are, in fact, supported by the kinds of evidence adduced in the sciences, once that evidence is rightly interpreted. It is doubtful, though, whether these intellectualist traditions capture the character of popular religious belief, the typical epistemic attitudes of religious believers ... But even putting popular religious belief to one side, there remain important senses in which intellectualist traditions are still *insulated from evidence*. First, of course, it is dubious (to put the matter gently) that these positions are really serious about following the evidence where it leads, as opposed to manipulating it to fit preordained ends. Second, and relatedly, in the case of the sciences, beliefs based on evidence are also *revisable* in light of the evidence; but in the intellectualist traditions in religious thought just noted, it never turns out that the fundamental beliefs are revised in light of new evidence. The whole exercise is one of post-hoc rationalization, as is no doubt obvious to those outside the sectarian tradition. Religious beliefs are *purportedly* supported by evidence, but they are still insulated from revision *in light of evidence*. (Leiter, *Why Tolerate Religion?*, 39–40; note omitted).

of belief that can or should be insulated from standards of evidence and reasons of the sciences.

But what's good for the goose is good the gander. Remember, the SR advocate also claims to ground his position on "common sense"[128] and that "the source and evidence for the truth lie in common human observation, experience, and reasoning,"[129] decrying that which is "impervious to ... empirical analysis ..."[130] But some views that claim to be consistent with SR and the deliverances of modern science seem not only inconsistent with common sense, experience, and reasoning, but incapable of being refuted by such avenues of knowledge. Take, for example, thinkers, such as Paul Churchland, who maintain that modern science establishes the truth of philosophical materialism, and thus we have no grounds to believe in any immaterial realities, including souls or minds. Writes Churchland: "The important point about the standard evolutionary story is that the human species and all of its features are the wholly physical outcome of a purely physical process.... If this is the correct account of our origins, then there seems neither need, nor room, to fit any non-physical substances or properties into our theoretical account of ourselves. We are creatures of matter. And we should learn to live with that fact."[131] But there is a sense in which this is inconsistent with common sense, experience, and reasoning. For Churchland intends his statements to be about something, which means his powers of reasoning allow him to grasp ideas that provide warrant for the propositional content of his statements. But the relationship between these ideas is logical, not spatial or material, and the power to grasp and offer these ideas as reasons for a conclusion requires intentionality, an ofness or aboutness (e.g., "This thought is about materialism"), something that cannot be had by a physical state. For this reason, Churchland maintains that intentionality and all our mental states literally do not exist.[132]

Churchland also tells us that "we should learn to live" with materialism, implying that we intellectually err if we do not do what we *ought to* do. This seems to be grounded in the more primitive notion that our mental powers are ordered toward the acquisition of truth, and thus to frustrate that end is inconsistent with our good. But such a normative judgment – grounded in

---

[128] Ibid., 34.

[129] Sherry, "Enlightening the Religion Clauses," 478.

[130] Gey, "Life After the Establishment Clause," 11.

[131] Paul Churchland, *Matter and Consciousness* (Cambridge, MA: MIT Press, 1984), 21.

[132] Paul Churchland, "Eliminative Materialism and the Propositional Attitudes," *Journal of Philosophy* 78 (1981): 67–90. Writes Churchland, "Eliminative materialism is the thesis that our common-sense conception of psychological phenomena constitutes a radically false theory, a theory so fundamentally defective that both the principles and the ontology of that theory will eventually be displaced, rather than smoothly reduced, by completed neuroscience. Our mutual understanding and even our introspection may then be reconstituted within the conceptual framework of completed neuroscience, a theory we may expect to be more powerful by far than the common-sense psychology it displaces, and more substantially integrated within physical science generally" (Ibid., 67).

ends and goods – implies final causality, which, like all our mental states, has no place in Churchland's materialism. Yet, despite its apparent inconsistency with common sense, experience, and reasoning, Churchland, like many other philosophical materialists who hold similar views, has not abandoned his materialism. (In Chapter 6, I explain how Richard Dawkins makes a similar mistake.)

Does it follow from this that Churchland's unwavering posture – seeming to contravene common sense, experience, and reasoning – means that philosophical materialism, or at least Churchland's version of it, is insulated from the ordinary standards of evidence and rational justification, and is therefore irrational? It depends. If one treats modern science as the measure of rationality, and if one believes that modern science requires belief in philosophical materialism, and philosophical materialism seems to be inconsistent with common sense, experience, and reasoning, then common sense, experience, and reasoning may not be rational. So, to be insulated from common sense, experience, and reasoning is not to be insulated from the ordinary standards of evidence and rational justification. And thus, Churchland's position is "rational." On the other hand, if one believes, as Gey, Sherry, and Leiter apparently do, that common sense, experience, and reasoning are of a piece with the standards and methods of modern science as well as the ordinary standards of evidence and rational justification, then philosophical materialism, or at least Churchland's version of it, may not be rational.

The point here is that there are just too many philosophical considerations that have to be addressed before one can confidently suggest that a claim, religious or otherwise, is insulated form the ordinary standards of evidence and rational justification. Ironically, then, by ignoring these considerations, the SR advocate insulates his position from just the sort of criticisms that may count against SR.

Christian theism, however, has shown itself to be quite resilient in responding to and engaging internal and external challenges. It has long been argued by many Christian thinkers from a variety of traditions that the idea of doctrinal development – the progressive changing of beliefs over time in response to a variety of external and internal challenges and insights – is *integral* to the Christian faith.[133] Thus, it is a mystery how Gey, Sherry, and Leiter, all claiming to distill the "essence of religion," could have missed it. Consider just four examples from the history of Christianity.

(1) One of the most important developments in Christian thought occurred as a consequence of its encounter with Greek philosophy. As some scholars have

---

[133] For the classic modern Catholic and Protestant accounts of doctrinal development, see respectively, John Henry Cardinal Newman, *An Essay on the Development of Christina Doctrine*, rev ed. (1878), forward Ian Kerr (Notre Dame, IN: University of Notre Dame Press, 1989); and James Orr, *The Progress of Dogma* (London: Hotter and Stoughton, 1901).

noted,[134] most Christian thinkers in the Church's first six centuries, rather than seeing pagan philosophical traditions as a threat, conscripted their insights to such an extent that the Early Church was able to formulate its most important creeds and resolve what otherwise would have been intractable theological issues. Later on, as Christianity moved into the Middle Ages and into the modern period,[135] the Church's philosophical inheritance continued to play an important role in the development of dogmatic and moral theology. Ironically, some writers, claiming to offer a more "scientific" understanding of theology,[136] fault the Church for *not* insulating itself from the influence of Greek philosophy.

(2) St. Thomas Aquinas, relying almost exclusively on Aristotle's view of biology, held that the human fetus did not receive its rational soul until several weeks after conception.[137] It was for centuries the dominant view of the Catholic Church as well as for many non-Catholic Christians. But as the science of embryology discovered more about human development, and biology

---

[134] See, e.g., Pope Benedict XVI, "Faith, Reason, and the University: Memories and Reflections" (12 September 2006), available at http://www.vatican.va/holy_father/benedict_xvi/speeches/2006/september/documents/hf_ben-xvi_spe_20060912_university-regensburg_en.html; Joseph Koterski, S. J., "Stories Are Not Enough: The Church's Choice to Make Use of Greek Philosophy," *Fellowship of Catholic Scholars Quarterly* 37.1/2 (Spring/Summer 2014): 4–11; John Mark Reynolds, *When Athens Met Jerusalem: An Introduction to Classical and Christian Thought* (Downers Grove, IL: InterVarsity Press, 2009), 221–245; Joseph Cardinal Ratzinger, *Introduction to Christianity*, originally published in German in 1968, trans. J. R. Foster (1969), with a new preface trans. Michael J. Miller (San Francisco: Ignatius Press, 2004), 103–150.

[135] See, e.g., John M. Rist, *What is Truth?: From the Academy to the Vatican* (New York: Cambridge University Press, 2008); Etienne Gilson, *God and Philosophy* (New Haven, CT: Yale University Press, 1941); and Etienne Gilson, *History of Christian Philosophy in the Middle Ages* (New York: Random House, 1955).

[136] See, e.g., Adolf Harnack, *History of Dogma, Volume I*, trans. Neil Buchanan (Grand Rapids, MI: Christian Classics Ethereal Library, 1894) cf. C. Wayne Glick, "Nineteenth Century Theological and Cultural Influences on Adolf Harnack," *Church History* 28.2 (June 1959): 157–182.

[137] See, e.g., Benedict Ashley and Albert Moraczewski, "Cloning, Aquinas, and the Embryonic Person," *National Catholic Bioethics Quarterly* 1.2 (Summer 2001): 189–201. Ashley and Moraczewski write:

> Aquinas ... did not know that the matter out of which the human body is generated is already highly organized at conception and endowed with the efficient and formal causality necessary to organize itself into a system in which, as it matures, the brain becomes the principal adult organ. Hence he was forced to resort to the hypothesis that the male semen remains in the womb, gradually organizing the menstrual blood, first to the level of vegetative life and then to the level of animal life, so as to be capable of the further self-development needed for ensoulment. But he also supposed that this entire process from its initiation was teleologically (final cause) predetermined to produce a human person, not a vegetable, an infra-human animal, or a mere embryonic collection of independent cells. That is why the Catholic Church has always taught that even if it were true that personal ensoulment takes place sometime after conception, nevertheless abortion at any stage is a very grave sin against the dignity of a human *person* (Ibid., 200).

rejected Aristotle's *biological* views, the Church, although never discarding Aquinas's metaphysics, embraced the view that an individual human being, with a rational soul, begins at conception.[138]

(3) Although the theory of evolution has been widely accepted in the academy, it has been rejected by some segments of the religious world, most notably among some (but by no means all) Fundamentalist and conservative Evangelical Protestants.[139] Nevertheless, the wider Christian world has engaged evolution rather impressively, showing respect for the deliverances of the natural sciences while pressing for philosophical modesty and rigor on the part of materialists who mistakenly believe that evolution is a defeater to theism.[140] The Catholic Church, for instance, has dealt with the creation/evolution question by making important and careful distinctions between science, metaphysics, and biblical hermeneutics.[141] Some Catholic authors, thoroughly committed to the Church and its teachings, have made some valuable contributions in understanding the relationship between science and theology and why the proposals by certain segments of the Christian world – for example, creationism and ID – may not be fruitful approaches.[142] Other thinkers, from a variety of Christian traditions,

---

[138] See, e.g., *Catechism of the Catholic Church*, 26–49, 1877–1948, 2104–2109, 2331–2400; Pope John Paul II, *Evangelium Vitae: The Gospel of Life* (25 March 1995), available at http://www.vatican.va/holy_father/john_paul_ii/encyclicals/documents/hf_jp-ii_enc_25031995_evangelium-vitae_en.html; John Paul II, *Fides Et Ratio*, 44–45,

[139] One has to be careful here, for there is a wide spectrum of views among Evangelical Protestants. See, for example, the helpful article by Presbyterian pastor, Tim Keller, "Creation, Evolution, and Christian Laypeople," BioLogos White Paper (2009 November), available at http://biologos.org/uploads/projects/Keller_white_paper.pdf.

[140] The work of the Reformed philosopher, Alvin Plantinga, is particularly illuminating in this regard. See, e.g., Alvin Plantinga, *Where the Conflict Really Lies: Science, Religion, and Naturalism* (New York: Oxford University Press, 2012); Daniel C. Dennett and Alvin Plantinga, *Science and Religion: Are They Compatible?* (New York: Oxford University Press, 2010).

[141] See, e.g., Pope Pius XII, *Humani Generis* (12 August 1950), available at http://www.vatican.va/holy_father/pius_xii/encyclicals/documents/hf_p-xii_enc_12081950_humani-generis_en.html; Pope John Paul II, "Message to the Pontifical Academy of Sciences: On Evolution" (22 October 1996), available at http://www.ewtn.com/library/PAPALDOC/JP961022.HTM; and Joseph Cardinal Ratzinger, *"In the Beginning ...": A Catholic Understanding of the Story of Creation and the Fall*, trans. Boniface Ramsey (Grand Rapids, MI: Eerdmans, 1986).

[142] See, e.g., Etienne Gilson, *From Aristotle to Darwin and Back Again: A Journey in Final Causality, Species, and Evolution* (San Francisco: Ignatius Press, 2009; John Lyon trans., 1984; originally published in French in 1971); Brad S. Gregory, "Science Versus Religion? The Insights and Oversights of the 'New Atheists'," *Logos: A Journal of Catholic Thought* 12.4 (2009): 17–55; Sr. Damien Marie Savino, FSE, "Atheistic Science: The Only Option?," *Logos: A Journal of Catholic Thought and Culture* 12.4 (2009): 56–73; William E. Carroll, "At the Mercy of Chance? Evolution and the Catholic Tradition," *Revue des Questions Scientifiques* 177 (2006): 179–204; William E. Carroll, "Creation, Evolution, and Thomas Aquinas," *Revue des Questions Scientifiques* 171 (2000): 319–47; Michael W. Tkacz, "Thomas Aquinas vs. the Intelligent Designers: What Is God's Finger Doing in My Pre-Biotic Soup?" in *Intelligent Design: Science or Religion? Critical Perspectives*, ed. Robert M. Baird & Stuart E. Rosenbaum (Amherst, NY: Prometheus Books, 2007): 275–282; Michael Tkacz, "The

have advanced similar efforts,[143] although in some cases showing a bit more sympathy for ID or at least the theoretical issues raised by it (while, however, engaging its critics).[144]

What this shows is that Christian thinkers – regardless of where they may stand on the intersection of theology and science – are having an important conversation among themselves and with those critics outside their communities, precisely because they do not believe that their theological beliefs are insulated from external challenges that may lead to true development and better understanding.

(4) The relationship between Christianity, its moral and political theologies, and the idea of religious liberty has clearly changed over time. As the late Avery Cardinal Dulles, S.J. has pointed out, "The problem of religious freedom, as understood today, has emerged only since the Enlightenment. In the Middle Ages, no doubt, the Church tolerated or authorized practices that strike us today as inconsistent with due respect for religious freedom ..."[145] The changing cultural and political landscape of post-Reformation Western Europe called for Christians to reassess how they thought church and state should interact. But the Protestant and Catholic communities did not have the luxury of just affirming religious liberty by fiat. If they were to affirm it, it had to be consistent with Scripture and (in the case of Catholics) Tradition (including the Church's prior authoritative pronouncements) and thus a legitimate development of doctrine. If theology is truly a knowledge tradition – and thus must take account of, and not insulate itself from, serious intellectual and cultural challenges – thoughtful Christians had to proceed in this fashion. And they did. The Catholic Church, for instance, grounds its defense of religious liberty in

Retorsive Argument for Formal Cause and the Darwinian Account of Scientific Knowledge," *International Philosophical Quarterly* 43 (2003): 159–66; Feser, *Aquinas*, 36–51, 110–120; Mark Ryland, "Intelligent Design Theory," in *New Catholic Encyclopedia Supplement*, ed. Robert L. Fastiggi (Farmington Hills, MI: Gale Publishing, 2009), I: 470–478; James A. Sadowsky, S. J., "Did Darwin Destroy the Design Argument?," *International Philosophical Quarterly*, 28 (1988): 95–104; Avery Cardinal Dulles, S. J., "God and Evolution," *First Things* 176 (October 2007): 19–24; and Machuga, *In Defense of the Soul*.

143 See, e.g., Simon Conway Morris, *Life's Solution: Inevitable Humans in a Lonely Universe* (Cambridge, UK: Cambridge University Press, 2003); and Francis Collins, *The Language of God: A Scientist Presents Evidence for Belief* (New York: The Free Press, 2006).

144 See, e.g., Bruce L. Gordon and William A. Dembski, eds., *The Nature of Nature: Examining the Role of Naturalism in Science* (Wilmington, DE: ISI Books, 2011); Del Ratzsch, *Nature, Science, and Design: The Status of Design in Natural Science*, Philosophy and Biology Series (Albany, NY: State University of New York Press, 2001); and Plantinga, *Where the Conflict Really Lies*.

145 Avery Cardinal Dulles, S. J., "*Dignitatis Humanae* and the Development of Catholic Doctrine," in *Catholicism and Religious Freedom: Contemporary Reflections on Vatican II's Declaration on Religious Liberty*, ed. Kenneth L. Grasso and Robert P. Hunt (Lanham, MD: Sheed & Ward, 2006), 43.

its rich theological anthropology, connecting this doctrinal development to the deliverances of its predecessors,[146] while other Christians have made a different sort of case.[147]

To conclude this section (2.2.B), it is abundantly clear that SR begs so many substantive questions that it is simply flat out wrong in affirming that (2.2.B.1) religious claims are unprovable, (2.2.B.2) religious claims are incontestable, and (2.2.B.3) religious claims cannot change or develop because they are insulated from the ordinary standards of evidence and rational justification.

### 2.2.C. SR Confuses Religion as Such with Particular Religions and Beliefs Tethered to Them

SR inhibits the critic of religion from getting his hands dirty. What I mean by this is that rather than having to assess each case offered by the religious believer for the policies she supports, the SR advocate can simply offer his understanding of religion as irrational and then note that the policy defended by the religious believer is tethered to that irrational tradition. This is precisely what I think Leiter does when he admits that there is a sense in which all commands of morality are categorical, but nevertheless argues that the ones that issue from religious beliefs, unlike their secular counterparts, are insulated from "standards of evidence and reasons in the sciences."[148] In this way, SR functions as a sort of epistemic exclusionary rule, disallowing any arguments for public consideration if obtained without a secular warrant.

As I pointed out in Section 2.2.B, the SR advocate ignores the voluminous number of arguments offered by religious believers, and in particular Christians, for the rationality of their theological beliefs and how these beliefs may be contested and are thus not insulated from external challenges. But even if we set aside those arguments and insights and concede to the SR advocate for the sake of argument that these theological beliefs are not amendable to reason or external challenges, it does not follow that attendant beliefs tethered to those theological beliefs are not themselves amenable to reason and external challenges.

[146] *The Declaration on Religious Freedom: Dignatitis Humanae* (7 December 1965), available at http://www.vatican.va/archive/hist_councils/ii_vatican_council/documents/vat-ii_decl_19651207_dignitatis-humanae_en.html. See also Hugo Rahner, S.J., *Church and State in Early Christianity*, originally published in German in 1961, trans. Leo Donald Davis, S.J. (San Francisco: Ignatius Press, 1992); John Courtney Murray, S.J., *We Hold These Truths: Catholic Reflections on the American Proposition* (Lanham, MD: Sheed & Ward, 1960); Robert Louis Wilken, *The Christian Roots of Religious Freedom* (Milwaukee: Marquette University Press, 2014).

[147] See, e.g., James E. Wood, Jr., E. Bruce Thompson, and Robert T. Miller, *Church and State in Scripture, History, and Constitutional Law* (Waco, TX: Baylor University Press, 1958).

[148] Leiter, *Why Tolerate Religion?*, 38.

Consider, for example, Jesus's command that one ought to love one's neighbor as oneself, the Golden Rule.[149] Suppose citizen X accepts that command because X believes that Jesus is God Incarnate and God should be obeyed because God can never be mistaken about his commands. By contrast, citizen Y, an agnostic, accepts the Golden Rule as well, but not based on the authority of Jesus. Rather, Y maintains that the Golden Rule is simply a variation of Immanuel Kant's Categorical Imperative that X accepts based on what he believes are reasonable arguments.[150] So, even though for the Christian the Golden Rule is tethered to Jesus's authority, a source that the SR advocate holds is irrational, one need not accept Jesus's authority in order to be rational in accepting the Golden Rule.

Moreover, some of the beliefs discussed in Section 2.2.B, although embraced by religious believers, are not, strictly speaking, dependent on the veracity of the believer's religion. The existence of the soul, for example, may be rationally defensible by philosophical argument even if it turns out that the believer's religion is false.[151]

Now let us consider a substantive policy question: abortion. As most everyone knows, opposition to legal abortion in the United States is disproportionally found among those who are theologically conservative religious believers, and a vast majority of those believers are Christians who identify themselves as Catholic or Evangelical Protestant. It is clear that the connection between their opposition to abortion and their religious beliefs is not merely tangential. As many prolife advocates – as diverse as St. Pope John Paul II[152] and Evangelical philosopher J. P. Moreland (who is neither a pope nor a saint)[153] – have conceded, their prolife convictions rely on a philosophical anthropology that arises from their theological beliefs about the nature of the human person.

As I noted earlier, Justice John Paul Stevens dismissed the constitutionality of the prolife position on abortion because it is a "religious tenet" that cannot in-principle have a "secular purpose." There is a sense in which Justice Stevens is correct, insofar as prolife advocates concede that their view is tethered to their theology of the human person. But there is a sense in which the Justice

---

[149] "In everything do to others as you would have them do to you; for this is the law and the prophets" (Matthew 7:12 – NRSV).

[150] There are several formulations of Kant's Categorical Imperative, the most well-known of which is: "Act only according to that maxim whereby you can, at the same time, will that it should become a universal law." (Immanuel Kant, *Grounding for the Metaphysics of Morals* [1785], with *On a Supposed Right to Lie Because of Philanthropic Concerns*, trans. James W. Ellington, 3rd ed. [Indianapolis: Hackett Publishing, 1993], 30).

[151] The secular philosopher Karl Popper, for example, rejected mind-body physicalism. See Popper, *Knowledge and the Body-Mind Problem*.

[152] Pope John Paul II, *Evangelium Vitae*.

[153] J. P. Moreland and Scott B. Rae, *Body & Soul: Human Nature and the Crisis in Ethics* (Dowers Grove, IL: InterVarsity Press, 2000).

is mistaken. Not only because there are self-identified unbelievers that oppose abortion because they believe the unborn are human persons,[154] but because the case for fetal personhood offered by religious believers is based on real arguments that may be assessed independently from one accepting the theological tradition from which their belief in fetal personhood arises. In order to appreciate this, let us carefully compare and contrast the differing views on the nature of prenatal life.

Those who support abortion rights – prochoice advocates – offer arguments in order to establish what they believe is the correct moral account of prenatal life. Prolifers, in response, offer contrary arguments for the purpose of showing that the prochoice position is mistaken. Both sets of advocates typically zero in on one question: Is the unborn a moral subject?[155] Prochoicers will answer this question in the negative, but the specificity of their answer will depend on what they believe is the point in its development at which the unborn becomes a moral subject. Some argue for a moderate position, arguing that the fetus becomes a moral subject (or a "person") when it becomes sentient,[156] which occurs sometime between sixteen and eighteen weeks after conception. Others argue that the fetus becomes a moral subject later in its gestation, at the onset of organized cortical brain activity,[157] which arises twenty-five to thirty-two weeks after conception. Yet, others locate this decisive moment at sometime after birth, arguing that even newborns are not moral subjects.[158] This is why prochoice advocates will refer to fetuses, prior to whichever decisive moment

[154] Doris Gordon (President, Libertarians for Life) and Nat Hentoff (writer, *The Village Voice*) are prolife atheists. See Doris Gordon, "Abortion Rights and Wrongs: Applying Libertarian Beliefs Correctly," available at http://www.fnsa.org/v1n2/gordon1.html (text) and http://www.fnsa.org/v1n2/gordon2.html (endnotes), and Nat Hentoff, "The Indivisible Fight for Life" (19 October 1986), available at http://groups.csail.mit.edu/mac/users/rauch/nvp/consistent/indivisible.html.

[155] There are exceptions, such as the work of Judith Jarvis Thomson ("A Defense of Abortion," *Philosophy and Public Affairs* 1.1 [1971]) and David Boonin (*A Defense of Abortion* [New York: Cambridge University Press, 2002] 133–281), both of whom concede for the sake of argument that the fetus is a person, but then go on to argue that the right to abortion is still justified. For a response, see Francis J. Beckwith, "Does Judith Jarvis Thomson Really Grant the Prolife View of Fetal Personhood in Her Defense of Abortion? A Rawlsian Assessment," *International Philosophical Quarterly* 54.4 (December 2014).

[156] See, e.g., L. W. Sumner, *Abortion and Moral Theory* (Princeton, NJ: Princeton University Press, 1981).

[157] See, e.g., Boonin, *A Defense of Abortion*. For a similar approach, see Kenneth Himma, "A Dualist Analysis of Abortion: Personhood and the Concept of Self *Qua* Experiential Subject," *Journal of Medical Ethics* 31.1 (2005): 48–55.

[158] See, e.g., Peter Singer and Helen Kuhse, "On Letting Handicapped Infants Die," in *The Right Thing to Do: Basic Readings in Moral Philosophy*, ed. James Rachels (New York: Random House, 1989); and Alberto Giubilini and Francesca Minerva, "After-Birth Abortion: Why Should the Baby Live?," *Journal of Medical Ethics* 39.5 (May 2013): 261–263.

these advocates embrace, as human beings that are *potential persons* but not actual persons.

Prolifers, with few exceptions,[159] argue that the unborn is a moral subject (i.e., a person) from the moment it comes into being at conception, because it is an individual human being and all human beings have a personal nature, even when they are not presently exercising the powers that flow from that nature's essential properties.[160] These essential properties include capacities for personal expression, rational thought, and moral agency. The maturation of these capacities are perfections of a human being's nature, and thus, contrary to what some prochoice critics claim,[161] the human fetus can be wronged even before it can know it has been wronged.

To understand the prolifer's point, consider this example.[162] (I offer similar illustrations in Chapters 4 and 5.) Imagine that a prochoice scientist wants to harvest human organs without at the same time harming human beings that are moral subjects, that is, persons. In order to accomplish this he first brings several embryos into being through in vitro fertilization. He then implants them in artificial wombs, and while they develop he obstructs their neural tubes so that they may never acquire higher brain functions, and thus they cannot become what the typical prochoice advocate considers "persons."[163]

---

[159] There are a few prolifers who argue that very early on in pregnancy (roughly during first the fourteen days after conception) the unborn is not yet an individual unified organism, because of the possibility of twinning, and thus is not a moral subject. See, e.g., Don Marquis, "The Moral-Principle Objection to Embryonic Stem-Cell Research," *Metaphilosophy* 38:2–3 (April 2007): 190–206.

[160] See, e.g., Stephen Napier, ed., *Persons, Moral Worth, and Embryos: A Critical Analysis of Pro-Choice Arguments* (Dordrecht: Springer, 2011); Robert P. George and Christopher Tollefsen, *Embryo: A Defense of Human Life*, 2nd ed. (Princeton, NJ: The Witherspoon Institute, 2011); Patrick Lee, *Abortion and Unborn Human Life*, 2nd ed. (Washington, DC: The Catholic University of America Press, 2010); Christopher Kaczor, *The Ethics of Abortion: Women's Rights, Human Life, and the Question of Justice* (New York: Routledge, 2011); Francis J. Beckwith, *Defending Life: A Moral and Legal Case Against Abortion Choice* (New York: Cambridge University Press, 2007); and Moreland and Rae, *Body & Soul*.

[161] "We take 'person' to mean an individual who is capable of attributing to her own existence some (at least) basic value such that being deprived of this existence represents a loss to her. This means that many nonhuman animals and mentally retarded human individuals are persons, but that all the individuals who are not in the condition of attributing any value to their own existence are not persons. Merely being human is not in itself a reason for ascribing someone a right to life." (Giubilini and Minerva, 2).

[162] The following is similar to a scenario suggested in Carol Kahn, "Can We Achieve Immortality?: The Ethics of Cloning and Other Life Extension Technologies," *Free Inquiry* (Spring 1989), 14–18.

[163] Boonin, for example, writes: "For on the account of the wrongness of killing that results from this modification of the original future-like-ours argument, the existence of other individuals makes a legitimate moral demand on us in virtue of their having at least some actual desires about how their lives go.... A human fetus has no such desires prior to the point at

Suppose, on hearing of this scientist's grisly undertaking, a group of pro-life radicals breaks into his laboratory and transports all the artificial wombs (with all the embryos in tact) to another laboratory located in the basement of the Vatican. While there, several prolife scientists inject the embryos with a drug that heals their neural tubes and allows for their brains to develop normally. After nine months, the former fetuses, now infants, are adopted by loving families.

If you think what the prolife scientists did was not only good but an act that justice requires, it seems that you must believe that embryos are beings of a personal nature ordered toward certain perfections that when obstructed results in a wrong. This is why prolife advocates would say that human embryos are not potential persons, but rather, that they are persons with potential.

The point here is not to defend the prolife position on abortion, or even to make a case against the variety of prochoice positions noted earlier. (This, in fact, will be the focus of Chapter 5.) But rather, it is to show that the pro-life position, although tethered to the philosophical anthropology of particular theological traditions, may be defended by rational arguments independent of the veracity of any of the traditions from which it hales.

Abortion, however, is not the only public policy issue about which reli-gious citizens have offered rational arguments that seem to be informed by, but do not require belief in, their theological creeds. These include critiques of same-sex "marriage,"[164] physician-assisted suicide,[165] and scientism[166] as well

---

which it has conscious experiences, and it has no conscious experiences prior to the point at which it has organized electrical activity in its cerebral cortex. It therefore has no such desires prior to the point at which it has organized electrical activity in its cerebral cortex" (Boonin, 125, 126).

[164] See, e.g., Sherif Girgis, Robert P. George and Ryan T. Anderson, *What is Marriage?: Man and Woman: A Defense* (New York: Encounter Books, 2012); Patrick Lee and Robert P. George, *Conjugal Union: What Marriage Is and Why It Matters* (New York: Cambridge University Press, 2014); David Bradshaw, "A Reply to Corvino," *Same Sex: Debating the Ethics, Science, and Culture of Homosexuality*, ed. John Corvino (Lanham, MD: Rowman & Littlefield, 1997), 17–30; Mary Geach, "Lying With the Body," *The Monist* 91.3–4 (July–October 2008): 523–557; Patrick Lee, "Marriage, Procreation, and Same-Sex Unions," *The Monist* 91.3–4 (July–October 2008): 422–438; John M. Finnis, "Law, Morality, and 'Sexual Orientation'," *Notre Dame Law Review* 69.5 (1994): 1049–1076; and Ryan T. Anderson, *Truth Overruled: The Future of Marriage and Religious Freedom* (Washington, DC: Regnery, 2015).

[165] See, e.g., John Keown, *Euthanasia, Ethics & Public Policy: An Argument Against Legalisation* (New York: Cambridge University Press, 2002).

[166] See, e.g., Plantinga, *Where the Conflict Really Lies*; Leon R. Kass, *Toward a Moral Natural Science: Biology and Human Affairs* (New York: Basic Books, 1988); Gregory, "Science Versus Religion?"; Carroll, "Creation, Evolution, and Thomas Aquinas"; and Edward Feser, "Blinded By Scientism," *Public Discourse: Ethics, Law, and the Common Good*, Online Publication of the Witherspoon Institute (9 March 2010), available at http://www.thepublicdiscourse.com/2010/03/1174.

as defenses of morals legislation[167] and the full political participation of citizens informed by their religious beliefs.[168]

## 2.3. CONCLUSION

It is clear that some courts and some legal theorists misrepresent the rational status of religious beliefs as well as their attendant moral and metaphysical notions. The judicial opinions we covered, most of which were issued in the mid to late 20th century, should not surprise us, because the jurists who authored them would not have been professionally acquainted with the literature on the rationality of religious belief that has been a staple of Anglo-American philosophy for nearly five decades.

What should surprise us are the legal theorists. A legal academy that is fully informed and intellectually serious about religion and religious beliefs should be one in which the same sort of care and deference afforded to scholarship involving speech, privacy, racial discrimination, and criminal justice would be extended without controversy to the theological traditions and beliefs many citizens in liberal democracies hold dear. But, as we have seen, one finds within the literature caricatures, straw men, and dismissals, claims about the religious views of these citizens that if they were about race, gender, or sexual orientation would be quickly and loudly dismissed by many of these same legal theorists as instances of bigotry borne of ignorance.

I am not suggesting, of course, that theism, or Christian theism in particular, does not have serious detractors who have offered fair-minded critiques of the arguments found in the literature mentioned earlier. But the presence of sincere and thoughtful critics of religion armed with counterarguments no more counts against the rationality of theism (and its attendant moral and metaphysical notions) than does the presence of sincere and thoughtful political libertarians and conservatives armed with counterarguments count against the rationality of social democracy.

I am also not suggesting that by showing that religion is not by nature irrational that therefore there are no irrational religious beliefs, or that there are

---

[167] See, e.g., Robert P. George, *Making Men Moral: Civil Liberties & Public Morality* (Oxford: Clarendon Press, 1993); Hadley Arkes, *Philosopher in the City: The Moral Dimensions of Urban Politics* (Princeton, NJ: Princeton University Press, 1981); and Francis A. Canavan, S. J., *The Pluralist Game: Pluralism, Liberalism, and the Moral Conscience* (Lanham, MD: Rowman & Littlefield, 1995).

[168] See, e.g., Christopher Eberle, *Religious Conviction in Liberal Politics* (New York: Cambridge University Press, 2002); Bryan McGraw, *Faith in Politics: Religion and Liberal Democracy* (New York: Cambridge University Press, 2010); Robert P. George, *A Clash of Orthodoxies: Law, Religion, and Morality in Crisis* (Wilmington, DE: ISI Books, 2001); and Nicholas Wolterstorff, "Why We Should Reject What Liberalism Tells Us about Speaking and Acting in Public for Religious Reasons," in *Religion and Contemporary Liberalism*, ed. Paul Weithman (Notre Dame, IN: Notre Dame University Press, 1997), 162–181.

not legitimate philosophical and Constitutional questions that one may raise against religiously informed legislation.

What I am suggesting is that there is simply no justification for a court or a legal theorist to issue a negative judgment on the rationality of all religious beliefs and their attendant notions, and then employ that judgment as an immutable standard by which to exclude a priori all such beliefs from serious consideration in policy disputes. Although one could argue that the Establishment Clause of the First Amendment was intended to "separate church and state," even if those precise words do not appear in the Constitution, it hardly follows from this that it was intended as an epistemological litmus test by which a court or a legal theorist may capriciously sequester faith from reason.

# 3

# Theological Exclusionary Rule: The Judicial Misuse of Religious Motives

> The Religion then of every man must be left to the conviction and conscience of every man; and it is the right of every man to exercise it as these may dictate. This right is in its nature an unalienable right. It is unalienable, because the opinions of men, depending only on the evidence contemplated by their own minds cannot follow the dictates of other men: It is unalienable also, because what is here a right towards men, is a duty towards the Creator. It is the duty of every man to render to the Creator such homage and such only as he believes to be acceptable to him. This duty is precedent, both in order of time and in degree of obligation, to the claims of Civil Society. Before any man can be considered as a member of Civil Society, he must be considered as a subject of the Governour of the Universe: And if a member of Civil Society, who enters into any subordinate Association, must always do it with a reservation of his duty to the General Authority; much more must every man who becomes a member of any particular Civil Society, do it with a saving of his allegiance to the Universal Sovereign. We maintain therefore that in matters of Religion, no man's right is abridged by the institution of Civil Society and that Religion is wholly exempt from its cognizance. True it is, that no other rule exists, by which any question which may divide a Society, can be ultimately determined, but the will of the majority; but it is also true that the majority may trespass on the rights of the minority.
>
> James Madison (1751–1836)[1]

In several federal cases concerning whether particular statutes or policies violate the First Amendment's prohibition of religious establishment, both the United States Supreme Court and other federal courts have rejected the constitutionality of these laws and policies on the grounds that they have an exclusively religious purpose. Aspects of the courts' analyses in some of these cases rely on the apparent religious *motives* of the statute's or policy's sponsors and/

---

[1] James Madison, *Memorial and Remonstrance against Religious Assessments* (20 June 1785), available at http://press-pubs.uchicago.edu/founders/documents/amendI_religions43.html.

or citizen-supporters as the basis by which the courts infer that the law or policy in question has a religious *purpose*.

I argue in this chapter that this sort of analysis may violate the spirit of the No Religious Test Clause section of Article VI of the U.S. Constitution. I say "the spirit," because this clause was a limit on the federal government and not on local or state governments, which, at the time of the American Founding, were free to have religious tests for public office. It was only in the 20th century that the U.S. Supreme Court would apply the spirit of Article VI by incorporating the First Amendment's Free Exercise and Establishment Clauses through the Fourteenth Amendment.[2] By doing so, the Court prohibited governments from punishing or rewarding citizens based on their beliefs. So, when I say "the spirit of Article VI" or "Article VI's spirit" I am referring to the now universal prohibition of religious tests for public office.

Ironically, as I argue in this chapter, the contemporary judiciary fails to appreciate that it in fact may be engaging in a violation of Article VI's spirit when it embraces a mode of analysis, when applied to the origin and purpose of statutes and policies, that is based on a conflation of the terms "motive" and "purpose" as well as a mistake in thinking that the reasons employed to justify laws and policies are the same as the beliefs that motivate the persons who support them. And because of these confusions, the judiciary in effect limits the enumerated powers of legislators and provides a perverse incentive for both citizens and legislators to pretend that their motives are not religious in order to convince a skeptical judiciary that the laws and policies they support have secular purposes. Learning from the judiciary's example, activists now draw pejorative attention to the apparent religious motives of citizens and legislators in order to shore up popular support against, and influence future cases on, legislation they think violates the Establishment Clause of the First Amendment.[3]

---

[2] *See* Laurence H. Tribe, *American Constitutional Law*, 2nd ed. (Westbury, NY: Foundation Press, 1988), 1155 n.1 (2nd ed. 1988); and Erwin Chemerinksy, *Constitutional Law: Principles and Policies* (New York: Aspen, 1997), 971–972. The Court first incorporated the freedom of speech and press clauses, eventually incorporating the entire First Amendment. *See* Gitlow v. New York 268 U.S. 652, 666 (1925) (freedom of speech and press "are among the fundamental personal rights and 'liberties' protected by the Due Process Clause of the Fourteenth Amendment from impairment by the states"); *see also* Near v. Minnesota 283 U.S. 697, 707 (1931) ("It is no longer open to doubt that the liberty of the press and of speech is within the liberty safeguarded by the due process clause of the Fourteenth Amendment from invasion by state action"); De Jorge v. Oregon 299 U.S. 353, 364 (1937) ("The right of peaceable assembly is a right cognate to those of free speech and free press as fundamental"); Cantwell v. Connecticut 310 U.S. 296, 303–304 (1940) ("The First Amendment declares that Congress shall make no law respecting an establishment of religion or prohibiting the free exercise thereof. The Fourteenth Amendment has rendered legislatures of the States as incompetent as Congress to enact such laws"); and Everson v. Board of Education 330 U.S. 1, 15–16 (1947) (noting the Establishment Clause applies to the States through the Fourteenth Amendment).

[3] For example, Barbara Forrest writes: "At heart, proponents of intelligent design are not motivated to improve science but to transform it into a theistic enterprise that supports religious faith."

In order to make my case, I assess (3.1) the No Religious Test Clause and the First Amendment, (3.2) the difference between motive and purpose, and (3.3) the distinction between belief and action. After (3.4) reviewing two cases in which federal courts employ a religious motive analysis, I (3.5) respond to a possible objection to my argument. I then conclude that the religious motive analysis targets beliefs and thus violates the spirit of Article VI when applied to lawmakers, and is an illegitimate assessment of belief when applied to either legislators or ordinary citizens.

## 3.1. THE NO RELIGIOUS TEST CLAUSE AND THE FIRST AMENDMENT

Article VI of the U.S. Constitution states that "no religious Test shall ever be required as a Qualification to any Office or public Trust under the United States."[4] According to Daniel Dreisbach, this "provision generated energetic debate in the state ratifying conventions."[5] For it was widely believed at the time of the American Founding that certain religious traditions and systems of belief in comparison to others were more conducive to protecting and sustaining republican government and civil society.[6] Dreisbach quotes Luther Martin in this regard: "[I]t should be at least decent to hold out some distinction between Christianity and downright infidelity or paganism."[7] However, supporters of Article VI's religious test ban, notes Dreisbach, "framed the debate in terms of

(Barbara Forrest, "The Newest Evolution of Creationism: Intelligent Design is About Politics and Religion, Not Science," in *Natural History* 111.3 [April 2002]: 80.) Joined by two coauthors, Professor Forrest has also offered a lengthy legal assessment of the teaching of intelligent design (ID) in public schools in which she stresses the "religious motives" of many ID supporters as dispositive for rejecting the teaching of ID in public schools as constitutionally permissible. *See* Steven G. Gey, Matthew J. Brauer, and Barbara Forrest, "Is it Science Yet?: Intelligent Design Creationism and the Constitution," FSU College of Law, Public Law Research Paper No. 125 (September 2004), 79–93, *available at* http://ssrn.com/abstract=590882. The ID controversy is the focus of Chapter 6 of this book.

[4] U.S. Constitution, article VI.

[5] Daniel L. Dreisbach, "In Search of a Christian Commonwealth: An Examination of Selected Nineteenth-Century Commentaries on References to God and the Christian Religion in the United States Constitution," *Baylor Law Review* 48 (Fall 1996): 927, 949.

[6] As Philip Hamburger points out when explaining the reaction of the Danbury Baptists to the Letter sent to them by then-President Thomas Jefferson, "[I]t may be useful to begin by considering the [Baptists'] awkward situation.... [E]stablishment ministers [i.e., those ministers supported state religious establishments] had long accused dissenters of advocating separation, whether of church from state or religion from government.... Of course, Baptists merely sought disestablishment and did not challenge the widespread assumption that republican government depended upon the people's morals and thus upon religion." (Phillip Hamburger, *Separation of Church and State* [Cambridge, MA: Harvard University Press, 2002], 165).

[7] Dreisbach, "In Search of a Christian Commonwealth," 950 (citing *Debates in the Several State Conventions, on the Adoption of the Federal Constitution*, vol 5, ed. Jonathan Elliot [1859], 385–386), *available online* http://oll.libertyfund.org/titles/madison-the-debates-on-the-adoption-of-the-federal-constitution-vol-5.

religious liberty."[8] Take for example the defense offered by a Connecticut delegate to the Constitutional Convention, Oliver Ellsworth:

My countrymen, the sole purpose and effect of it [i.e., Article VI] is to exclude persecution, and to secure to you the important right of religious liberty.... In our country every man has a right to worship God in that way which is most agreeable to his conscience. If he be a good and peaceable person[,] he is liable to no penalties or incapacities on account of his religious sentiments; or in other words, he is not subject to persecution.[9]

As Dreisbach notes, the federal ban on religious tests was not the result of a consensus of delegates rejecting such bans in principle. For religious tests and/ or oaths were found in almost all state constitutions during the time of the Revolutionary War, and some of these state tests and oaths were fashioned and championed by some of the delegates at the Constitutional Convention who supported a federal prohibition of religious tests and oaths.[10] This suggests that federalism concerns, and the specific concern that state religious tests and oaths not be superseded by national tests, were factors in the passage of the federal ban.[11] The common understanding at the time did not maintain that religious liberty and religious disestablishment were inconsistent with state religious tests and oaths for public office, because it was widely believed, as I noted earlier, that the role of a public official required a certain moral character that could best (or only) be sustained in a citizen who had been inculcated with certain religious beliefs.[12] Nevertheless, given the historical milieu in which the Constitution's drafters found themselves, the radical and groundbreaking nature of Article VI cannot be overstated, even though it seems modest by

---

[8] Dreisbach, "In Search of a Christian Commonwealth," 950.

[9] Oliver Ellsworth, "The Landholder," *Connecticut Courant* (17 December 1787), VII, reprinted in *Essays on the Constitution of the United States Published During its Discussion by the People, 1787–1788*, ed. Paul L. Ford (New York: B. Franklin, 1970),167–168, as quoted in Dreisbach, "In Search of a Christian Commonwealth," 950.

[10] Dreisbach, "In Search of a Christian Commonwealth," 950.

[11] Ibid., 950–951. Michael McConnell writes:

At the federal level, restrictions of this sort were barred by Article VI of the Constitution, which provides that "no religious Test shall ever be required as a Qualification to any Office or public Trust under the United States." This is the only explicit "religious liberty" provision of the original Constitution. It proved, however, to be one of the more controversial features of the document. Many Americans considered it too risky a proposition to allow Catholics or non-Christians to hold office. What if they introduced the Inquisition? The provision ultimately proved acceptable less because of opposition to test oaths than to concerns that test oaths at the federal level might reflect the views of some other religious faction than one's own. As with so many matters, federalism offered a solution to otherwise deeply divisive problems. (Michael W. McConnell, "Establishment and Disestablishment at the Founding, Part I: Establishment of Religion," 44 *William & Mary Law Review* 44 [April 2003], 2178–2179).

[12] Dreisbach, "In Search of a Christian Commonwealth," 950–951. See also, Gerard V. Bradley, "The No Religious Test Clause and the Constitution of Religious Liberty: A Machine That Has Gone of Itself," *Case Western Law Review* 37 (1987): 681–687.

today's standards. For it "was a bold and significant departure from the prevailing practices in Europe, as well as most of the states."[13] Dreisbach goes on to explain:

Religious tests had long been a favored instrument for preserving the political power of established churches and denying equal political opportunity to adherents of other creeds. The test ban was not strictly a "disestablishment" measure since there was no formal establishment to abolish. However, the test ban preempted the prospect of a national ecclesiastical establishment by removing a useful mechanism for a religious denomination to exert control over the political processes. Moreover, the ban opened the door for members of minority sects to become full and equal participants in the democratic enterprise. The ban was thus calculated to secure religious liberty, deter religious persecution, ensure sect equality before the law, and promote independence of the federal government from ecclesiastical domination and interference.[14]

Despite the historical significance of the inclusion of Article VI in the Constitution of the early republic, the *text* of the religious test ban has become more or less a dead letter because the Supreme Court has found the prohibition of religious tests and oaths in the Free Exercise and/or Establishment Clauses and have applied them to the states by incorporation of the First Amendment through the Fourteenth Amendment.[15] For instance, in *Torcaso v. Watkins* (1961), the Supreme Court declared as unconstitutional a Maryland law that required a declaration of belief in God's existence as a condition for holding public office.[16] Justice Hugo Black wrote in the Court's unanimous opinion:

We repeat and again reaffirm that neither a State nor the Federal Government can constitutionally force a person to "profess a belief or disbelief in any religion." ... This Maryland religious test for public office unconstitutionally invades the appellant's freedom of belief and religion and therefore cannot be enforced against him.[17]

Although he leaves out any such citation, Justice Black in this passage seems to be relying on an interpretation of the First Amendment he first offered over a decade earlier in *Everson v. Board of Education* (1947),[18] in which he states: "No person can be punished for entertaining or professing religious beliefs or disbeliefs ..." Four years earlier, Justice Robert Jackson, seeming to embrace the same rationale, writes in *West Virginia Board of Education v. Barnette* (1943):[19] "If there is any fixed star in our constitutional constellation, it is that no official, high or petty, can prescribe what shall be orthodox in politics, nationalism, religion, or other matters of opinion or force citizens to confess by word or act their faith therein." The principle that seems to ground

---

[13] Dreisbach, "In Search of a Christian Commonwealth," 951.
[14] Ibid.
[15] See footnote 2.
[16] Torcaso v. Watkins 367 U.S. 488 (1961).
[17] Ibid., 495.
[18] *Everson*, 330 U.S. 1 (1947).
[19] West Virginia Board of Education v. Barnette 319 U.S. 624, 642 (1943).

this rationale has its origin in what was once called "freedom of conscience": *no citizen's religious beliefs may be employed by the government to disqualify that citizen from either public office in particular or political participation in general.* Although a minority view at the time of the American Founding, Thomas Jefferson articulates it well in his Bill for Establishing Religious Freedom:

That our civil rights have no dependence on our religious opinions, any more than our opinions in physics or geometry; that, therefore, the proscribing of any citizen as unworthy of the public confidence by laying upon him an incapacity of being called to offices of trust and emolument, unless he profess or renounce this or that religious opinion, is depriving him injuriously of those privileges and advantages to which in common with his fellow-citizens he has a natural right.[20]

So, what was first a constitutional prohibition of religious tests and oaths for only federal offices – partly motivated by both sustaining federalism and protecting local religious tests and oaths from federal supersession – eventually was extended to all public offices in every jurisdiction of the United States. It is no exaggeration to say that the ban on religious tests and oaths for public office is now a fixed principle of America's constitutional framework, and, as I argue later, that principle is no less violated when a legislator's powers are obstructed by a religious test *after* he or she enters public office than it is when he or she is excluded on religious grounds from holding public office altogether. It seems clear as well that this principle has been extended, through the contemporary interpretation of the Free Exercise and Establishment Clauses,

---

[20] *A Bill for Establishing Religious Freedom* (1786), reprinted in Michael W. McConnell, John Garvey and Thomas Berg, *Religion and the Constitution* (New York: Aspen, 2002), 70. However, James Madison's defense of freedom of conscience is more explicit than Jefferson's. Madison writes:

> Because we hold it for a fundamental and undeniable truth, "that Religion or the duty which we owe to our Creator and the manner of discharging it, can be directed only by reason and conviction, not by force or violence." The Religion then of every man must be left to the conviction and conscience of every man; and it is the right of every man to exercise it as these may dictate. This right is in its nature an unalienable right. It is unalienable; because the opinions of men, depending only on the evidence contemplated by their own minds, cannot follow the dictates of other men: It is unalienable also; because what is here a right towards men, is a duty towards the Creator. It is the duty of every man to render to the Creator such homage, and such only, as he believes to be acceptable to him.... We maintain therefore that in matters of Religion, no man's right is abridged by the institution of Civil Society, and that Religion is wholly exempt from its cognizance.... Because it is proper to take alarm at the first experiment on our liberties. We hold this prudent jealousy to be the first duty of citizens, and one of the noblest characteristics of the late Revolution. The freemen of America did not wait till usurped power had strengthened itself by exercise, and entangled the question in precedents. They saw all the consequences in the principle, and they avoided the consequences by denying the principle. We reverse this lesson too much, soon to forget it. Who does not see that the same authority which can establish Christianity, in exclusion of all other Religions, may establish with the same ease any particular sect of Christians, in exclusion of all other Sects? (Madison, *Memorial and Remonstrance*).

to prohibiting the government from punishing or rewarding citizens for "entertaining or professing beliefs or disbeliefs."[21]

## 3.2. THE DISTINCTION BETWEEN BELIEF AND ACTION: FREEDOM OF BELIEF AS AN ULTIMA FACIE RIGHT

The Supreme Court has, in several opinions, concluded that holding a *religious belief* is an ultima facie right. Unlike prima facie fundamental rights – for example, freedom of speech, free exercise of religion – that may be trumped by the government's compelling state interest, religious beliefs as such *may never* be proscribed or serve as the basis of punishment or reward by the government.[22] This seems to be what Thomas Jefferson had in mind when he told the Danbury Baptists in his famous letter to them "that the legitimate powers of government reach actions only, & not opinions."[23]

In *McDaniel v. Paty* (1978), the Supreme Court held that "[t]he Free Exercise Clause categorically prohibits government from regulating, prohibiting, or rewarding religious *beliefs as such*."[24] The Court was relying on a notion it clearly articulated fifteen years earlier in *Sherbert v. Verner* (1963):

*The door of the Free Exercise Clause stands tightly closed against any governmental regulation of religious beliefs as such.* Government may neither compel affirmation of a repugnant belief, nor penalize or discriminate against individuals or groups because they hold religious views abhorrent to the authorities, nor employ the taxing power to inhibit the dissemination of particular religious views. On the other hand, the Court has rejected challenges under the Free Exercise Clause to governmental regulation of certain overt acts prompted by religious beliefs or principles, for "even when the action is in accord with one's religious convictions, (it) is not totally free from legislative restrictions." The conduct or actions so regulated have invariably posed some substantial threat to public safety, peace or order.[25]

The jurisprudential paternity of these holdings can be found in the Jefferson-influenced *Reynolds v. United States* (1878): "Laws are made for the government of actions, and while they cannot interfere with mere religious

---

[21] *Everson*, 330 U.S., 15–16.

[22] *See* Church of the Lukumi Babalu Aye, Inc. v. City of Hialeah 508 U.S. 520, 533 (1993):

> Although a law targeting religious *beliefs as such* is never permissible, if the object of a law is to infringe upon or restrict *practices* because of their religious motivation, the law is not neutral and it is invalid unless it is justified by a compelling interest and is narrowly tailored to advance that interest. (citations omitted) (emphasis added).

[23] Letter from Thomas Jefferson to the Danbury Baptists (January 1, 1802), in *The Library of Congress Information Bulletin* 57.6 (June 1998), available at http://www.loc.gov/loc/lcib/9806/danpre .html (last visited 18 July 2014).

[24] 435 U.S. 618, 626 (1978) (citing Sherbert v. Verner 374 U.S. 398, 406 [1963]) (emphasis added).

[25] 374 U.S. 402–403 (citations omitted) (emphasis added) (quoting Braunfeld v. Brown 366 U.S. 599, 603 [1961]).

beliefs and opinions, they may with practices."[26] Clearly, the judiciary and other branches of government are not restricted from assessing the *actions* of the country's constituent governments and their citizens,[27] and the *reasons* offered by these governments and citizens to support these actions.[28] But the *beliefs* of both citizens and lawmakers are not legitimate objects of assessment by the state, including by its courts.[29]

The Supreme Court, at least on one occasion, has expressed skepticism in being able to clearly demarcate between beliefs and actions. In *Wisconsin v. Yoder* (1972), the Court claimed that the case "does not become easier because respondents were convicted for their 'actions' in refusing to send their children to the public high school; in this context belief and action cannot be neatly confined in logic-tight compartments."[30] Nevertheless, I am not convinced that the distinction between belief and practice – as articulated by Jefferson and in *Reynolds* – was rejected in *Yoder*. In *Yoder*, the Court assessed the question of whether Wisconsin's refusal to exempt Amish children from the state's compulsory education requirement could be upheld because the law only touched the actions and not the beliefs of the Amish. But, as the Court points out, the education of the Amish community's children is one of those cases in which belief and action are tightly intertwined, because the community's view of education is inexorably connected to Amish theology's views on humanity, the social order, knowledge, and the good life.[31] Nevertheless, the Court did *not* reject the Jeffersonian principle – affirmed in *Reynolds*, *McDaniel*, and *Sherbert* – that *mere* belief ("belief as such," as the Court calls it) could not be the object of state interference, which is essential to the case I am making in this chapter. After all, if the state of Wisconsin had targeted the Amish's religious beliefs *as such*, rather than the community's refusal to conform to the state's compulsory education policy, the state would have probably lost on summary judgment in the trial court.

---

[26] 98 U.S. 145, 166 (1878).

[27] Consider, for example, in light of the First Amendment, the Court's assessment of the *actions* of teacher-led, government-authorized, school prayer, *see* Engel v. Vitale 370 U.S. 421, 424–425 (1962), as well as a university's refusal *to act* by not funding printing costs for a religious publication that was similarly situated to school-funded secular publications, *see* Rosenberger v. Rectors and Visitors of the University of Virginia 515 U.S. 819, 823–827 (1995).

[28] Consider, for example, the *reasons* offered by the state to justify teacher-led, government-authored, school prayer, *see* Engel, 370 U.S. at 430–431, and the *reasons* offered by a university for its refusal to fund the printing costs of a religious publication that was similarly situated to school-funded secular publications, *see* Rosenberger, 515 U.S. at 830–831. In both cases, the Court assessed the reasons offered by the state and ruled that they were inadequate to justify the policies under the First Amendment.

[29] "Thus, the particular phraseology of the Constitution of the United States confirms and strengthens the principle, supposed to be essential to all written constitutions, that a law repugnant to the Constitution is void; *and that courts*, as well as other departments, *are bound by that instrument.*" (Marbury v. Madison 5 U.S. 137, 180 [1803] [emphasis added]).

[30] 406 U.S. 205, 220 (1972).

[31] Ibid., 209–219.

## 3.3. MOTIVES AS BELIEFS

So far, I have shown that two principles of American constitutional law are well-established: (1) a religious test or oath for office (and by extension, a religious test for the rights and powers of citizenship in general) is forbidden by the Constitution; (2) the government, including the judiciary, is categorically forbidden from limiting a citizen's political rights on the basis of her religious beliefs.

In this section, I argue that motives are types of beliefs. This is important for the case I am making, because I want to argue that the judiciary's religious motive analysis runs afoul of the two well-established constitutional principles defended earlier. In order to make this case, I offer two points: (A) I argue that purposes and motives are conceptually distinct. (I do this because, as I discuss in Section 3.4, the judiciary oftentimes confuses the purpose of a piece of legislation with the motive of the legislators or citizens who support it); (B) I explain why motives are types of beliefs.

### 3.3.A. Purposes and Motives Are Conceptually Distinct

Consider a modest example derived from a familiar case. Imagine that it is 1802, you are a leader in the Danbury Baptist Church in Connecticut, and you are not pleased that your state has levied a tax to support its established church, Congregationalism. Although Connecticut does allow Baptists and other citizens to request that the state redirect their tax money to their own churches, the process requires that "they first ... obtain, fill out, and properly file an exemption certificate."[32] And because "Baptists [are] a harassed minority, some communities [make] it difficult for them to receive these exemptions,"[33] which is why you and your fellow Baptists share your complaint with President Thomas Jefferson. The President replies in what has become a famous letter. In that reply, Jefferson writes that he agrees "with you that religion is a matter which lies solely between Man & his God, that he owes account to none other for his faith or his worship, that the legitimate powers of government reach actions only, & not opinions."[34] Jefferson goes on to announce his reverence for the American people's embracing of that portion of the First Amendment that declares that Congress "should 'make no law respecting an establishment of religion, or prohibiting the free exercise thereof,' thus building a wall of *separation between Church & State.*"[35]

---

[32] Derek H. Davis, "Thomas Jefferson and the 'Wall Of Separation' Metaphor," *Journal of Church and State* 45 (Winter 2003): 10.

[33] Ibid.

[34] Ibid.

[35] Letter from Thomas Jefferson to the Danbury Baptists (1 January 1802) (emphasis added).

Suppose that you agree with the president's sentiments and wish that your state, Connecticut, would include religion clauses in its constitution similar to those found in the Federal Constitution and extolled by the president in his reply. So, in principle you support religious free exercise for all faiths including your own. You see, correctly, that *the purpose* of such a constitutional amendment would be to increase religious liberty for all by forbidding the state to establish a religion and support it financially by taxing those of contrary faiths. However, your *motive* for advancing this constitutional amendment is so that the state may relieve your religion's adherents of a financial burden that is inhibiting evangelism. That is to say, your motive for supporting this constitutional amendment is religious: you believe that it is a good thing for people to convert to the Baptist faith and the current legal arrangement in your state makes such conversions more difficult. But that is not a complete account of your motive. It also has a state-restricting aspect to it. For you have no intention in establishing the Baptist faith as the state's official religion, even if you had the opportunity and power to do so, because you sincerely hold to the theological belief that faith resulting from coercion, however minimal, is not authentic faith. So, your motive for supporting a state constitutional amendment that protects religious liberty and forbids religious establishment is unequivocally to advance a particular understanding of religious truth. Nevertheless, the purpose of the proposed amendment is consistent with a liberal view of religious freedom and antiestablishment, which, by any account, is secular. So, we have a case in which a particular law's purpose is secular while the motive of its supporter is purely religious. And yet, it seems odd to say that this law, because of the motive of its supporter, would violate religious establishment. After all, the law, motivated by religious beliefs, *forbids* religious establishment.

Now imagine that you are a resident of Virginia, and you, with the help of the president, convince your fellow citizens that the state should place in its constitution an amendment that consists of religious liberty and antiestablishment clauses identical to the amendment proposed in Connecticut. Suppose, however, that your motive for proposing this amendment is not religious at all. Rather, your beliefs in religious liberty and antiestablishment are motivated by the belief that a good community is one that ought to rid itself of any vestiges of a bygone era in which citizens persecuted each other for political power so that the state may endorse, establish, and support a particular ecclesiastical body. Although the purpose and wording of the amendment offered in Virginia is identical to the one the Baptists are suggesting for Connecticut, the one in Virginia is motivated by what most people would consider nonreligious beliefs while the one in Connecticut is religiously motivated. Yet, the motive of the supporters of each adds nothing to the content and purpose of the amendment. Thus, a law's purpose and a legislator's (or citizen's) motive are conceptually distinct.

### 3.3.B. Motives Are Types of Beliefs

A motive is a type of *belief* that is causally effective in contributing to the bringing about of an action *by an agent* (i.e., a citizen). A motive, of course, is not a sufficient condition to bring about an action by an agent, because an agent may hold a number of beliefs that, although potentially causally effective, never contribute to bringing about an action for a variety of reasons including the absence of other conditions such as the agent's failure to exercise the power to act. For example, if I am a citizen with libertarian political beliefs, I would be motivated to support legislation that would eradicate the public school system if such legislation were proposed by the lawmakers in my state. But because no such legislation has been proposed – that is, a condition for my acting is absent – my motive is merely a potentially causally effective contributory condition for me to bring about an action, namely, to offer financial and political support for the legislation.

A motive, however, is not the act or policy itself, and neither is the motive the reason *that justifies the particular policy or action*. At best, a motive may *explain why* an agent supports a particular policy, but an explanation is neither the policy itself nor the justification for the policy. For example, one's belief in God may be *explained* by one's belief that one ought to follow the religious tradition of one's family, but the belief itself – "God exists" – and the *justification for* that belief – for example, the cosmological argument (a version of which we briefly reviewed in Chapter 2) or one's personal encounter with God – are separate matters altogether and should be assessed as such. To discount the veracity of $belief_1$ on the grounds that one may offer another $belief_2$, a motive, as a causally contributory condition that helps account for how $belief_1$ arose in the believer's noetic structure is to commit the genetic fallacy.[36]

Consider the role of motives on questions of public policy and law and their relation to the policy or law in question and the reasons for it. Two people, for instance, can have the exact same motive for two contrary policies or acts, for example, Bob opposes, and Fred supports, welfare reform because each is motivated by a desire to help the poor. Moreover, one policy or act may be supported by citizens with contrary motives, for example, Bob opposes welfare reform because he is motivated to help the poor; Tom opposes welfare reform because he is motivated to get reelected and most of his constituents oppose welfare reform. In addition, one policy or act may be supported by two citizens

[36] The genetic fallacy occurs when the origin of a viewpoint or argument, rather than its merits, is employed to dismiss it out of hand. Although the origin of an idea may play a part in assessing its merits (e.g., I might reject Trent's advice because he justifies it by appealing to the authority of the Ouji Board, from which he claims to have acquired the advice), the genetic fallacy is committed when an idea is dismissed based on its origin even though the origin of the idea is not a necessary condition for the veracity of the reasons for belief in it.

with the same motive but each justifies the policy or act for different reasons, for example, Bob and Sid both oppose welfare reform because each is motivated to help the poor, but Bob justifies the policy by showing that a similar policy in California failed whereas Sid justifies the policy by appealing to what he thinks are sound principles of social justice.

A motive in many ways is a belief properly basic to one's personal constitution, character, and inner life and cannot be "unbelieved" by an act of will in the way that one may willingly and without much difficulty offer different reasons or purposes for the same policies and acts one may advance throughout one's life. Consider, for example, some of our firmest convictions. Virtually all citizens who hold unwavering beliefs about the immorality of torture, the government's obligation to help the poor, and even the idea of human equality found in the Declaration of Independence,[37] would find it next to impossible to discard these beliefs even if they realized that they could not come up with a knock-down drag-out argument that would convince a torturer, an ethical egoist, or a white supremacist that she is wrong.

Within constitutional law, these distinctions are important. Let me reiterate some points raised earlier. The Supreme Court holds that "[t]he Free Exercise Clause categorically prohibits government from regulating, prohibiting, or rewarding religious *beliefs* as such."[38] This is because the Court makes a distinction between belief and practice: "Laws are made for the government of actions, and while they cannot interfere with mere religious beliefs and opinions, they may with practices."[39] Although the government (including the judiciary) may assess its own *actions* and those of its citizens, as well as the reasons for those actions, given the Supreme Court's religious jurisprudence, it may not assess religious motives *if* motives are beliefs. This seems to be the principle on which Justice Brennan relies in his concurring opinion in *McDaniel v. Paty* (1978): "Government may not inquire into the religious beliefs and motivations of officeholders – it may not remove them from office merely for making public statements regarding religion, or question whether their legislative actions stem from religious convictions."[40]

## 3.4. RELIGIOUS MOTIVE ANALYSIS

In this section I critically examine two federal court cases in which government acts were declared unconstitutional because of the motivation of its legislative and/or citizen supporters. Although these are very different cases, nevertheless,

---

[37] "We hold these truths to be self-evident, that all men are created equal, that they are endowed by their Creator with certain unalienable Rights, that among these are Life, Liberty and the pursuit of Happiness." (Declaration of Independence [4 July 1776])
[38] *McDaniel*, 435 U.S. 626 (emphasis added).
[39] *Reynolds*, 98 U.S. 166.
[40] *McDaniel*, 435 U.S. 641 (Brennan, J., concurring).

when critically examined in light of the conceptual distinctions we have established, they reveal how the religious motive analysis is inconsistent with the principles of religious liberty that have guided the federal courts since the American Founding.

Although there are, of course, other cases that I could have conscripted for our purposes here, the following two are representative of the reasoning found in virtually all of the cases in which courts try to divine the "religious motives" of citizens and legislators in order to determine whether the law, ordinance or policy in question has a "religious purpose."

### 3.4.A. *Selman v. Cobb County School District (2005)*

In March 2002, the school board of Cobb County, Georgia, ordered that a cautionary sticker be placed on science textbooks covering the topic of evolution. The sticker states: "This textbook contains material on evolution. Evolution is a theory, not a fact, regarding the origin of living things. This material should be approached with an open mind, studied carefully and critically considered."[41] A group of parents whose children attend Cobb County schools went to court to challenge the constitutionality of this warning.[42] On 13 January 2005, U.S. District Judge Clarence Cooper agreed that the sticker violates the Establishment Clause of the First Amendment.

There are, of course, problems with this sticker that are not of the constitutional sort. First, calling evolution a theory "regarding the origin of living things" may be misleading if one is talking about biological evolution, which concerns how living things that already exist change over time. Second, the claim that evolution is "not a fact" is inconsistent with the school board's call for critical thinking. The board cannot say that evolution is not a fact and at the same time suggest to students that they should have an open mind on the subject, because having an open mind requires that they critically consider the possibility that evolution is a fact. Thus, one can see why these parents would not be pleased with the board's policy. However, what concerns us here is the court's legal analysis of the policy and how that analysis targets religious motives

Judge Cooper begins his opinion with some important clarifications. He points out that the court's opinion deals with a narrow question – the constitutionality of the sticker's content – and does not address the many other issues that animate the differing factions in this debate. For Judge Cooper, this case is not about the relationship between science and religion or even the proper classification of evolution as a theory or a fact.[43] He then applies to the

---

[41] Selman v. Cobb County School District 390 F. Supp. 2d, 1286, 1292. (2005).
[42] Ibid., 1288.
[43] Ibid.

narrow question the three-prong test laid out by the Supreme Court in *Lemon v. Kurtzman* (1971): "First, the statute must have a secular legislative purpose; second, its principal or primary effect must be one that neither advances nor inhibits religion; finally, the statute must not foster 'an excessive government entanglement with religion.' "[44] A statute or policy that fails any one of these prongs violates the Establishment Clause.

The Cobb County sticker passes the first prong because it has two secular purposes, writes the judge. First, the sticker "fosters critical thinking by encouraging students to learn about evolution to make their own assessment regarding its merit."[45] Second, the sticker is an attempt to present evolution "in a manner that is not unnecessarily hostile" in order to "reduce offense to students and parents whose beliefs may conflict with the teaching of evolution."[46]

In determining whether the sticker passes Lemon's second prong (the "principal or primary effect must be one that neither advances nor inhibits religion"), Cooper conscripts the rationale behind the Supreme Court's endorsement test:[47] If a statute or policy creates a perception that the state is either endorsing or disfavoring a religion, the action is unconstitutional. As Justice Sandra Day O'Connor, who first proposed the test, notes in *Lynch v. Donnelly* (1984), the concern here is whether the disputed law or policy sends "a message to nonadherents that they are outsiders, not full members of the political community, and an accompanying message to adherents that they are insiders, favored members of the political community."[48] In *Wallace v. Jaffree* (1985), Justice O'Connor argues that a statute violates the Establishment Clause if an objective observer fully informed of all the facts "would perceive it as a state endorsement" of religion.[49] (We will encounter this application of the endorsement test in Chapter 6 when we examine the reasoning of Judge John E. Jones III in the 2005 case of *Kitzmiller v. Dover*.)[50]

Judge Cooper concludes that the sticker fails this test, although this judgment is *not* based on the "views or reactions held by the Plaintiffs or the numerous citizens and organizations who wrote to the Board."[51] Rather, it is based on "the view of a disinterested, reasonable observer."[52] Such a person, fully conversant with the history of opposition to Darwin's idea, would recognize that the assertion "evolution is a theory, not a fact" has its origin in anti-evolution

---

[44] Lemon v. Kurtzman 403 U.S. 602, 612–613 (1971) (citation of quote omitted) (striking down as unconstitutional statutes in Pennsylvania and Rhode Island that involved public aid programs to private school teachers, some of whom were parochial school teachers); *see Selman*, 390 F. Supp. 2d, 1298–1301.

[45] *Selman*, 390 F. Supp. 2d, 1305.

[46] Ibid.

[47] Ibid., 1305–1310.

[48] 465 U.S. 668, 688 (1984) (O'Connor, J., concurring).

[49] 472 U.S. 38, 67 (1985) (O'Connor, J., concurring).

[50] Kitzmiller v. Dover Area Sch. Dist., 400 F. Supp. 2d, 707, 722 (M.D. Pa. 2005).

[51] *Selman*, 390 F. Supp. 2d, 1306.

[52] Ibid.

literature published by creationists.[53] Thus, an informed, reasonable observer would view the sticker as endorsing a particular view of evolution espoused by the religiously motivated citizens and public officials of Cobb County. This, according to Judge Cooper, tells citizens who are staunch supporters of "evolution that they are political outsiders."[54] The judge writes:

In this case, the Court believes that an informed, reasonable observer would interpret the Sticker to convey a message of endorsement of religion. That is, the Sticker sends a message to those who oppose evolution for religious reasons that they are favored members of the political community, while the Sticker sends a message to those who believe in evolution that they are political outsiders.... Further, the informed, reasonable observer would be aware that citizens and parents largely motivated by religion put pressure on the School Board to implement certain measures that would nevertheless dilute the teaching of evolution, including placing a disclaimer in the front of certain textbooks that distinguished evolution as a theory, not a fact. Finally, the informed, reasonable observer would be aware that the language of the Sticker essentially mirrors the viewpoint of these religiously-motivated citizens.[55]

This analysis fails for several reasons. First, it seems inconsistent with the analysis under Lemon's first prong, which affirms that one of the sticker's secular purposes is to reduce offense to religious citizens. In other words, religious citizens advanced, through their government representatives, their goal of reducing hostility to certain religious beliefs, and the court acknowledges that such a goal constitutes a secular purpose that passes Lemon's first prong. Yet somehow the policy does not survive under Lemon's second prong for precisely the same reason that the court had just approved it under the first prong.

Consequently, this reasoning presents a Catch-22 that makes it nearly impossible for religious citizens to remedy public policies that they believe are uniquely hostile to their beliefs. For who but the citizens who take religious offense would be the most vocal critics of such policies and the most visible proponents of ways to mitigate their effects? Thus, it is difficult to believe that the judge is suggesting that the very citizens who desire to remedy a religious offense in their public school curricula, which they perceive as hostile to their

---

[53] Ibid., 1306–1307. *Creationism*, as understood by American courts and popular culture, is synonymous with *young-earth creationism*. This view, according to Phillip E. Johnson (who is not a young-earth creationist), is associated with the "term 'creation-science,' as used in the Louisiana law [that required 'balanced treatment' between evolution and creationism, and struck down in Edwards v. Aguillard, 482 U.S. 578 (1987)], [and] is commonly understood to refer to a movement of Christian fundamentalists based upon an extremely literal interpretation of the Bible. Creation-scientists do not merely insist that life was *created*; they insist that the job was completed in six days no more than ten thousand years ago, and that all evolution since that time has involved trivial modifications rather than basic changes.... [Young-earth creationism] attributes the existence of fossils to Noah's flood. (Phillip E. Johnson, *Darwin on Trial* [Downers Grove, IL: InterVarsity Press, 1991], 4).

[54] *Selman*, 390 F. Supp. 2d, 1305.

[55] Ibid., 1306–1307.

beliefs, cannot themselves lobby their government. Yet if political representatives respond to their concerns (just as elected officials might respond to citizens objecting to school policies for nonreligious reasons or even to citizens calling for the teaching of evolution), such a response would, under Judge Cooper's reasoning, raise Establishment Clause concerns. The result is to impose a special burden on the political activity of religious citizens, a burden not placed on secular political participation.

Second, what makes this opinion particularly strange is not that Judge Cooper is relying on the actual motives of religious citizens to dismiss the textbook disclaimer as unconstitutional, although he does indeed do that. Rather, the strangeness of this opinion lies in the judge's relying on what an imaginary third-party (the "reasonable observer") believes about the motives of the law's citizen-supporters based on the history and common understanding of the debate over evolution. Here, the First Amendment has been completely turned on its head. Rather than serving as a protector of believing-citizens and a bulwark against religious prejudice, the coercive power of the First Amendment's Establishment Clause, according to Judge Cooper, is *triggered* for the purpose of limiting the political actions of religious citizens *whenever* secular citizens are thought to *believe* (by a nonexistent "reasonable observer") that the political views of their religious neighbors are the result of a type of belief, a religious motive, even if the law under scrutiny has a bona fide secular purpose and is supported by secular reasons. So, in this case, the government rewards secular citizens for their hypothetical (although not necessarily actual) beliefs about religious citizens (as concluded by a nonexistent "rational observer") and punishes religious citizens because of what secular citizens are thought to perceive about what the religious citizens believe (as concluded by a nonexistent "rational observer"). But if government cannot touch beliefs, as the judiciary's understanding of the First Amendment unequivocally affirms (see Sections 3.2 and 3.3 of this chapter), then this opinion is inconsistent with the Constitution. For its major premise relies entirely on the *beliefs* of citizens (both real and imagined) including some of these citizens' beliefs about other citizens' beliefs and their religious content.

### 3.4.B. *Wallace v. Jaffree (1985)*

In this case,[56] the U.S. Supreme Court struck down as unconstitutional an Alabama statute that *permitted*, but did not require, the following to take place in its public schools:

At the commencement of the first class of each day in all grades in all public schools the teacher in charge of the room in which each class is held may announce that a period of

---

[56] *Wallace*, 472 U.S. 38.

silence not to exceed one minute in duration shall be observed for meditation or voluntary prayer, and during any such period no other activities shall be engaged in.[57]

This portion of the code is one of three parts brought to the attention of the Court. The first – which required meditation and did not mention prayer[58] – was not challenged by the appellees. The third – "enacted in 1982, which authorized teachers to lead 'willing students' in a prescribed prayer to 'Almighty God ... the Creator and Supreme Judge of the world'"[59] – had been struck down by the Court a year earlier.[60]

So the Court in this case dealt only with the statute that permitted teachers to start class with a moment of silence that may include either meditation or prayer. Unlike the third portion of the code, it did not specifically permit teachers to lead students in a particular prayer, but rather merely allowed teachers to set aside a minute at the commencement of the day in which the instructor informs her students that they may meditate or pray as a result of their own initiative. The Court, nevertheless, struck down the statute because it violated the purpose prong of the Lemon test. And the reason for this, the Court opines, is that the law's chief sponsor, State Senator Donald Holmes, was motivated by a desire, as he states in his own words, "to return voluntary prayer to our public schools.... [I]t is a beginning and a step in the right direction."[61] Moreover, because "Senator Holmes

---

[57] Alabama Code § 16-1-20.1 (1984), as quoted in *Wallace*, 472 U.S., 40 note 2.

[58] The unchallenged provision reads:

> At the commencement of the first class each day in the first through the sixth grades in all public schools, the teacher in charge of the room in which each such class is held shall announce that a period of silence, not to exceed one minute in duration, shall be observed for meditation, and during any such period silence shall be maintained and no activities engaged in. (Alabama Code § 16-1-20 [1984])

[59] *Wallace*, 472 U.S., 40, quoting Alabama Code § 16-1-20.2 (1984) (note omitted). This former provision in its entirety states:

> From henceforth, any teacher or professor in any public educational institution within the state of Alabama, recognizing that the Lord God is one, at the beginning of any homeroom or any class, may pray, may lead willing students in prayer, or may lead the willing students in the following prayer to God: Almighty God, You alone are our God. We acknowledge You as the Creator and Supreme Judge of the world. May Your justice, Your truth, and Your peace abound this day in the hearts of our countrymen, in the counsels of our government, in the sanctity of our homes and in the classrooms of our schools in the name of our Lord. Amen. (Alabama Code § 16-1-20.2 [1984])

[60] Wallace v. Jaffree 466 U.S. 924 (1984).

[61] *Wallace*, 472 U.S. at 43. The Court quoted from a statement that Senator Holmes inserted into the legislative record:

> Gentlemen, by passage of this bill by the Alabama Legislature our children in this state will have the opportunity of sharing in the spiritual heritage of this state and this country. The United States as well as the State of Alabama was founded by people who believe in God. *I believe this effort to return voluntary prayer* to our public schools for its return to us to the original position of the writers of the Constitution, this local philosophies and beliefs

unequivocally testified that he had 'no other purpose in mind,' "[62] the Court concluded that "the record not only provides us with an unambiguous affirmative
answer [as to the religious purpose of the statute], but it also reveals that the
enactment of [it] was not motivated by any clearly secular purpose – indeed, the
statute had *no* secular purpose."[63]

Three problems emerge from the Court's analysis, the second and third of
which are germane to this chapter's thesis. First, Senator Holmes's motives may
not represent the motives of his colleagues who voted to pass the legislation
for which he was the primary sponsor.[64] After all, as I noted earlier, legislators
support bills for a variety of motives, including a desire to get reelected, to
please a particular constituency, or to advance the public good. Thus, a plausible, though admittedly debatable, reading of Senator Holmes's comments
may show that even his so-called religious motive was not entirely religious.
One could say that he was motivated by a desire to advance a notion of the
public good that he believes is connected to America's religious heritage and its
importance in the moral formation of the school-age members of civil society.
Holmes states that "by passage of this bill by the Alabama Legislature our children in this state will have the opportunity of sharing in the spiritual heritage
of this state and this country. The United States as well as the State of Alabama
was founded by people who believe in God."[65] He, apparently, sees in this a
wisdom in which the young people of his state should have the opportunity to
voluntarily partake: "Since coming to the Alabama Senate I have worked hard
*on this legislation to accomplish the return of voluntary prayer in our public
schools and return to the basic moral fiber.*"[66]

Second, even if Senator Holmes had only a religious motive for sponsoring
this bill, it does not follow from this that the legislation itself may not have a
valid secular purpose. As I pointed out earlier, motives and purposes are conceptually distinct. For this reason, to employ the concepts interchangeably, as

---

> hundreds of Alabamians have urged my continuous support for permitting school prayer.
> Since coming to the Alabama Senate I have worked hard *on this legislation to accomplish the
> return of voluntary prayer in our public schools and return to the basic moral fiber.* (Ibid., 57
> n. 43 [emphasis added by the Court])

[61] Ibid., 43 (note omitted).

[63] Ibid., 56.

[64] Chief Justice Warren Burger says as much:

> As even the appellees concede ... there is not a shred of evidence that the legislature as a
> whole shared the sponsor's motive or that a majority in either house was even aware of the
> sponsor's view of the bill when it was passed. The sole relevance of the sponsor's statements,
> therefore, is that they reflect the personal, subjective motives of a single legislator. No case in
> the 195-year history of this Court supports the disconcerting idea that postenactment state-
> ments by individual legislators are relevant in determining the constitutionality of legislation.
> (Ibid., 86–87 [Burger, J., dissenting] [citation omitted])

[65] Ibid., 57 n.43.

[66] Ibid. (emphasis added by the Court).

the Court does in its reasoning in *Wallace*, is to offer an analysis that is fundamentally flawed. After all, even if Senator Holmes were motivated to sponsor this legislation in order to pave the way for the eventual reinstitution of unconstitutional teacher-led prayer in public schools, as the Court suggests,[67] it does not follow that the law in question in fact violates the same principle on which the Court relied when it declared teacher-led prayer unconstitutional.[68] A legislator's motive for an unconstitutional goal does not mean that a particular law he sponsors as the first step toward reaching that goal is itself unconstitutional. A proposed law that prohibits elementary school teachers from playing hard-core pornographic videos to their students may be the "first step" in a long-term legislative conspiracy to eventually pass laws that ban Plato, Shakespeare, and Milton from the public school classroom. But that hardly makes the initial law unconstitutional.

That is, the law and its purpose and the reasons for it, and not Senator Holmes's motives, are the proper objects of analysis. For one could without much difficulty *both* grant that Senator Holmes's motives are purely and unambiguously religious *and at the same time* construct a plausible secular purpose for this legislation that would not be inconsistent with the language of the statute.[69] For example, because religious free exercise is part of the secular Constitution, one could argue that Alabama's statute is simply informing its public school students that they may, if they so choose, exercise this religious freedom by engaging in voluntary prayer. As Justice Byron White eloquently points out in his dissenting opinion, if more than half of his brethren would "approve statutes that provided for a moment of silence but did not mention prayer,"[70] then where precisely would his brethren come down in the case of a teacher who answered "yes" when asked by a student if she could silently pray during the approved moment of silence?[71] And if the giving of that answer by a state actor, the teacher, is permissible, then why is it not permissible for the

---

[67] The Court writes:

> The sponsor of the bill that became § 16-1-20.1, Senator Donald Holmes, inserted into the legislative record – apparently without dissent – a statement indicating that the legislation was an "effort to return voluntary prayer" to the public schools. Later Senator Holmes confirmed this purpose before the District Court. In response to the question whether he had any purpose for the legislation other than returning voluntary prayer to public schools, he stated: "No, I did not have no other purpose in mind." (Ibid., 56–57 [notes omitted]).

[68] See generally *Engel*, 370 U.S.

[69] As the Court states elsewhere:

> The cardinal principle of statutory construction is to save and not to destroy. We have repeatedly held that as between two possible interpretations of a statute, by one of which it would be unconstitutional and by the other valid, our plain duty is to adopt that which will save the act. (NLRB v. Jones & Laughlin Steel Corp., 301 U.S. 1, 30 [1937])

[70] *Wallace*, 472 U.S. at 91 (White, J., dissenting).
[71] Ibid.

Alabama legislature to provide precisely the same answer before the question is asked?[72] Moreover, because earlier cases against school-sponsored prayer may have led some citizens to mistakenly believe that *all prayer* is prohibited in public schools, another purpose of this legislation is to remedy that misconception by showing that the state is not hostile to religious free exercise when voluntarily engaged in by its citizens.[73]

Third, and most importantly, the Court offers an extended lesson on the freedom of conscience before it directly assesses the issue before it.[74] This lesson includes a sizeable litany of quotes from prior cases and important figures in American history,[75] some of which are quoted earlier in this chapter (including in footnotes). The purpose of this portion of the Court's opinion is to scold the District Court for it's "remarkable conclusion that the Federal Constitution imposes no obstacle to Alabama's establishment of a state religion."[76] The Court concludes its lesson with these words:

Just as the right to speak and the right to refrain from speaking are complementary components of a broader concept of individual freedom of mind, so also the individual's freedom to choose his own creed is the counterpart of his right to refrain from accepting the creed established by the majority. At one time it was thought that this right merely proscribed the preference of one Christian sect over another, but would not require equal respect for the conscience of the infidel, the atheist, or the adherent of a non-Christian faith such as Islam or Judaism. *But when the underlying principle has been examined in the crucible of litigation, the Court has unambiguously concluded*

---

[72] Ibid.

[73] Chief Justice Burger, in fact, makes this point in his dissent:

Even if an individual legislator's after-the-fact statements could rationally be considered relevant, all of the opinions fail to mention that the sponsor also testified that one of his purposes in drafting and sponsoring the moment-of-silence bill was to clear up a widespread misunderstanding that a schoolchild is legally prohibited from engaging in silent, individual prayer once he steps inside a public school building.... That testimony is at least as important as the statements the Court relies upon, and surely that testimony manifests a permissible purpose. (Ibid., 87 [Burger, J., dissenting] [citation omitted])

[74] "Before analyzing the precise issue that is presented to us, it is nevertheless appropriate to recall how firmly embedded in our constitutional jurisprudence is the proposition that the several States have no greater power to restrain the individual freedoms protected by the First Amendment than does the Congress of the United States" (Ibid., 48–49).

[75] Ibid., 48–55.

[76] Ibid., 48. The offending portion of the District Court opinion states: "Because the establishment clause of the First Amendment to the United States Constitution does not prohibit the state from establishing a religion, the prayers offered by the teachers in this case are not unconstitutional. Therefore, the Court holds that the complaint fails to state a claim for which relief could be granted." (Jaffree v. Board of School Comm'rs of Mobile County 554 F. Supp. 1104, 1128 [SD Ala. 1983]). The District Court's judgment was stayed by Justice Lewis F. Powell, justice for the Eleventh Circuit. See Jaffree v. Board of School Comm'rs of Mobile County 459 U.S. 1314 (1983) (in chambers). The Eleventh Circuit overturned the District Court's opinion on appeal. See Jaffree v. Wallace 705 F. 2d, 1526 (1983), *en banc hearing denied*, 713 F. 2d, 614 (1983).

*that the individual freedom of conscience protected by the First Amendment embraces the right to select any religious faith or none at all.* This conclusion derives support not only from the interest in respecting the individual's freedom of conscience, but also from the conviction that religious beliefs worthy of respect are the product of free and voluntary choice by the faithful, and from recognition of the fact that the political interest in forestalling intolerance extends beyond intolerance among Christian sects – or even intolerance among "religions" – to encompass intolerance of the disbeliever and the uncertain.[77]

What is ironic about this summary is that it is inconsistent with the Court's religious motive analysis found elsewhere in the same opinion. As I have already noted, motives are types of beliefs; citizens, including legislators, have an ultima facie right to their beliefs such that the state ought not reward or punish them for having these beliefs; and a statute's purpose and the reasons for it are conceptually distinct from the motives of the statute's supporters in both the legislature and in the citizenry. Therefore, when the Court claims that a statute or policy violates the Establishment Clause because of a legislator's or a citizen's religious motives, it is in fact limiting one of the enumerated powers of that legislator or the political rights of that citizen *solely* based on the religious quality of *beliefs* that contribute causally to the exercise of each individual's political powers and rights.

Concerning citizens who hold public office, the Court's religious motive analysis functions as a de facto religious test in violation of the Supreme Court's application of the First Amendment (through the Fourteenth Amendment) to the states, because it implicitly limits the powers of those legislators. The fact that the legislators have already assumed office does not seem to be relevant, because a religious test violation would occur if a state passed a law that forbade only Catholic elected officials from voting on matters concerning human reproduction. Therefore, a religious test that limits a citizen's right to exercise the powers of public office – whether to limit all her powers by forbidding her to hold office or to limit some of her powers after she holds office – is nevertheless an impermissible religious test for public office. Moreover, just because a court, rather than a legislature or an executive branch, offers the test and targets a legislator's religious motive, rather than her ecclesiology or her creedal commitments, does not make it any less a government action or any less a religious test for public office.

When the religious motive analysis is applied to citizens in general, it shows, as the Supreme Court notes in *Wallace*, disrespect for "the individual's freedom of conscience"[78] and "freedom of mind,"[79] for it results in a subtle coercion of, and provides an incentive to, religiously-motivated citizens to publicly pretend as if they do not have the motives they in fact have. It punishes these

---

[77] *Wallace*, 472 U.S., 52–54 (notes omitted) (emphasis added).
[78] Ibid., 53.
[79] Ibid., 52.

citizens because of their beliefs, for their political freedom as citizens to shape their communities is being limited by a judicial prohibition of laws and policies that happen to have proponents who are motivated exclusively by their religious beliefs. In addition, the religious motive analysis provides sustenance to a political culture in which citizens are taught that any public disclosure of their beliefs, that motivate these citizens to support a legislative proposal, may result in the judiciary's rejection of that legislation regardless of its content or the reasons offered for the proposal.

### 3.5. AN OBJECTION

A strong objection to my analysis is that the U.S. Supreme Court has legitimately employed motive in its assessment of statutes in racial discrimination cases.[80] Thus, if the Court may legitimately cite racist motives to invalidate an apparently neutral statute, then there is nothing awry in a court employing similar reasoning in religion cases.

The case that most strongly supports this argument is *Hunter v. Underwood*, a 1985 case in which the Supreme Court struck down a 1901 Alabama statute that "provides for the disenfranchisement of persons convicted of, among other offenses, 'any crime ... involving moral turpitude.' "[81] The Court pointed out that in 1875 Alabama had passed a typical disenfranchisement statute that included only felonies. It "denied persons 'convicted of treason, embezzlement of public funds, malfeasance in office, larceny, bribery, or other crime punishable by imprisonment in the penitentiary' the right to register, vote or hold public office."[82] This was replaced by the 1901 statute, which had been adopted at the 1901 Alabama Constitutional Convention, the purpose of which was in fact to "establish white supremacy in the state," according to the convention's president in his opening address.[83]

The evidence is overwhelming that the 1901 statue was crafted in such a way that "the crimes selected for inclusion in § 182 [that were not in the 1875 statute] were believed by the delegates [of the Alabama convention] to be more frequently committed by blacks."[84] So, although the language of the statute was racially neutral, it was intended to disenfranchise blacks solely on racial grounds. For this reason, the statute was struck down as a violation of the Equal Protection Clause of the Fourteenth Amendment.

---

[80] This objection was raised to me by Jack Wade Nowlin during the question-and-answer session of an 18 October 2010 lecture I was invited to deliver at the University of Mississippi School of Law, where Nowlin serves as a Professor of Law.

[81] Hunter v. Underwood 471 U.S. 222, 223 (1985), quoting Art. VIII, § 182, of the Alabama Constitution of 1901.

[82] Ibid., 226, quoting Art. VIII, § 3, of the Alabama Constitution of 1875.

[83] Ibid., 229, quoting John B. Knox from the Official Proceedings of the Constitutional Convention of the State of Alabama, May 21st, 1901, to September 3rd, 1901, p. 8 (1940).

[84] Ibid., 226.

Although *Hunter* is the best example of a case that may count against my critique of the courts' religious motive analysis in religion clause cases, there are two reasons why I think it comes up short. First, it is not clear that motive is doing as much work in this opinion as the Court thinks it is doing. After all, if the 1901 convention had simply reaffirmed the 1875 statute, and the subsequent application of that statute had in fact resulted in a disproportionate number of blacks being disenfranchised, the conventioneers' white supremacist motives, however despicable, could not have served as grounds to declare the racially neutral statute unconstitutional. Why then did the Court strike down the 1901 statute? The answer is simple. It was not *really* racially neutral. Its *content* was crafted by the conventioneers for the precise purpose of disenfranchising more blacks than the 1875 statute could accomplish, and it succeeded in doing so.[85] The 1901 law was an example of what I call *conceptual gerrymandering*, a practice by which lawmakers pick out a characteristic disproportionately found among one minority group and then craft a law that disenfranchises all those who happen to have that characteristic. The characteristic serves as a proxy for race or any other protected classification. In contrast, in the religious motive cases covered in Section 3.4, the designs of the legislation were virtually irrelevant. What mattered almost exclusively to the jurists were the religious motives of those who advanced the legislation, and in one case (*Selman v. Cobb County School District*) it was "the motives" of the supporters *as perceived* by a fictional "rational observer" through the interpretative framework of the history of the debates over the teaching of evolution in public schools.

Consider this example. Suppose a state legislature, months after the opening of the state's first Catholic parish, passes a facially neutral statute that prohibits the distribution and consumption of wine, but only on Sunday. Imagine that this legislature had convened a special session to pass this bill in order to "establish Protestant supremacy in the state." In such a scenario, the legislators' motives would simply serve as a hermeneutical key to help explain the contours of the legislation, which was in fact intended to punish Catholics.

This sort of conceptual gerrymandering is also found in the famous 1886 case of *Yick Wo v. Hopkins* (1886),[86] in which the Supreme Court dealt with an 1880 San Francisco ordinance that did not allow one to operate a laundry in a wooden building without first receiving approval to do so by the Board of Supervisors. However, if one operated a laundry in a brick or stone building, no such permission was necessary. It turns out, according to Gerald Gunther

[85] "The registrars' expert estimated that, by January, 1903, section 182 had disfranchised approximately ten times as many blacks as whites. This disparate effect persists today. In Jefferson and Montgomery Counties, blacks are by even the most modest estimates at least 1.7 times as likely as whites to suffer disfranchisement under section 182 for the commission of nonprison offenses." (Ibid., 277 quoting Underwood v. Hunter 730 F. 2d, 614, 620 [1984])

[86] Yick Wo v. Hopkins 118 U.S. 356 (1886).

and Kathleen Sullivan, that "[t]he Board granted permits to operate laundries in wooden buildings to all but one of the non-Chinese applicants, but to none of about 200 Chinese applicants. A Chinese alien who had operated a laundry for many years was refused a permit and imprisoned for illegally operating a laundry."[87] In the Court's opinion, Justice Stanley Matthews writes:

[T]he facts shown establish an administration directed so exclusively against a particular class of persons as to warrant and require the conclusion that, whatever may have been the intent of the ordinances as adopted, they are applied by the public authorities charged with their administration, and thus representing the State itself, with a mind so unequal and oppressive as to amount to a practical denial by the State of that equal protection of the laws which is secured to the petitioners, as to all other persons, by the broad and benign provisions of the Fourteenth Amendment to the Constitution of the United States. Though the law itself be fair on its face and impartial in appearance, yet, if it is applied and administered by public authority with an evil eye and an unequal hand, so as practically to make unjust and illegal discriminations between persons in similar circumstances, material to their rights, the denial of equal justice is still within the prohibition of the Constitution.[88]

Although it was a facially neutral ordinance, its textual contours (which granted almost absolute discretion to the Board of Supervisors) were crafted so that the city government may intentionally discriminate against those of Chinese ancestry, which constituted the ethnicity of roughly 75 percent of those who operated laundries in wooded buildings.[89]

Given the facts in *Hunter v. Underwood*, it is very much like *Yick Wo* and the fictional Catholic wine case: the design of the legislation – to intentionally discriminate against a minority group – is what is wrong with it. Although the legislators' motives help us to interpret the legislation's design, it is ultimately its design that is the reason that the Court strikes down the statute. This is why the Court – in several other cases – has been reluctant to employ motive to strike down as unconstitutional laws and policies that either have a disparate impact on minorities when no racist motivation could be proved[90] or have

---

[87] Gerald Gunther and Kathleen Sullivan, *Constitutional Law*, 13th ed. (Westbury, NY: Foundation Press, 1997), 750.

[88] *Yick Wo*, 118 U.S., 373–374.

[89] "It is also admitted to be true, as alleged in the petition, that on February 24, 1880, 'there were about 320 laundries in the city and county of San Francisco, of which about 240 were owned and conducted by subjects of China, and of the whole number, viz., 320, about 310 were constructed of wood, the same material that constitutes ninetenths of the houses in the city of San Francisco[']" (Ibid., 358–359; quoting from facts admitted on the record).

[90] See, e.g., Washington v. Davis 426 U.S. 229 (1976) (upheld a District of Columbia Metropolitan Police Department personnel test for promotion even though the results excluded black applicants disproportionally from promotion); and Arlington Heights v. Metropolitan Housing Development Corp., 429 U.S. 252 (1977) (even though a Village of Arlington Heights denial of a zoning request to build low-income housing disproportionally affected racial minorities, there was no evidence that the village's purpose was to intentionally engage in racial discrimination).

no racially discriminatory design even though the lawmakers may have been motivated by racial animus.[91]

A second reason why this objection fails is that the race cases and the religion cases are actually analogous in a way that is consistent with my critical analysis of the religious motive test: racially motivated legislation designed to discriminate against minorities is similar to the courts' religious motive test insofar as the latter seems designed to limit the political participation of religious citizens based on certain beliefs they harbor. In the race cases the issue in play is whether minorities are treated with equal respect and dignity as citizens under the Constitution, while in the religious motive cases the issue in play is whether citizens' religious beliefs provide warrant for a court to not treat those citizens with equal respect and dignity under the Constitution. Paradoxically, then, the race cases actually provide support for my critique of the religious motive test.

## 3.6. CONCLUSION

Citizens and legislators are often motivated by their religious beliefs to influence the institutions of government and to craft laws and policies that affect the trajectory of their communities. Oftentimes these policies and laws are proposed in order to remedy what these citizens and legislators think is a wrong or an injustice, and sometimes these laws and policies are offered to merely advance what these citizens and legislators believe is the public good. In a liberal democracy, the religious motives of these citizens and legislators should never serve as a basis by which the courts reject as unconstitutional the laws and policies that likely would have not been offered by these citizens and legislators if not for their motives. Although one could construct a good philosophical argument against this judicial practice, as some indeed have,[92] it is not necessary. For, as I have argued in this chapter, the principles against the religious motive analysis are already firmly embedded in our constitutional jurisprudence.

---

In 2015, the U. S. Supreme Court dealt with disparate impact analysis in the application of the Fair Housing Act. Because the case concerned statutory interpretation and not constitutional analysis, it is not germane to our concerns in this chapter. See Texas Department of Housing and Community Affairs v. The Inclusive Communities Project, Inc. 135 S. Ct. 2507 (2015).

[91] Palmer v. Thompson 403 U.S. 217 (1971) (Upheld a Jackson, Mississippi ordinance that closed down four of the city's public swimming pools, and surrendered the lease of a fifth, soon after a court's decree to desegregate all the city's public facilities).

[92] See generally Nicholas Wolterstorff's contributions to Robert Audi and Nicholas Wolterstorff, *Religion in The Public Square* (Lanham, MD: Rowman & Littlefield, 1997).

# PART II

# DIGNITY AND PERSONHOOD

4

# Dignity Never Been Photographed: Bioethics, Policy, and Steven Pinker's Materialism

> Sick man lookin' for the doctor's cure
> Lookin' at his hands for the lines that were
> And into every masterpiece of literature
> for dignity ...
>
> Someone showed me a picture and I just laughed
> Dignity never been photographed
> I went into the red, went into the black
> Into the valley of dry bone dreams
>
> So many roads, so much at stake
> So many dead ends, I'm at the edge of the lake
> Sometimes I wonder what it's gonna take
> To find dignity
>
> Bob Dylan (1941–)[1]

> We are moving towards a dictatorship of relativism which does not recognize anything as for certain and which has as its highest goal one's own ego and one's own desires.
>
> Joseph Cardinal Ratzinger (the future Pope Benedict XVI) (1927–)[2]

In March 2008, the President's Council on Bioethics published a volume entitled, *Human Dignity and Bioethics*.[3] It consists of essays penned by council members as well as other scholars and practitioners invited to contribute. As

---

[1] Bob Dylan, "Dignity." © 1991 Special Rider Music.
[2] "Homily of His Eminence Joseph Cardinal Ratzinger, Dean of the College of Cardinals," in the Mass Pro Eligendo Romano Pontifice (18 April 2005), available at http://www.vatican.va/gpII/documents/homily-pro-eligendo-pontifice_20050418_en.html.
[3] President's Council on Bioethics, *Human Dignity and Bioethics: Essays Commissioned by the President's Council on Bioethics* (Washington, DC: www.bioethics.gov, 2008), available at http://www.bioethics.gov/reports/human_dignity/human_dignity_and_bioethics.pdf.

one would guess, the idea of human dignity and what it means for bioethics, both in theory and in practice, is the theme that dominates each of the works included in this impressive volume. But for those who have been following or participating in the interdisciplinary and multidisciplinary world of secular bioethics during the past several decades, the insertion of the idea of "human dignity," or even the word "dignity," as the anthropological foundation of bioethics is highly unusual.[4] Much of the cutting edge literature in bioethics, with few exceptions, tends to employ the language of modern political theory and contemporary analytic political philosophy and jurisprudence. So, for example, one finds in these cutting-edge works discussions about the meaning and implementation of the principles of autonomy, justice, nonmaleficence, and beneficence, as well as calls for the application of these principles to what constitutes physician neutrality, informed consent, and patients' rights. This project often goes by the name *principlism*. There is, of course, much that this project has contributed to the study and practice of bioethics. For each principle and its application has a long and noble pedigree about which many of us hold a variety of opinions. But what distinguishes principlism from the concept of "human dignity," and what makes this central concern of the council's volume so astounding, is that advocates of principlism typically intend for it to be a means by which a physician, ethics committee, nurse practitioner, general counsel, etc., *need not* delve into the metaphysical question for which "human dignity" is offered as a partial answer, namely, "Who and what are we, and can we know it?"[5]

To put it another way, if bioethics commits itself to the idea that "human dignity" is essential to its practice, as the President's Council suggests, it follows that bioethics must embrace a philosophy of the human person, a philosophical anthropology, if you will, that can provide substantive content to the notion of "human dignity." But such a suggestion seems to run counter to two ideas that are dominant in the secular academy: (1) Political Liberalism (PL), and (2) Scientific Materialism (SM).

*Political Liberalism* (PL) is, roughly, the view that a state that aspires to justice and fairness ought not to embrace one view of the human person as

---

[4] Although proponents of voluntary active euthanasia and physician-assisted suicide sometimes employ the slogan "death with dignity" in advancing their case in the public square, their use of the word "dignity" is not being employed with any rich anthropological beliefs in mind. In fact, their entire approach to the issue eschews any reliance on such beliefs, often portraying them as unjustified "religious constraints" on the liberty or autonomy of the patient who wants to kill himself. See, e.g., Emily Jackson's contribution to Emily Jackson and John Keown, *Debating Euthanasia* (Oxford: Hart Publishing, 2012).

[5] There are, of course, exceptions to this, such as the Christian principlisms of Scott B. Rae and David B. Fletcher. See Scott B. Rae, *Moral Choice: An Introduction to Ethics*, 3rd ed. (Grand Rapids, MI: Zondervan, 2009); and David B. Fletcher, "Response to Nigel de S. Cameron's Bioethics and the Challenge of a Post-Consensus Society," *Ethics & Medicine: An International Journal of Bioethics* 11:1 (Spring 1995).

the correct view because to do so would be to violate the principles essential to liberal democracy. It's most well-known advocate is the late John Rawls (1921–2002),[6] whose ideas about state neutrality and fairness have been applied by both him and others to a variety of contemporary issues including abortion and same-sex marriage, each of which is covered in greater detail in Chapters 5 and 7. Because PL is essential to the cultural infrastructure of contemporary secular bioethics, the principles central to principlism, such as autonomy and justice, are almost all procedural in their application. That is, when they are applied and practiced correctly, they commit the relevant medical personnel and institution to as minimal an understanding of the human person and her good as possible, with autonomy doing virtually all of the heavy lifting.

Consider, for example, how the principle of nonmaleficence is presented by the standard text in the field, *Principles of Biomedical Ethics* by Tom Beauchamp and James Childress.[7] "[T]he principle of nonmaleficence," they write, "obligates us to abstain from causing harm to others."[8] But, with few exceptions, Beauchamp and Childress are reluctant to say that a fully informed and competent patient can actually harm herself if she noncoercively chooses a course of "treatment," with which her physician freely cooperates, and that she believes is consistent with her own view of the good life. For example, they ask us to "consider the actions of physician Timothy Quill," who prescribed "the barbiturates desired by a forty-five-year-old patient who had refused a risky, painful, and often unsuccessful treatment for leukemia. She had been his patient for many years, and members of her family had, as a group, come to this decision with his counsel. She was competent and had already discussed and rejected all available alternatives for the relief of suffering."[9] After briefly mentioning some problems raised by critics of Dr. Quill as well as the fact that he had tried to minimize his legal liability by lying to the medical examiner, Beauchamp and Childress write that they "do not criticize Quill's basic intentions, his patient's decision, or their relationship." For "physicians such as Quill do not act wrongly in assisting competent patients, at their request, to bring about their deaths."[10]

What is true of autonomy and nonmaleficence is largely true of the other principles as well. They are often presented as almost entirely procedural with minimal substantive content. Now, as I point out later, I think that this is actually false. I believe that secular bioethics does commit its practitioners to a substantive understanding of the human person and the human good, one that

---

[6] John Rawls, *Political Liberalism*, rev. ed. (New York: Columbia University Press, 1996).

[7] Tom Beauchamp and James Childress, *Principles of Biomedical Ethics*, 7th ed. (New York: Oxford University Press, 2013).

[8] Ibid., 150.

[9] Ibid., 184.

[10] Ibid., 184, 185.

is as contested and controversial as the so-called "religious" views for which principlism is often thought of as a neutral arbiter.[11] What I am suggesting here, however, is that this is not how its supporters present, or in some cases understand, their position.

The second idea, *Scientific Materialism* (SM), is, roughly, the view that because science concerns itself only with material and efficient causes, and because science is the best or only way of knowing, therefore, any claim that cannot be accounted for under that rubric either is not real or cannot be known to be real.[12] Consequently, under SM, philosophies of the human person that affirm nonmaterial properties like "human dignity" cannot be a true description of reality. Thus, such philosophies of the human person, although they may be privately embraced and practiced by individual citizens in accordance with their own religious sensibilities or believed on the basis of utility,[13] may never serve as the basis on which a society may regulate research and practices of bioethical controversy, such as embryonic stem-cell research, physician-assisted suicide, abortion, or reproductive technologies.

As one would suspect, given these definitions, advocates of PL and SM offer them as neutral and uncontested concepts that provide a fair, impartial, and scientifically respectable foundation for the practice of medical ethics in

---

[11] See Tristram Engelhardt, Jr., "Public Discourse and Reasonable Pluralism: Rethinking the Requirements of Neutrality," in *Handbook on Bioethics and Religion*, ed. David E. Guinn (New York: Oxford University Press, 2006), 169–198.

[12] Although I reject Scientific Materialism (SM) as a worldview, it would be a mistake to believe that I also reject methodological naturalism (MN) in the hard sciences, although there was a time I was not too sure about the latter. (See, e.g., Francis J. Beckwith, *Law, Darwinism, and Public Education: The Establishment Clause and the Challenge of Intelligent Design* [Lanham, MD: Rowman & Littlefield, 2003], 92–116.) I have since that time changed my mind. As I argue in Chapter 6, I part ways with both the New Atheists and the Intelligent Design advocates, both of whom, ironically, seem to believe that the deliverances of the natural sciences can in-principle refute or confirm the existence of God as well as a variety of other beliefs connected to theism such as the existence of final and formal causes in nature. Although MN is proper to the natural sciences, it does not entail or require SM. For as I argue in this chapter as well as Chapter 6, one can make a reasonable case for certain philosophical notions congenial to theism that do not require the rejection of one deliverance of the natural sciences.

[13] Writes Steven Pinker: "[E]thical theory requires idealizations like free, sentient, rational, equivalent agents whose behavior is uncaused, and its conclusions can be sound and *useful* even though the world, as seen by science, does not really have uncaused events.... A human being is simultaneously a machine and a sentient free agent, depending on the purpose of the discussion, just as he is also a taxpayer, an insurance salesman, a dental patient, and two hundred pounds of ballast on a commuter airplane, depending on the purpose of the discussion. The mechanistic stance allows us to understand what makes us tick and how we fit into the physical universe. When those discussions wind down for the day, we go back to talking about each other as free and dignified human beings." (Steven Pinker, *How the Mind Works* [New York: W. W. Norton, 1997], 55, 56) (emphasis added).

a pluralistic society of competing religious and secular worldviews.[14] Despite their intuitive appeal to many in the academic and professional cultures in which secular bioethics is dominant, I want to argue that these views are not neutral and uncontested concepts. Rather, they support an account of the common good and the human person that answers precisely the same questions that the so-called contested worldviews, including so-called religious perspectives, attempt to answer. In order to make my case, I employ as my point of departure several comments that appeared in a 2008 article published in *The New Republic*, "The Stupidity of Dignity," authored by Harvard University psychology professor, Steven Pinker.[15]

Following the lead of bioethicist, Ruth Macklin, who published a 2003 editorial entitled, "Dignity is a Useless Concept,"[16] Professor Pinker maintains that "dignity" adds nothing of importance to bioethics:

The problem is that "dignity" is a squishy, subjective notion, hardly up to the heavy-weight moral demands assigned to it.... Ruth Macklin ... [has] argued that bioethics has done just fine with the principle of personal autonomy – the idea that, because all humans have the same minimum capacity to suffer, prosper, reason, and choose, no human has the right to impinge on the life, body, or freedom of another. This is why informed consent serves as the bedrock of ethical research and practice, and it clearly rules out the kinds of abuses that led to the birth of bioethics in the first place, such as Mengele's sadistic pseudoexperiments in Nazi Germany and the withholding of treatment to indigent black patients in the infamous Tuskegee syphilis study. Once you recognize the principle of autonomy, Macklin argued, "dignity" adds nothing.[17]

Pinker seems to be making two claims: (I) "Dignity" cannot be adequately defined because it is a subjective notion, and thus cannot inform our moral judgments, and (II) "dignity" is unnecessary because the principle of personal autonomy can do all the work that dignity is procured by its advocates to handle.

In what follows, I assess each claim as well as some of Pinker's sub-claims. Although I do not directly offer and defend a particular understanding of intrinsic human dignity, I offer several counterexamples and clarifications that rely on what I believe is an understanding of human dignity embraced by many members of the President's Council on Bioethics as well as other scholars from a variety of religious and philosophical perspectives. I conclude that the view embraced by Pinker and his allies – and the cluster of ideas that they are convinced is entailed by it – is not the only one that rational reflection has the power and insight to deliver.

---

[14] See Jeffrey W. Bulger, "An Approach Towards Applying Principlism," *Ethics & Medicine: An International Journal of Bioethics* 25.2 (Summer 2009).

[15] Steven Pinker, "The Stupidity of Dignity," *The New Republic* Vol. 238 Issue 9 (28 May 2008): 28–31.

[16] Ruth Macklin, "Dignity is a Useless Concept," *British Medical Journal* 327 (20 December 2003): 1419–1420.

[17] Pinker, "The Stupidity of Dignity," 28.

## 4.1. DIGNITY IS SUBJECTIVE

Pinker argues that the concept of dignity is too subjective, and thus is relative, fungible, and harmful. On each count, Pinker fails to make his case.

### 4.1.A. Dignity Is Relative

Human dignity is relative, argues Pinker, because people and cultures have disagreed on the propriety of a variety of behaviors and whether or not those who engage in them are acting in a dignified fashion. For example, what constitutes proper dress or culinary practices, whether modesty requires knee-high stockings, or whether licking an ice cream cone in public is a case of bad gastronomic form, are matters of wide and varied opinions across cultures and across time.[18] This, according to Pinker, constitutes definitive evidence against the idea that human dignity is intrinsic to the person and thus not reducible to the flux of unguided nature, historical epochs, and/or social institutions.

This argument can be challenged on at least three grounds: (1) disagreement is not sufficient to reject intrinsic human dignity, (2) disagreement between cultures, ironically, counts against Pinker's position, and (3) Pinker confuses relative practices and beliefs about which social indignities may arise with the idea that intrinsic human dignity is an essential property had by human beings by nature.

(1) It does not follow from the fact that there are differing understandings of human dignity that there is no such thing as intrinsic human dignity or that no one has authentic or even approximate knowledge of it. The fact that Mother Teresa and Margaret Sanger, for example, had different conceptions of human dignity does mean that neither one was right. The premise – "people disagree on what constitutes human dignity" – is not sufficient to support the conclusion, "therefore, intrinsic human dignity is either not known or non-existent." It may, of course, turn out that Pinker is correct. But the mere fact of disagreement cannot logically ground his claim.

Moreover, if disagreement over the meaning of a concept entails its relativity, this is true of autonomy as well, Pinker's suggested replacement for dignity. Writes Christopher Kaczor:

---

[18] "One doesn't have to be a scientific or moral relativist to notice that ascriptions of dignity vary radically with the time, place, and beholder. In olden days, a glimpse of stocking was looked on as something shocking. We chuckle at the photographs of Victorians in starched collars and wool suits hiking in the woods on a sweltering day, or at the Brahmins and patriarchs of countless societies who consider it beneath their dignity to pick up a dish or play with a child. Thorstein Veblen wrote of a French king who considered it beneath his dignity to move his throne back from the fireplace, and one night roasted to death when his attendant failed to show up. [Leon] Kass finds other people licking an ice-cream cone to be shamefully undignified; I have no problem with it." (Pinker, "The Stupidity of Dignity," 30).

[Immanuel] Kant, the originator of the contemporary emphasis on autonomy, considered it always contrary to autonomy, the self-given universal law of practical reason, to commit suicide or to have sexual activity of any kind outside of a marriage between one man and one woman. Contemporary advocates of using autonomy as the basis for ethics reject these positions with scorn. Now autonomy is used to attempt to justify physician-assisted suicide as well as freedom of "sexual expression." So, if dignity cannot be used in bioethics because it has been understood in various ways over the ages, this standard likewise excludes appealing to autonomy in bioethical disputes.[19]

What's good for the goose is good for the gander. If disagreement over autonomy's meaning entails that it cannot be employed in assessing bioethical decisions, then neither can autonomy, given the disagreement over its meaning.

(2) Pinker makes a claim – disagreement about what constitutes human dignity means there is no truth on the matter – that undermines his own position. After all, some of us believe that Pinker's view is mistaken. We, in other words, *disagree* with Pinker over whether intrinsic human dignity exists and whether any of us can have knowledge of it if, in fact, it does exist. Some of us indeed believe that intrinsic human dignity is real and knowable, whereas others of us, like Pinker, do not. But, according to Pinker, disagreement over the question of human dignity means that one ought to believe that there is no truth on the matter. Thus, Pinker himself ought to abandon his own position about human dignity's relativity as the truth on the matter, because some of us, after all, disagree with it. What's more, the principle that seems to ground his proposition does not itself garner universal agreement – whenever people disagree on the matter of X, there is truth on the matter of X – and thus on its own grounds must be rejected. As Hadley Arkes points out concerning a similar argument in support of moral relativism, "My disagreement establishes that the proposition does not enjoy a universal assent, and by the very terms of the proposition, that should be quite sufficient to determine *its own invalidity*."[20]

(3) Conceptually, Pinker is confusing the "dignity" we often associate with social practices, and what they may or may not mean to the community, with the idea of dignity as a philosophical or theological concept that refers to an intrinsic property had by human persons from the moment they come into being. The former, no one doubts, is in a sense relative. But as many have pointed out,[21]

[19] Christopher Kaczor, "The Importance of Dignity: A Reply to Steven Pinker," *Public Discourse: Ethics, Law, and the Common Good*, Online Publication of the Witherspoon Institute (31 January 2012), available at http://www.thepublicdiscourse.com/2012/01/4540/.

[20] Hadley Arkes, *First Things: An Inquiry Into the First Principles of Moral and Justice* (Princeton NJ: Princeton University Press, 1986), 132.

[21] See, e.g., Arkes, *First Things*, 134–158; C. S. Lewis, *Mere Christianity* (a revised and amplified edition, with a new introduction, of the three books, *Broadcast Talks, Christian Behaviour, and Beyond Personality*) (San Francisco: HarperCollins, 2001; originally published in 1952), 5–6; and Timothy Mosteller, *Relativism: A Guide for the Perplexed* (New York: Continuum, 2008), 43–57.

these social practices are often relative to that which is nonrelative. That is, the sorts of practices offered by Pinker as evidence of dignity's relativity typically acquire their meaning and justification because of their power to actualize and protect deeper and apparently unchanging truths. C. S. Lewis provides several illustrations to make this point:

I know that some people say the idea of a Law of Nature or decent behaviour known to all men is unsound, because different civilisations and different ages have had quite different moralities.

But this is not true. There have been differences between their moralities, but these have never amounted to anything like a total difference. If anyone will take the trouble to compare the moral teaching of, say, the ancient Egyptians, Babylonians, Hindus, Chinese, Greeks and Romans, what will really strike him will be how very like they are to each other and to our own. Some of the evidence for this I have put together in the appendix of another book called *The Abolition of Man*; but for our present purpose I need only ask the reader to think what a totally different morality would mean. Think of a country where people were admired for running away in battle, or where a man felt proud of double-crossing all the people who had been kindest to him. You might just as well try to imagine a country where two and two made five. Men have differed as regards what people you ought to be unselfish to – whether it was only your own family, or your fellow countrymen, or everyone. But they have always agreed that you ought not to put yourself first. Selfishness has never been admired. Men have differed as to whether you should have one wife or four. But they have always agreed that you must not simply have any woman you liked.[22]

By contrast, the philosophical or theological concept of dignity – that it is an intrinsic essential property had by human persons from the moment they come into being – is not something its defenders claim can be discovered by mere empirical observation of cultural practices, as Pinker seems to think, for he limits his critique to recording just such observations. But, just as the country singer Johnny Lee once sang of his vain search for love in "single bars" and with "good time lovers,"[23] Pinker is looking for dignity in all the wrong places.

According to those who champion the idea of intrinsic human dignity, it is something that we come to know when we reflect upon the nature of human

---

[22] Lewis, *Mere Christianity*, 5–6.
[23] From the song, "Lookin' for Love" by Johnny Lee:

> I spent a lifetime lookin' for you
> Single bars and good time lovers were never true
> Playing a fools game, hopin' to win
> Tellin' those sweet lies and losin' again.
>
> I was lookin' for love in all the wrong places
> Lookin' for love in too many places
> Searchin' her eyes, lookin' for traces
> Of what I'm dreamin' of
> Hoping to find a friend and a lover
> I'll bless the day I discover,
> You – lookin' for love.

persons, their properties and powers, as well as the goods to which they are ordered and contribute to a human being's flourishing.[24] And yet, much like everything else about which we believe, the idea of intrinsic human dignity is deeply embedded in our cultural, jurisprudential, and religious traditions. (Hence, the Catholic Church's connection of human dignity with the *imago dei*, the image of God: "God has imprinted his own image and likeness on man [cf. Gen 1:26], conferring upon him an incomparable dignity.... In effect, beyond the rights which man acquires by his own work, there exist rights which do not correspond to any work he performs, but which flow from his essential dignity as a person."[25]) Thus, it is sometimes very difficult to understand human dignity apart from the institutions, laws, mores, practices, and beliefs in which the idea of human dignity finds expression, protection, and application.[26] This is why, for example, for most people the parable of the Good Samaritan, the charitable work of Mother Teresa, or Martin Luther King Jr.'s speech at the Lincoln Memorial resonate with them more than Immanuel Kant's categorical imperative.[27] And yet, human dignity is not reducible to the institutions, laws, mores, practices or beliefs in which and by which it is often recognized. For we can think of clear-cut cases in which and by which such institutions and practices have in fact not adequately protected human dignity, such as in the cases of Nazi Germany, Stalinist Russia, and American slavery. This is because human dignity is an intrinsic property had by all human beings by nature. And much more follows from this insight.

Intrinsic human dignity, if it indeed exists, cannot be a degreed property like rationality, moral virtue, intelligence, height, or weight. For at whatever *degree* each is manifested, that degree is accidental and not essential to the sort of thing that has that property. For by their very nature these properties change, develop, diminish or cease to be actual over time for the human being who has them. But that means that the human being as a whole is prior to its accidental properties, for the human being subsists as a unified being through all the changes it undergoes. Of course, because the human being is by nature a rational moral animal – as I explain more thoroughly in Chapter 5 – these accidental properties are grounded in the human being's essential properties,

---

[24] See, e.g., J. P. Moreland, *The Recalcitrant Imago Dei: Human Persons and the Failure of Naturalism* (London: SCM Press, 2009); Patrick Lee and Robert P. George, "The Nature and Basis of Human Dignity," *Ratio Juris* 21.2 (June 2008): 173–193; and John Finnis, *Fundamentals of Ethics* (Washington, DC: Georgetown University Press, 1983).

[25] Pope John Paul II, *Centesimus Annus* (1 May 1991), 11, available at http://www.vatican.va/holy_father/john_paul_ii/encyclicals/documents/hf_jp-ii_enc_01051991_centesimus-annus_en.html.

[26] See, e.g., Alasdair MacIntyre, *After Virtue* (Notre Dame, IN: University of Notre Dame Press).

[27] There are several formulations of Kant's Categorical Imperative, the most well-known of which is: "Act only according to that maxim whereby you can, at the same time, will that it should become a universal law." (Immanuel Kant, *Grounding for the Metaphysics of Morals* [1785], with *On a Supposed Right to Lie Because of Philanthropic Concerns*, trans. James W. Ellington, 3rd ed. [Indianapolis: Hackett Publishing, 1993], 30).

such as the ultimate capacities to exercise rationality and moral choice as well as to have a height or a weight. Thus, if the human being is ontologically prior to its accidental properties, its intrinsic dignity cannot be one of those accidental properties. Moreover, if any of the human being's accidental properties were the ground of its dignity, dignity would no longer be an intrinsic and essential property that is actualized in any being that exemplifies human nature. It would also mean that we would have to abandon the idea of human equality and draw the conclusion that no two human beings have the same degree of dignity.[28]

Because human dignity is not a degreed property, it cannot develop and/or atrophy. For that reason, it is not a material property that has mass or extension. Moreover, because human dignity is intrinsic to every being that exemplifies human nature, it is not the sort of property that is local, in the sense that it depends on the mature actualization of particular human powers and properties, such as intelligence, rational faculties, moral choice, etc. Rather, human dignity is a global property, one that applies to the human being as a whole. That is, human dignity is the essential property had by the unified entity of a particular sort that maintains absolute identity through change, including the development, growth, and flourishing, as well as the decline and diminishing, of her numerous accidents and powers. This is why it is difficult to sustain

---

[28] Lee and George, for example, argue that a human being is intrinsically valuable and possesses intrinsic dignity because it is a being with a rational nature, that is, one that has the basic natural capacity for rationality from the moment it comes into existence (Lee and George, "The Nature and Basis of Human Dignity"). In making their case they argue that this basic natural capacity is not an accidental property:

> On this position every human being, of whatever age, size, or stage of development, has inherent and equal fundamental dignity and basic rights. If one holds, on the contrary, that full moral worth or dignity is based on some accidental attribute, then, since the attributes that could be considered to ground basic moral worth (developed consciousness, etc.) vary in degree, one will be led to the conclusion that moral worth also varies in degrees.

> It might be objected against this argument, that the basic natural capacity for rationality also comes in degrees, and so this position (that full moral worth is based on the possession of the basic natural capacity for rationality), if correct, would also lead to the denial of fundamental personal equality.... However, the criterion for full moral worth is having a nature that entails the capacity (whether existing in root form or developed to the point at which it is immediately exercisable) for conceptual thought and free choice – not *the development* of that basic natural capacity to some degree or other. The criterion for full moral worth and possession of basic rights is not the possession of a capacity for conscious thought and choice considered as an accidental attribute that inheres in an entity, but being a certain kind of thing, that is, having a specific type of substantial nature. Thus, possession of full moral worth follows upon being a certain type of entity or substance, namely, a substance with a rational nature, despite the fact that some persons (substances with a rational nature) have a greater intelligence, or are morally superior (exercise their power for free choice in an ethically more excellent way) than others. Since basic rights are grounded in being a certain type of substance, it follows that having such a substantial nature qualifies one as having full moral worth, basic rights, and equal personal dignity. (Lee and George, "The Nature and Basis of Human Dignity," 190; citation omitted)

the idea of "human dignity" as an intrinsic property of the whole being if one maintains that the human being is merely a collection of material parts rather than a real unified substance whose parts work in concert for the good of the whole. In sum, its champions claim that human dignity is an intrinsic, immaterial, nonempirical,[29] nondegreed, and essential property had by human beings by nature.

But remember, the second of the two foundational ideas maintained by Pinker and his allies is SM, the view that affirms, as I noted earlier, that because science concerns itself only with material and efficient causes, and because science is the best or only way of knowing, therefore, any claim that cannot be accounted for under that rubric either is not real or cannot be known to be real. This, of course, excludes the possibility that there exists, or we can have knowledge of, an immaterial, nondegreed, nonempirical, intrinsic property such as human dignity.[30] As Pinker asserted in his 2003 testimony before the President's Council on Bioethics:

The idea of humans as possessing some immaterial essence that categorically distinguishes them from animals, I think, is going to come under – is going to become less and less credible, and there will be, I think, a crisis among the religious faiths that depend critically on the assumption that there is some nonmaterial essence.... I think there's going to be a rethinking of ethical issues, such as responsibility and justice and equality, not that it will evaporate.... On the contrary, I think they will focus our ethical discussions on what we most value, what we want moral guidelines to do.[31]

In his 1997 book, *How the Mind Works*, Pinker is more explicit in his commitment to SM:

The traditional explanation of intelligence is that human flesh is suffused with a non-material entity, the soul, usually envisioned as some sort of ghost or spirit. But the theory faces an insurmountable problem: How does the spook interact with solid matter? How does an ethereal nothing respond to flashes, pokes, and beeps and get arms and legs to move? Another problem is the overwhelming evidence that the mind is the activity of the brain. The supposedly immaterial soul, we know now, can be bisected with a knife,

---

[29] In one sense, some champions of intrinsic human dignity would say human dignity is empirically detectable insofar as our awareness of that property arises when our minds grasp the nature of the human being, an exercise of an intellectual power that *begins with* sense experience. The problem is that thinkers, like Pinker, who consider themselves empiricists, naturalists, and so on have a deficient understanding both of what counts as "empirical" and of how to detect it. What they mean by "empirical" is associated with the Empricism that developed out of the work of David Hume (1711–1776), namely, that which is knowable is merely passively received sense perception of a universe that seems to be nothing more than matter in motion.

[30] See, e.g., Margaret Urban Walker, "Introduction: Groningen Naturalism in Bioethics," in *Naturalized Bioethics: Toward Responsible Knowing and Practice*, ed., Hilde Lindemann, Marian Verkerk, and Margaret Urban Walker (New York: Cambridge University Press, 2009), 1–20.

[31] Meeting Transcript (6 March 2003), President's Council on Bioethics, available at http://www.bioethics.gov/transcripts/march03/mar6full.html.

altered by chemicals, started or stopped by electricity, and extinguished by a sharp blow or by insufficient oxygen.[32]

(Oddly, Pinker is raising questions about the Cartesian view of the soul, which has rarely been defended by religious believers as their view. For such believers often rely on Aristotelian understandings of the soul to illuminate and support what they learn from divine revelation. This is why, as some have noted,[33] this non-Cartesian view does not fall prey to the "insurmountable" problems that Pinker raises.)

And now we see why Pinker's epistemological and metaphysical commitments limit his analysis of human dignity to wardrobes and eating habits – empirical claims derived from sense perception that can be observed and quantified – when in fact the human dignity embraced by its advocates is not that sort of property. This is why, for Pinker, ethics is "what we most value, what we want moral guidelines to do."[34] By contrast, for the supporter of intrinsic human dignity, ethics is the normative standard by which we assess the rightness of what we value and what guidelines we want. But this option is not open for Pinker. He is committed to an evolutionary naturalist account of ethics that maintains that what we value emerges from inherited behavioral dispositions, although these dispositions, he admits, provide no moral grounds for why an agent ought to behave consistently with those dispositions in the future.[35] So, he offers us an account of morality that is bereft of any duties we may have to obey it.

---

[32] Pinker, *How the Mind Works*, 64.

[33] Edward Feser, *Aquinas: A Beginner's Guide* (Oxford: Oneworld, 2009), 131–173; David Oderberg, "Hylomorphic Dualism," in *Personal Identity*, ed. Ellen Frankel Paul, Fred D. Miller, Jr., and Jeffrey Paul (New York: Cambridge University Press, 2005), 70–99.

[34] Meeting Transcript (6 March 2003), President's Council on Bioethics, available at http://www .bioethics.gov/transcripts/march03/mar6full.html Pinker writes elsewhere: "The foundation of individual rights is the assumption that people have wants and needs and are authorities on what those wants and needs are" (Pinker, *How the Mind Works*, 48).

[35] "[M]oral emotions are designed by natural selection to further the long-term interests of individuals and ultimately their genes" (Pinker, *How the Mind Works*, 406). Writes Pinker:

> Our organs of computation are a product of natural selection. The biologist Richard Dawkins called natural selection the Blind Watchmaker; in the case of the mind, we can call it the Blind Programmer. Our mental programs work as well as they do because they were shaped by selection to allow our ancestors to master rocks, tools, plants, animals, and each other, ultimately in the service of survival and reproduction.

> Natural selection is not the only cause of evolutionary change. Organisms also change over the eons because of statistical accidents in who lives and who dies, environmental catastrophes that wipe out whole families of creatures, and the unavoidable by-products of changes that *are* the product of selection. But natural selection is the only evolutionary force that acts like an engineer, "designing" organs that accomplish improbable adaptive outcomes (a point that has been made forcefully by the biologist George Williams and by Dawkins)....

> Nature does not dictate what we should accept or how we should live our lives.... I do know that happiness and virtue have nothing to do with what natural selection designed us to accomplish in our ancestral environment. They are for us to determine. In saying this I am

Ironically, Pinker's suggestion that SM ought to be the metaphysical principle that guides our bioethics violates the first foundational idea that he and his allies embrace: PL. That is, because proponents of SM attempt to answer the same fundamental question that contrary points of view attempt to answer on matters bioethical – who and what are we and can we know it? – a regime, whether political or legal, that proclaims SM as its official position on the nature of human persons and our knowledge about them violates PL's requirement for worldview neutrality. Although he claims in one place that "a free society disempowers the state from enforcing a conception of dignity on its citizens,"[36] Pinker nevertheless seeks to shape policy in a direction that recognizes only those views informed exclusively by SM.

### 4.1.B. Dignity Is Fungible

According to Pinker, dignity is often set aside or trumped when another good is at stake. He writes:

The Council ... treat[s] dignity as a sacred value, never to be compromised. In fact, every one of us voluntarily and repeatedly relinquishes dignity for other goods in life. Getting out of a small car is undignified. Having sex is undignified. Doffing your belt and spread-eagling to allow a security guard to slide a wand up your crotch is undignified. Most pointedly, modern medicine is a gantlet of indignities. Most readers of this article have undergone a pelvic or rectal examination, and many have had the pleasure of a colonoscopy as well. We repeatedly vote with our feet (and other body parts) that dignity is a trivial value, well worth trading off for life, health, and safety.[37]

Pinker is confusing awkward or embarrassing situations or events – which in our verbal nomenclature we call "indignities" – with a violation of a person's intrinsic human dignity, which, as we have already seen, its proponents maintain is an intrinsic moral property had by human beings by nature. This understanding of human dignity means, among other things, that human beings and their caregivers should treat the human person consistently with his or her own good as a person and not merely as a means to some apparently good end. So,

---

no hypocrite, even though I am a conventional straight white male. Well into my procreating years I am, so far, voluntarily childless, having squandered my biological resources reading and writing, doing research, helping out friends and students, and jogging in circles, ignoring the solemn imperative to spread my genes. By Darwinian standards I am a horrible mistake, a pathetic loser, not one iota less than if I were a card-carrying member of Queer Nation. But I am happy to be that way, and if my genes don't like it, they can jump in the lake.

(Ibid., 36, 52). See also Steven Pinker, "The Moral Instinct," *New York Times Magazine* (13 January 2008), available at http://www.nytimes.com/2008/01/13/magazine/13Psychology-t.html?_r=1&pagewanted=all.

[36] Pinker, "The Stupidity of Dignity," 30.
[37] Ibid.

according to that understanding, a violation of human dignity would occur if a physician were to *discourage* her patient to undergo a routine pelvic or rectal examination because of the "indignities" described by Pinker. This is because the good of the patient is compromised when he or she willingly abandons her own good in order to avoid a mild indignity that is by its nature not intrinsically immoral.

Moreover, as Kaczor points out, Pinker's own suggested alternative to dignity, autonomy, is fungible as well:

Soldiers give up autonomy when they enlist for military service. Employees give up autonomy when they sign contracts agreeing to perform certain services and refrain from doing other activities that constitute a conflict of interest. Police officers, FBI agents, and politicians relinquish autonomy when they swear to enforce the laws of our nation. Lawyers and psychologists give up autonomy in speech in preserving client or patient confidentiality. Do the actions of these people reveal that autonomy is a trivial value, well worth trading off for money, public order, confidentiality, the good of raising children, or health?[38]

So, just as undergoing mild indignities for the sake of trying to acquire an intrinsic good for oneself does not mean that the idea of human dignity is trivial, voluntarily giving up one's autonomy for the sake of advancing the common good or living within the ethical contours of a noble profession does not entail the triviality of autonomy.

### 4.1.C. Dignity Is Harmful

Pinker maintains that dignity is harmful. That is, of course, an odd thing to say because willing the good of the human person – as human dignity requires – cannot, by definition, be harmful. What then does Pinker mean? What he means is that throughout human history, governments, and especially religious groups, have committed unspeakable crimes against people in the name of enforcing their version of "dignity" on others. He writes:

Every sashed and bemedaled despot reviewing his troops from a lofty platform seeks to command respect through ostentatious displays of dignity. Political and religious repressions are often rationalized as a defense of the dignity of a state, leader, or creed: Just think of the Salman Rushdie fatwa, the Danish cartoon riots, or the British schoolteacher in Sudan who faced flogging and a lynch mob because her class named a teddy bear Mohammed. Indeed, totalitarianism is often the imposition of a leader's conception of dignity on a population, such as the identical uniforms in Maoist China or the burqas of the Taliban.[39]

Pinker is no doubt correct that there are, and have been, despots who employ the language of "dignity" for the purpose of violating the intrinsic human

---

[38] Kaczor, "The Importance of Dignity: A Reply to Steven Pinker," n.p.
[39] Pinker, "The Stupidity of Dignity," 30.

dignity of their citizens. But that's not an argument against the claim made by many contributors to the council's report that a human being possesses intrinsic dignity by nature. Pinker is simply making the observation that political and religious leaders sometimes debase language for the purpose of achieving unjust ends. Who disagrees with that?

Nevertheless, a supporter of intrinsic human dignity could find Pinker's examples to be useful illustrations of what happens when a culture or civilization abandons or does not fully embrace the idea of intrinsic human dignity. In fact, one such supporter, St. Pope John Paul II, whose name is mentioned in the council's report over fifteen times, makes this very point in his 1995 encyclical *Evangelium Vitae*:

> It is true that history has known cases where crimes have been committed in the name of "truth." But equally grave crimes and radical denials of freedom have also been committed and are still being committed in the name of "ethical relativism." When a parliamentary or social majority decrees that it is legal, at least under certain conditions, to kill unborn human life, is it not really making a "tyrannical" decision with regard to the weakest and most defenceless of human beings? Everyone's conscience rightly rejects those crimes against humanity of which our century has had such sad experience. But would these crimes cease to be crimes if, instead of being committed by unscrupulous tyrants, they were legitimated by popular consensus?[40]

Thus, the rhetorical trick that Pinker brings to our attention – using the language of "good ends" to justify violating or ignoring a person's intrinsic dignity – was brought to the world's attention in 1995 by a Slavic Pope who knew something about what it means for a regime to embrace ideologies that violate human dignity. As a citizen of Poland, he survived the totalitarian adventures of two such regimes: Nazi Germany and the Soviet Union.[41]

Pinker is certainly right to bring to our attention this disreputable practice of employing the language of dignity as a means to sequester true justice from one's policy deliberations. For this reason, let me suggest yet another example, but one often ignored by Pinker and others who embrace similar views on intrinsic human dignity.

Consider the eugenics movement of the twentieth century. Its members offered a scientific research program that they were confident would secure certain desirable ends: human excellence, social improvement, and the eradication of a variety of mental and physical pathologies. The eugenicists offered the promise of a brave new future free of misery and disease, one that might fail to be realized if the citizenry stood in the way and continued thinking of

---

[40] John Paul II, *Evangelium Vitae: Encyclical Letter on the Value and Inviolability of Human Life* (25 March 1995), 20, available at http://www.newadvent.org/library/docs_jpo2ev.htm (1 March 2013).

[41] George Weigel, *Witness to Hope: The Biography of John Paul II* (New York: HarperCollins, 1999).

the targets of eugenicists as persons with intrinsic dignity. Take, for example, the following comments that appeared in an article published in 1914 in the *Virginia Law Review*:

Could there be general welfare, or would the blessings of liberty to us and our posterity be secured, if there were not restraint upon the human object of the sterilization laws as already passed? Can there be the full blessings of liberty, or full domestic tranquility, if those civilly unfit are allowed to procreate their species and scatter their kind here and there and everywhere amongst our people? ...We bestow care upon the breeding of our chickens, horses and cattle; is not the human being worthy of equal care? Nature provides certain immutable laws. It is the duty of our scientists to develop those laws for the benefit of mankind. And if by research it has been found that sterilization will prevent the procreation of idiots, criminals and degenerates, is it not the duty of the legislatures to enact laws which will bring it about? Has it not been for ages an undenied principle that the few must suffer for the good of the many? And when we cause these few to suffer, does it not foster and promote the preamble proclaiming the object of our Constitution?[42]

Pinker, ironically, offers the same type of rhetorically charged parade of utopian promises – human excellence, social improvement, and the eradication of a variety of mental and physical pathologies – in order to justify several practices such as embryonic stem-cell research and "therapeutic human cloning."[43] He suggests by his comments that researchers and scientists should not take into consideration the moral status of their research subjects (human embryos) or how that research may change the way we think of ourselves, our children, and the other members of our community. Those who think otherwise are labeled "theocons." Writes Pinker:

[T]heocon bioethics flaunts a callousness toward the billions of nongeriatric people, born and unborn, whose lives or health could be saved by biomedical advances. Even if progress were delayed a mere decade by moratoria, red tape, and funding taboos (to say nothing of the threat of criminal prosecution), millions of people with degenerative diseases and failing organs would needlessly suffer and die. And that would be the biggest affront to human dignity of all.[44]

---

[42] J. Miller Kenyon, "Sterilization of the Unfit," *Virginia Law Review* 1 (1913–1914): 461–462, 466.

[43] "This spring [2008], the President's Council on Bioethics released a 555-page report, titled *Human Dignity and Bioethics*. The Council, created in 2001 by George W. Bush, is a panel of scholars charged with advising the president and exploring policy issues related to the ethics of biomedical innovation, including drugs that would enhance cognition, genetic manipulation of animals or humans, therapies that could extend the lifespan, and embryonic stem cells and so-called 'therapeutic cloning' that could furnish replacements for diseased tissue and organs. Advances like these, if translated into freely undertaken treatments, could make millions of people better off and no one worse off. So what's not to like? The advances do not raise the traditional concerns of bioethics, which focuses on potential harm and coercion of patients or research subjects. What, then, are the ethical concerns that call for a presidential council?" (Pinker, "The Stupidity of Dignity," 28).

[44] Ibid., 31.

Although Pinker's language is far more urbane and politically correct than the crude suggestions made by his eugenicist predecessor in 1914, the moral substance is the same: utilitarian considerations, rather than the question of intrinsic human dignity, ought to serve as the basis by which we assess our scientific work on human subjects. Like the 1914 eugenicist, Pinker is asking us to set aside or diminish the question of the moral status of ourselves and our research subjects and focus exclusively on the promised end of eradicating all illness and imperfection.

Moreover, as Kaczor notes, Pinker completely ignores the harm that can arise from the exercise of autonomy:

[I]t is even more obvious that autonomy can be harmful. Consider the case of Desmond Hatchett who, before the age of thirty, exercised his sexual autonomy by fathering twenty-one children with eleven different women. Exercising her reproductive autonomy in similarly irresponsible fashion, Nadya Suleman, unemployed and unmarried, used in vitro fertilization to add eight more babies to join her other six young children at home. Drug abusers exercise their autonomy in harming themselves physically and mentally, often to the point where they become a drain on society. Politicians regularly exercise their autonomy in such a way as to cause unreasonable taxes, unfair laws, and unjust wars for their own political gain. Indeed, misuse of autonomy causes more harm, arguably much more harm, than misuse of dignity.[45]

Thus, if the misuse of the concept of human dignity means that it is of no value in bioethical judgments, then we can say the same about autonomy and on those grounds reject it as a suggested replacement for human dignity.

## 4.2. DIGNITY IS UNNECESSARY

Having dealt with Pinker's claim that dignity is too subjective, I want to now assess his claim that dignity is unnecessary – that the principle of autonomy can do all the work for which dignity has been conscripted by its advocates. Here is Pinker's argument, as I quoted earlier at the beginning of this chapter:

Ruth Macklin ... [has] argued that bioethics has done just fine with the principle of personal autonomy – the idea that, because all humans have the same minimum capacity to suffer, prosper, reason, and choose, no human has the right to impinge on the life, body, or freedom of another. This is why informed consent serves as the bedrock of ethical research and practice, and it clearly rules out the kinds of abuses that led to the birth of bioethics in the first place, such as Mengele's sadistic pseudoexperiments in Nazi Germany and the withholding of treatment to indigent black patients in the infamous Tuskegee syphilis study. Once you recognize the principle of autonomy, Macklin argued, "dignity" adds nothing.[46]

---

[45] Kaczor, "The Importance of Dignity: A Reply to Steven Pinker," n.p.
[46] Ibid., 28.

There are several reasons why I do not think this argument works: (1) autonomy presupposes dignity, but is not identical to it, (2) dignity has greater explanatory power than does autonomy in accounting for certain wrongs, (3) nonautonomous human beings can have their dignity violated, and (4) it has problems accounting for autonomy as a power had by a rational agent.

### 4.2.A. Autonomy Is Not Identical to Dignity

What if, while on a panel discussion at a meeting of the American Psychological Association, someone turned to Pinker and shouted, "Please sit down and shut up. I am right and you are wrong. And that's that." I suspect that Pinker would find this treatment grossly inappropriate, one not consistent with the sort of respect a man of his accomplishments and stature should be afforded in such a public venue. He would indeed be correct. But why would he think so? Is there something about him that requires others to treat him with respect and deference? Perhaps it is his accomplishments. That seems partly right. But what precisely is it about his accomplishments that demands our respect? It seems to me that they are impressive because they are the consequence of the development of natural gifts that a person with such gifts is morally required to hone and perfect and not to waste on frivolity. After all, if in another possible world Steven Pinker$_2$ had in fact spent his adult years as a couch potato collecting welfare checks, eating Cheetos, and watching Jerry Springer until he died as an obese loner in a Central Texas trailer park, we would rightfully lament the incredible waste of native abilities that not only disrupted Mr. Pinker's own good but the common good as well. So, we would say that Steven Pinker$_2$, by living a life of laziness and self-indulgence, did not properly respect himself. He would, by all accounts, have exercised his personal autonomy, and yet he did so in a way inconsistent with the intrinsic purposes of a being of his nature. So, the exercise of autonomy not only cannot adequately ground human dignity; it can be exercised inconsistently with that dignity.

Thus, we would be correct in saying that in a sense one ought not respect people like Steven Pinker$_2$ who, when given the opportunity to hone and nurture certain gifts waste these potentials in a life of sloth and depravity. But the "respect" not owed here is not the respect about which defenders of human dignity write. It is a second-order respect that is *earned* by persons who properly employ and nurture those natural talents that are not equitably distributed among human beings (and thus come in degrees and thus cannot be the basis of first-order respect, or human dignity). But the withholding or lavishing of second-order respect on a particular being makes sense only in light of the *sort of being* it is by nature, that is, a being who has certain intrinsic capacities and purposes that if prematurely disrupted by either its own agency or another agent, result in an injustice. So, the human being who wastes his talents is one who does not respect his natural gifts or the basic capacities whose maturation and proper employment make possible the flourishing of talent and skill.

That is, the idea that certain perfections grounded in basic capacities have been impermissibly obstructed from maturing is assumed in the very judgment one makes about human beings and the way in which they should treat themselves (as in the case of Steven Pinker$_2$) or be treated by others (as in the case of the actual Steven Pinker who was told to shut up and sit down). Thus, both Steven Pinker and Steven Pinker$_2$ possess intrinsic human dignity, even if Steven Pinker objects to our assessment about the grounds by which we should accord him the respect to which he believes he is entitled. And in neither case is the principle of autonomy doing any of the real work.

### 4.2.B. Dignity Has Greater Explanatory Power Than Does Autonomy

According to Pinker, "[I]nformed consent serves as the bedrock of ethical research and practice, and it clearly rules out the kinds of abuses that led to the birth of bioethics in the first place, such as Mengele's sadistic pseudoexperiments in Nazi Germany."[47] Although it is true that the Nazi victims were not provided with informed consent, it does not follow that the absence of that informed consent is the reason why the Nazi research was wicked.

After all, suppose we discovered that half of the Nazis' victims had come to believe Adolph Hitler's rhetoric and concluded that they were in fact to blame for all that was wrong with Germany. And imagine that some of them willingly became Mengele's guinea pigs and the remaining went to the gas chambers because of their love for the Fatherland. These courses of action would be entirely voluntary, an exercise of the principle of autonomy. Yet, the reason why these people were gassed was precisely the same reason why the nonvoluntary victims were gassed. A bad reason to do evil does not become less of a bad reason simply because the victim voluntarily participates in his own unjustified homicide. Replacing intrinsic dignity with autonomy actually diminishes that wrong, for it turns an intrinsic wrong into a conditional one. So, ironically, if this analysis is correct, it is autonomy and not dignity that is not a necessary condition for assessing the wickedness of these acts. Thus, it is the idea that human beings have intrinsic dignity that best accounts for our understanding of the wrongness of the Nazi atrocities.

I am, of course, not suggesting that autonomy does not matter for ethics. Consent, for example, is a necessary condition for the licitness of a marriage. There is, after all, such a thing as unjust coercion. Rather, what I am arguing is that the moral life cannot be *reduced* to mere autonomy, as Pinker believes should be done. For, as we have seen, when Pinker's reduction is applied to actual atrocities, our attention subtly shifts from what seems true at first sight – the intrinsic dignity of the human person – to the deflated alternative which the modern mind thinks it can substitute without remainder: the conditional will of the individual chooser.

---

[47] Ibid.

The implication of this is clear: there is no human good to which we are ordered and to which our wills should conform. Good is merely what we prefer, and to which we direct our wills. But in that case, we possess no *intrinsic* dignity, because such a property would be a good independent of what we will and under which our preferences should be ruled. In effect, mere autonomy is the abolition of human dignity.

### 4.2.C. Nonautonomous Beings Can Have Their Dignity Violated

Not only can the principle of autonomy not fully account for the wrongness of the Nazi atrocities, it also cannot account for the wrongness of intentionally creating nonautonomous human beings for apparently noble purposes. It seems that only intrinsic human dignity can do that. Consider this example. (In order to tap into the same intuitions while addressing the issue of abortion, I offer similar illustrations in Chapters 2 and 5.) Imagine an embryologist manipulates the development of an early embryo-clone in such a way that what results is an infant without higher brain functions, but whose healthy organs can be used for ordinary transplant purposes or for spare parts for the person from whom the embryo was cloned.[48] Given the dominant accounts of moral personhood in the literature – views that claim that a being's possession of protected moral status is contingent upon some presently held property or immediately exercisable mental capacity to function in a certain way[49] – it is not clear how intentionally creating such deformed beings for a morally good purpose is morally wrong. It certainly cannot be that the embryo-clone's autonomy is violated, because it has not reached a point in its development at which it can exercise autonomy. In fact, the whole point of tinkering with the embryo-clone's development is so that it will not become autonomous.

Suppose, in response, someone nevertheless argues that this is morally wrong because the embryo is entitled to his higher brain functions. But as bioethicist Dan Brock argues, "this body clone" could not arguably be harmed because of its "lack of capacity for consciousness."[50] Yet, he concedes that "most people would likely find" the practice of purposely creating permanently nonsentient human beings "appalling and immoral, in part because here the cloned later twin's capacity for conscious life is destroyed *solely as a means* to benefit another."[51] This intuition, however, only makes sense if the cloned twin is entitled to his higher brain functions. But according to

---

[48] Carol Kahn offers this proposal in her essay, "Can We Achieve Immortality?: The Ethics of Cloning and Other Life Extension Technologies," *Free Inquiry* (Spring 1989), 14–18.

[49] See, e.g., David Boonin, *A Defense of Abortion* (New York: Cambridge University Press).

[50] David W. Brock, "Cloning Human Beings: An Assessment of the Ethical Issues Pro and Con," in National Bioethics Advisory Commission, *Cloning Human Beings*, vol. 2 (Rockville, MD: The Commission, 1997), E8 (hereinafter, NBAC 2) (emphasis in original).

[51] Ibid., E9.

the view embraced by Pinker, the principle of autonomy is adequate for the purpose of determining whether scientific research is ethical. But the presentient embryo is not autonomous, because it cannot consciously choose. So, the entitlement account does not do the trick if autonomy is the ground of dignity, as Pinker claims. Moreover, imagine if a group of anti-cloning activists broke into the laboratory, abducted the tinkered-with embryo-clones, reversed the tinkering, and allowed the embryos to develop normally until they became healthy newborns and then were adopted by loving families. It seems perfectly reasonable to say that the anti-cloning activists had acted justly toward the embryo-clone, while the scientist who had originally tinkered-with the embryo-clone had not. It seems to me, therefore, that the moral principle supporting this judgment would have to look something like this: it is *prima facie* wrong to destroy the physical structure necessary for the realization of a human being's basic, natural capacity for the exercisability of a function that is a perfection of its nature.[52] But there are two problems for Pinker if he accepts this: (1) autonomy is totally absent from this account, and thus it shows that the principle of autonomy cannot do the sort of work he claims it can do, and (2) it means that human beings have certain natural ends that are perfections of their nature, an idea at home with the philosophical anthropology embraced by proponents of intrinsic human dignity.

## 4.2.D. Autonomy as a Power Had by a Rational Agent

According to Pinker, because "all humans have the same minimum capacity to suffer, prosper, reason, and choose, no human has the right to impinge on the life, body, or freedom of another."[53] But according to Pinker's account of the human person, all our faculties, including the cognitive faculties by which we reason, arrived in their present state as a result of blind nonrational forces combined with natural selection and/or perhaps other material causes.[54] In that

---

[52] This prima facie principle does not mean it would be wrong to destroy or amputate a diseased body part for the benefit of the whole person. In such a case, one can appeal to the *principle of totality*, which receives its meaning from what we know of the human person's good as a whole. Writes David Oderberg, the principle of totality "is simply a reflection of the evident metaphysical truth that the parts of a thing are subordinated to the thing itself; in the moral sphere, this is mirrored by the idea that the fundamental unit of concern is the human being, so that the parts of the person are morally important only insofar as they contribute to the person's normal functioning. If the person can only survive without a certain part, then the part must go even if the functioning is thereafter impaired" (David S. Oderberg, *Moral Theory: A Non-Consequentialist Approach* [Oxford: Blackwell, 2000], 78–79).

[53] Pinker, "The Stupidity of Dignity," 28.

[54] Writes Pinker:

> Our organs of computation are a product of natural selection. The biologist Richard Dawkins called natural selection the Blind Watchmaker; in the case of the mind, we can call it the Blind

case, what grounds would provide warrant for Pinker to claim that his cognitive faculties, including his rational powers, are functioning properly? Alvin Plantinga has raised a similar question in what he calls *an evolutionary argument against naturalism.*[55] I will briefly summarize Plantinga's argument while applying it to Pinker's case.

Here's the problem for Pinker: If he provides reasons for his belief that his cognitive faculties are functioning properly he must rely on those very cognitive faculties in order to arrive at those reasons. However, Pinker tells us that everyone's cognitive faculties, including his, arrived in their present state as a result of blind nonrational forces combined with natural selection and/ or perhaps other material causes. But, as Plantinga points out, "[e]volution is interested, not in true belief, but in survival or fitness." Thus, "[i]t is ... unlikely that our cognitive faculties have the production of true belief as a proximate or any other function, and the probability of our faculties' being reliable (given naturalistic evolution) would be fairly low."[56] Thus, "any argument" Pinker "offers" for the reliability of his cognitive faculties "is in this context delicately

Programmer. Our mental programs work as well as they do because they were shaped by selection to allow our ancestors to master rocks, tools, plants, animals, and each other, ultimate in the service of survival and reproduction.

Natural selection is not the cause of evolutionary change. Organisms also change over the eons because of statistical accidents in who lives and who dies, environmental catastrophes that wipe out whole families of creatures, and the unavoidable by-products of changes that *are* the product of selection. But natural selection is the only evolutionary force that acts like an engineer, "designing" organs that accomplish improbable adaptive outcomes (a point that has been made forcefully by the biologist George Williams and by Dawkins). (Pinker, *How The Mind Works*, 36)

55 Alvin Plantinga, *Warrant and Proper Function* (New York: Oxford University Press, 1993), 216–237.
56 Ibid., 219. Philosopher Anthony O'Hear makes a similar observation:

In the Darwinian view, even our reason is simply an instrument of survival. It was not given to us to unearth the ultimate truth about things but simply to find our way around the savannah well enough to survive and reproduce. That we have a disinterested power to seek and the ability to find the truth for its own sake is as much of an illusion as our faith that our moral sense is truly altruistic and other-regarding. It may, be like our moral faith, a useful illusion, for purposes of survival and reproduction, in that having the illusion may encourage us to uncover facts that aid survival. But it is an illusion none the less, foisted on us by our genes, that we are really engineered by nature to discover ultimate, universally valid truth. Neither our sense nor evolution in general provides any guarantee that what our investigations reveal is the real truth, as opposed to a set of notions useful for a time in the struggle for existence, which of course, leaves a question over the Darwinian notion itself that we are basically survival machines. Is that real truth or merely a notion useful in the struggle for survival? The Darwinian account, seeing our knowledge, as everything else about us, in terms simply of selective advantage, gives us no hope for deciding. (Anthony O'Hare, *After Progress: Finding the Old Way Forward* [London: Bloomsbury, 1999], 68)

circular or question-begging."[57] Although it is not *formally* circular in the sense that the conclusion appears in the argument's premises, it is, writes Plantinga, "*pragmatically* circular in that it purports to give a reason for trusting our cognitive faculties, but is itself trustworthy only if those faculties (at least the ones involved in its production) are indeed trustworthy." Thus, Pinker or your garden-variety naturalist "subtly assumes the very proposition" he "proposes to argue for." In other words, "[o]nce I come to doubt the reliability of my cognitive faculties, I can't properly try to allay that doubt by producing an *argument*; for in doing so I rely on the very faculties I am doubting."[58] Thus, one of the grounds that Pinker offers for the principle of autonomy – the minimal capacity to reason – is not an obvious deliverance of reason, because it seems, according to the arguments of Plantinga and several other thinkers,[59] difficult to sustain while embracing a materialist and evolutionary naturalist account of the human person.[60]

[57] Plantinga, *Warrant and Proper Function*, 234.

[58] Ibid. Plantinga suggests that the idea of properly functioning cognitive faculties makes the most sense if they were designed by a being for that purpose. That is, "naturalistic epistemology flourishes best in the garden of supernaturalistic metaphysics. Naturalistic epistemology conjoined with naturalistic metaphysics leads *via* evolution to skepticism or to violation of canons of rationality; conjoined with theism it does not. The naturalistic epistemologist should therefore prefer theism to metaphysical naturalism" (Plantinga, *Warrant and Proper Function*, 237). For a response to Plantinga's case, see Branden Fitelson and Elliot Sober, "Plantinga's Probability Arguments Against Evolutionary Naturalism," in *Intelligent Design Creationism and Its Critics: Philosophical, Theological, and Scientific Perspectives*, ed. Robert T. Pennock (Cambridge, MA: MIT Press, 2001).

[59] In addition to Plantinga's work, see William Hasker, *The Emergent Self* (Ithaca, NY: Cornell University Press, 1999); Stewart Goetz and Charles Taliaferro, *Naturalism* (Grand Rapids, MI: Eerdmans, 2008), 25–96; Richard Swinburne, *The Evolution of the Soul*, 2nd ed. (New York: Oxford University Press, 1997); Moreland, *The Recalcitrant Imago Dei*, especially 41–103; J. P. Moreland, *Consciousness and the Existence of God: A Theistic Argument* (New York: Routledge, 2009); J. P. Moreland, "The Argument from Consciousness," in *The Blackwell Companion to Natural Theology*, ed. William Lane Craig and J. P. Moreland (Oxford, UK: Wiley-Blackwell, 2009), 282–343; Victor Reppert, "The Argument from Reason," in *The Blackwell Companion to Natural Theology*, 344–390; Keith Yandell, "A Defense of Dualism," *Faith and Philosophy* 12 (October 1995): 548–66; Charles Taliaferro, "Animals, Brains, and Spirits," *Faith and Philosophy* 12 (October 1995): 567–81; and Ric Machuga, *In Defense of the Soul: What It Means to Be Human* (Grand Rapids, MI: Brazos Press, 2002)

[60] I say "evolutionary *naturalism*" to distinguish it from theistic evolution or other understandings of evolution that are non-naturalist. Because it is often mistakenly assumed that evolution is in-principle inconsistent with final or formal causes, many people, including some Christians, have come to believe that evolution per se is a defeater to the belief that the universe is designed. I address this error in Chapter 6. See also Etienne Gilson, *From Aristotle to Darwin and Back Again: A Journey in Final Causality, Species, and Evolution* (San Francisco: Ignatius Press, 2009; John Lyon trans., 1984; originally published in French in 1971); Francis S. Collins, *The Language of God: A Scientist Presents Evidence for Belief* (New York: The Free Press, 2006); and Alvin Plantinga, *Where The Conflict Really Lies: Science, Religion, and Naturalism* (New York: Oxford University Press, 2011), 3–31.

## 4.3. CONCLUSION

Pinker, like many secular academics, rejects notions such as "human dignity" because they are tightly tethered to understandings of the human person that spring from religious traditions. That, in itself, would be a good reason for Pinker and his allies to reject the idea of human dignity if and only if they could convincingly show that religious traditions and their attendant metaphysical and epistemological beliefs are obviously irrational and thus not necessary for the practice of bioethics. But, as we have seen, at least in terms of the belief in human dignity, at least one of those beliefs is neither obviously irrational nor obviously unnecessary.

# 5

# Personhood, Prenatal Life, and Religious Belief

Today there exists a great multitude of weak and defenceless human beings, unborn children in particular, whose fundamental right to life is being trampled upon. If, at the end of the last century, the Church could not be silent about the injustices of those times, still less can she be silent today, when the social injustices of the past, unfortunately not yet overcome, are being compounded in many regions of the world by still more grievous forms of injustice and oppression, even if these are being presented as elements of progress in view of a new world order.

St. Pope John Paul II (1920–2005)[1]

My suggestion, then, is that we accord the life of a fetus no greater value than the life of a nonhuman animal at a similar level of rationality, self-consciousness, awareness, capacity to feel, etc. Since no fetus is a person, no fetus has the same claim to life as a person. We have yet to consider at what point the fetus is likely to become capable of feeling pain. For now it will be enough to say that until that capacity exists, an abortion terminates an existence that is of no "intrinsic" value at all.

Peter Singer (1946–)[2]

The political and legal disputes over embryonic stem cell research, cloning, and abortion are some of the most contentious in public life. But, as I noted in both the introduction and Chapter 2, the question that any resolution to these disputes must address – when does a human being become a subject of moral concern? – is sometimes assessed in a way that suggests that the prolife answer to this question – that a human being is a moral subject from

---

[1] John Paul II, *Evangelium Vitae: Encyclical Letter on the Value and Inviolability of Human Life* (25 March 1995), 5, available at http://www.newadvent.org/library/docs_jpo2ev.htm (1 March 2013).
[2] Peter Singer, *Practical Ethics*, 2nd ed. (New York: Cambridge University Press, 1993), 151.

conception or soon thereafter – is a religious one and thus not a deliverance of rational argument. In this chapter I show that this is a mistake, and that its advocates seem to confuse a position that is tightly tethered to a theological tradition with a position incapable of being supported by rational argument. Why they make this mistake is unclear, although I suspect that it has more to do with commonly held, although rarely questioned, beliefs about the positions held by religious citizens rather than a charitable and careful assessment of the actual grounds on which the religious citizens hold the positions they do. This was clearly evident in the Secular Rationalism we assessed in Chapter 2.

In this present chapter, however, I will focus on disputes about the beginning of human life and whether the prolife position held by many religious citizens should be excluded from public life because, as its critics claim, it is not the deliverance of rational argument. (5.1) I first deal briefly with the issue of embryonic stem cell research and Sherry F. Colb's claim that because those citizens who oppose the federal funding of such research do so on religious grounds, it would violate the separation of church and state for the government to incorporate their understanding into the law. (5.2) I then move on to engage certain philosophical criticisms of the prolife view on unborn human life that is embraced by so many religious citizens. By doing this, I show how the prolife view is no different than contrary views that attempt to offer an account of the value of nascent life. And for that reason, the prolife view cannot be excluded from the public square simply because it is tightly tethered to a theological tradition. (5.3) I end this chapter with a brief discussion of some of the issues concerning the 2014 U.S. Supreme Court case, *Burwell v. Hobby Lobby Stores, Inc.*[3] This case involved two closely held family-run companies, Hobby Lobby and Conestoga Wood Specialties, that objected to a regulation, issued by the Secretary of Health Human Services (HHS) under powers given to her by the 2010 Affordable Care Act,[4] that required for-profit companies to include in their employee health insurance plans birth control methods that the owners believe may at times function as abortifacients, that is, they kill human embryos soon after conception. In a 5-4 opinion, the Court, applying the 1993 Religious Freedom Restoration Act (RFRA),[5] ruled in favor of Hobby Lobby and Conestoga Wood. After briefly reviewing the Supreme Court's holding, I argue that the Court mistakenly implies by its description of the businesses' objection to the mandate that their objection could not in principle be a deliverance of reason. This, unfortunately, reinforces habits of thought about religion that lead to not taking rites seriously.

---

[3] Burwell v. Hobby Lobby Stores, Inc., 134 S. Ct. 2751 (2014).
[4] Patient Protection and Affordable Care Act (2010), Public Law, 111–148.
[5] Religious Freedom Restoration Act (1993), Public Law 103–141.

## 5.1. EMBRYONIC STEM CELL RESEARCH

Stem cells are found in all animals, including human beings.[6] In adults, stem cells serve the function of repairing damaged tissue.[7] For example, "hematopoietic stem cells" are "a type of cell found in the blood."[8] Their purpose is to repair the tissue of a damaged part of the organ of which they are a part, for adult stem cells are differentiated.[9] However, stem cells found in the early embryo – before its cells differentiate into the cells of particular organs – "retain the special ability to develop into nearly any cell type."[10] The embryo's germ cells, "which originate from the primordial reproductive cells of the developing fetus," possess similar properties.[11]

Few doubt the potential of human stem cell research and the possibilities it offers for finding cures for numerous diseases such as Parkinson's and Alzheimer's.[12] But the real issue that animates opponents of this research, and raises deep ethical questions, is how these cells are obtained and from what entity they are derived. According to the National Bioethics Advisory Commission's (NBAC) 1999 report, these stem cells can be derived from four sources:

- human fetal tissue following elective abortion (EG cells) [Embryonic germ cells],
- human embryos that are created by *in vitro* fertilization (IVF) and that are no longer needed by couples being treated for infertility (ES cells) [Embryonic stem cells],
- human embryos that are created by IVF with gametes donated for the sole purpose of providing research material (ES cells), and
- potentially, human (or hybrid) embryos generated asexually by somatic cell nuclear transfer or similar cloning techniques in which the nucleus of an

---

[6] National Institutes of Health, *Stem Cell Information, Stem Cell Basics, Introduction: What are stem cells, and why are they important?*, available at http://stemcells.nih.gov/info/basics/pages/basics1.aspx (accessed 16 September 2014).

[7] National Institutes of Health, *Stem Cell Information, Stem Cell Basics, What are the unique properties of all stem cells?*, http://stemcells.nih.gov/info/basics/pages/basics2.aspx (accessed 16 September 2014).

[8] National Bioethics Advisory Commission, *Ethical Issues in Human Stem Cell Research: Volume I Report and Recommendations of the National Bioethics Advisory Commission* i (NBAC Sept. 1999) [hereinafter NBAC I, *Stem Cell*].

[9] Ibid.

[10] Ibid.

[11] Ibid

[12] National Institutes of Health, *Stem Cell Information, Stem Cell Basics, What are the potential uses of human stem cells and the obstacles that must be overcome before these potential uses will be realized?*, available at http://stemcells.nih.gov/info/basics/pages/basics6.aspx (accessed 17 September 2014).

adult human cell is introduced into an enucleated human or animal ovum (ES cells).[13]

Since the publication of the 1999 report, research on adult stem cells has shown much more promise in the research for which embryonic stem cells were procured.[14] Thus, we can now add a fifth source of stem cells for research. However, with the exception of the first and fifth sources, no embryo is intentionally killed as a direct consequence of acquiring its stem cells.[15] This is why many citizens who otherwise support stem-cell research oppose both *embryonic* stem-cell research as well as the federal funding of it.[16] For, according to these citizens, embryos are full-fledged members of the human community and thus the government at least ought not to underwrite their demise for the sake of another's good. Moreover, these citizens' belief about the nature of embryos is shaped significantly by theological traditions that are the result of a philosophical anthropology informed by both Scripture and philosophical reflection.[17]

For this reason, supporters of embryonic stem cell research and its government funding have drawn attention to the theological roots of the bioethical views of these citizens and have concluded that their policy proposals are in violation of the First Amendment's establishment clause. Take, for example, the comments of Cornell law professor, Sherry F. Colb:

Religious freedom is an essential right in this country. Religion and religious organizations have often provided compassion and support to those in need. Observant members of religious groups have a fundamental constitutional right to practice their respective religions – a right enumerated explicitly in the First Amendment.... But as strongly as our Constitution protects religion, it forbids our government from becoming a religious one ...

---

[13] NBAC I, *Stem Cell*, i–ii.

[14] Gina Kolata, "*Scientists Bypass Need for Embryo to Get Stem Cells,*" *New York Times* (21 November 2007): A1; Gina Kolata, "Man Who Helped Start Stem Cell War May End It," *New York Times* (22 November 2007): A1.

[15] Although the first source is a fetus that dies as a consequence of elective abortion, it is from its germ cells that the stem cells are derived. Thus, the fetus dies as a result of the abortion and not the taking of its stem cells. Of course, this raises other ethical questions having to do with the proper respect owed to nascent human life and whether it is ever morally permissible to will the death of such a human being for any reason. However, the use of its germ cells to acquire stem cells for research is not what brings about the fetus' death.

[16] See, e.g., Robert P. George and Christopher Tollefsen, *Embryo: A Defense of Human Life* (New York: Doubleday, 2008).

[17] See, e.g., John Paul II, *Evangelium Vitae*; Congregation for the Doctrine of the Faith, *Instruction Dignitas Personae on Certain Bioethical Questions* (Washington, DC: U.S. Conference of Catholic Bishops, 2008); J.P. Moreland & Scott B. Rae, *Body & Soul: Human Nature & the Crisis in Ethics* (Downers Grove, IL: InterVarsity Press, 2000).

... [T]he idea that full-fledged human life begins at conception – is a religious notion, and it is one to which some, but not all, religions subscribe.

The idea of "ensoulment" is, of course, a purely religious concept. The notion that life begins at conception is counterintuitive if understood in secular terms.

In a secular world, because an embryo lacks the capacity to think, to experience joy, and to suffer pain or distress, it accordingly lacks legal entitlements that could possibly trump or even equal the interest in saving lives and curing disease through research. A secular perspective, then, would unequivocally approve of stem cell research....

Only a religious view would equate a clump of undifferentiated cells the size of a pinprick with a fully formed human being – deeming both equivalent "life." Proceeding on the basis of this equation, ... wrongfully imposes a religious perspective on all citizens, regardless of their religious belief or lack thereof.[18]

The sort of analysis that Professor Colb offers is ubiquitous in both the professional and popular literature on the subject.[19] And like some of those other works, Colb's essay seems to commit two mistakes: (1) It privileges, without adequate justification, what she calls the secular perspective; and (2) it mistakenly presents the so-called secular and religious perspectives as two different subjects rather than two different answers about the same subject.

Concerning the first, Colb claims that the secular perspective requires the law to protect only those human beings with interests that arise when they possess certain mental and physical capacities. She writes: "In a secular world, because an embryo lacks the capacity to think, to experience joy, and to suffer pain or distress, it accordingly lacks legal entitlements that could possibly trump or even equal the interest in saving lives and curing disease through research. A secular perspective, then, would unequivocally approve of stem cell research."[20] Although this is a widely held point of view defended by some of the finest minds in the academy,[21] it is not clear why we should embrace it as *the* secular perspective. After all, Aristotle (384–322 BCE),[22] whose views many religious people, including Thomas Aquinas (1225–1274),[23] have found congenial to their theological projects, offered a "secular" theory of ensoulment and

---

[18] Sherry F. Colb, "A Creeping Theocracy: How The U.S. Government Uses Its Power to Enforce Religious Principles," *FindLaw's Writ* (21 November 2001), http://writ.lp.findlaw.com/colb/20011121.html (accessed 9 March 2013).

[19] See, e.g., Lee M. Silver, *Challenging Nature: The Clash of Science and Spirituality at the New Frontiers of Life* (New York: HarperCollins, 2006); Richard Dawkins, *The God Delusion* (New York: Bantam Press 2006), 294–298; Paul D. Simmons, "Religious Liberty and Abortion Policy: *Casey* as "Catch-22," *Journal of Church and State* 42 (Winter 2000); Chris Mooney, *The Republican War on Science* (New York: Basic Books, 2005).

[20] Colb, n.p.

[21] See, e.g., David Boonin, *A Defense of Abortion* (New York: Cambridge University Press, 2002); Michael Tooley, *Abortion and Infanticide* (New York: Oxford University Press, 1983).

[22] See Aristotle, *De Anima (On the Soul)*, trans. Hugh Lawson-Tancred (New York: Penguin Books, 1986).

[23] See Thomas Aquinas, *On Human Nature*, ed. Thomas S. Hibbs (Indianapolis: Hackett, 1999).

a philosophical anthropology that do not rely on special revelation and religious dogma, but rather on empirical observation, philosophical reflection, and actual arguments. The contemporary supporters of Aquinas's Aristotelianism offer arguments of a similar sort,[24] and yet they are inconsistent with what Colb calls *the* secular perspective.

Thus, the contemporary religious or non-religious Aristotelian (or Thomist) can raise the question: why should one accept what Colb calls the secular understanding of human beings and their interests? After all, for the contemporary Aristotelian,[25] there is a sense in which embryos do have these interest-making capacities from the moment they come into being. From its genesis, the embryo possesses essential properties, which its being and constituent parts are intrinsically ordered to work in concert to bring to maturation.[26] For this reason, Colb is simply mistaken when she describes the embryo as "a clump of undifferentiated cells."[27] Even when the embryo's cells are undifferentiated (i.e., the cells are pluripotent and thus have the capacity to develop into virtually any cell type), the early embryo, as several scholars have pointed out,[28] functions as a substantial unity whose parts

---

[24] See, e.g., George and Tollefsen, *Embryo*; Patrick Lee, *Abortion and Unborn Human Life* (Washington, DC: Catholic University of America Press,1996); Francis J. Beckwith, *Defending Life: A Moral and Legal Case Against Abortion Choice* (New York: Cambridge University Press, 2007); Edward Feser, *Aquinas: A Beginner's Guide* (Oxford: Oneworld Publications, 2009); David Oderberg, *Real Essentialism* (New York: Routledge, 2008); and Christopher Kaczor, *The Ethics of Abortion: Women's Rights, Human Life, and the Question of Justice* (New York: Routledge, 2010); John Haldane and Patrick Lee, "Aquinas on Human Ensoulment, Abortion, and the Value of Human Life," *Philosophy* 78.2 (2003): 255–278.

[25] I am, of course, not suggesting that the historical Aristotle would be prolife if he were alive today and were fully aware of our contemporary knowledge of human embryology. I am not even suggesting that all contemporary Aristotelians should be prolife. Rather, I am offering Aristotelian metaphysics as one nonreligious understanding of human nature that has been employed by many prolifers to make their case. For a nice overview of the issues concerning Aristotle, abortion, and personhood, see Matthew Lu, "Aristotle on Abortion and Infanticide," *International Philosophical Quarterly* 53.1 (2013): 47–62.

[26] See George and Tollefsen, *Embryo*; Beckwith, *Defending Life*, chapters 4 and 6.

[27] Colb, n.p.

[28] See George and Tollefsen, *Embryo*; Beckwith, *Defending Life*, ch. 4; Lee, *Abortion and Unborn Human Life*, ch. 3; Benedict Ashley and Albert Moraczewksi, "Is the Biological Subject of Human Rights Present from Conception?," in *The Fetal Tissue Issue: Medical and Ethical Aspects*, ed. Peter J. Cataldo and Albert S. Moraczewksi (Braintree, MA: Pope John Center, 1994); Antony Fisher, "'When Did I Begin?' Revisited," *Linacre Quarterly* 58 (1991); Ann McLaren, "The Embryo," in *Reproduction in Mammals*, Book 2: *Embryonic and Fetal Development*, 2nd ed., ed. C.R. Austin & R.V. Short (New York: Cambridge University Press, 1982); Patrick Lee and Robert P. George, "The First Fourteen Days of Human Life," *The New Atlantis: A Journal of Technology & Society* no. 13 (Summer 2006): 61–67; A. A. Howsepian, "Lockwood on Human Identity and the Primitive Streak," *Journal of Medical Ethics* 23 (1997): 38–41; and A. A. Howsepian, "Four Queries Concerning the Metaphysics of Early Human Embryogenesis," *Journal of Medicine & Philosophy* 33 (2008): 140–157.

work in concert with one another for the growth, development, and continued existence of the whole.[29]

With these clarifications, Colb may now want to make the counterargument that excluding the early embryo from legal protection is still justified, but not because it lacks certain ultimate capacities for the actualization of certain powers, actions and experiences, for the standard embryo surely does not lack those ultimate capacities. Rather, she may want to argue that it is the present and immediate exercisability of those capacities that distinguishes protectable persons from early embryos, because the latter do indeed lack that power. This is clearly a more defensible position than Colb's initial argument. Yet, like her first argument, this revised one has its sophisticated detractors as well.[30] (In fact, much of the next section of this chapter deals precisely with those who defend some version of Colb's "revised" argument.)

Nevertheless, no matter which argumentative strategy she procures for her case, it is clear from the earlier analysis she can no longer present the embryonic stem cell debate as if it were a dispute between two different subjects – religious and secular understandings of embryonic stem-cell research – rather than what it really is about, two different answers to the same question: What is the nature of the unborn human being that will die as a consequence of extracting embryonic stem cells from it? Instead of confronting the arguments for the position she labels "religious," Colb seems to believe that if a position on a policy question can be labeled religious, it is no longer a position that may legitimately have a bearing on the public's deliberation on the issue. But that's putting the cart before the horse. For unless Colb first shows that no argument in principle can provide warrant for a view of embryonic personhood connected to a theological tradition, justice requires that we treat so-called religious and secular understandings of embryonic personhood as different answers to the same question.

After all, Colb offers an answer to a question of philosophical anthropology that religious traditions have also offered an answer. She makes her case by suggesting that because the early embryo lacks certain capacities (or in our revised version of her argument, certain present and immediately exercisable

---

[29] An often cited exception is the phenomenon of monozygotic twinning, which can occur within the first two weeks after conception. But even if every early embryo were to possess an intrinsically-directed potential for twinning – that may be triggered by some external stimulus – it would not follow that the early embryo is not a unified organism. It would only mean that the human being, early in her existence, possesses a current capacity that becomes latent after a certain level of development, just as some latent capacities become current later in the human being's existence (e.g., the ability to philosophize).

[30] See Beckwith, *Defending Life*; Francis J. Beckwith, "The Explanatory Power of the Substance View of Persons," *Christian Bioethics* 10 (2004); Lee, *Abortion and Unborn Human Life*; Patrick Lee, "The Pro-Life Argument from Substantial Identity: A Defense," *Bioethics* 18 (2004); Moreland & Rae, *Body & Soul*; George and Tollefsen, *Embryo*; Kaczor, *The Ethics of Abortion*.

capacities), the early embryo does not have interests. But by doing this, Colb is offering an account of the human being (i.e., a philosophical anthropology) in order to exclude early embryos from the realm of moral subjects. Not surprisingly, those who oppose Colb's position, mostly religious citizens, present arguments and counterarguments in order to first show that the early embryo is a moral subject and then from there show that killing that entity in the way that Colb suggests is unjustified. She responds to their position by calling it "religious," even although its advocates offer real arguments with real conclusions and real reasons.[31] Of course, these arguments and the beliefs they support are, for many of their advocates, religious, in the sense that they are integral to the development and understanding of their church's theology. But they are also offered as the deliverances of rational argument and not merely as commands of divine revelation. Consequently, the arguments of these believers should be assessed on their own merits as *arguments*.

In order to show how an advocate for this sort of prolife account of the human person engages critics of this view, in what follows I offer an analysis of a critical review of my 2007 book, *Defending Life: A Moral and Legal Case Against Abortion Choice*.[32] As this analysis should make clear, the prolife account of the human person, although tightly tethered to a theological tradition, is no less a deliverance of reason than the position that Colb describes as "secular."

## 5.2. DEFENDING LIFE

My point of departure will be Dean Stretton's 2008 *Journal of Medical Ethics* review of *Defending Life*.[33] In *Defending Life* I offer a defense of fetal personhood, which I call the *substance view*.[34] According to the substance view, the human being is a particular type of living organism – a rational moral animal[35] – that remains identical to herself as long as she exists, even if she is not presently exhibiting the functions, behaviors, or current abilities to immediately engage in the activities that we typically attribute to active and mature rational moral animals. Because the human being is a rational moral animal, she is a person of intrinsic moral worth as long as she exists. As I note in *Defending Life*:

---

[31] See, e.g., the works cited in footnote 30.

[32] Beckwith, *Defending Life*.

[33] Dean Stretton, "Critical Notice" – *Defending Life: A Moral and Legal Against Abortion Choice," Journal of Medical Ethics* 34 (2008): 793–797.

[34] Beckwith, *Defending Life*, chapters 4 and 6.

[35] In *Defending Life* and other works I use the term "rational moral agent" rather than "rational moral animal." However, I have come to the conclusion over the past couple of years that the latter more accurately captures the prolife understanding of human nature, since it maintains that the human being is a physical substance (with an immaterial form and some immaterial powers and properties) rather than merely an immaterial mind attached to a physical body.

When I say that the prenatal human being is a person I mean to say that she is just as much a bearer of rights as any person whose rights-bearing status is uncontroversial, e.g., her mother, you, or me. That is, the prenatal human being is entitled to all the rights to which free and equal persons are entitled by virtue of being free and equal persons. So, for example, one cannot deprive the standard fetus of her life without the sort of justification we would expect if we were depriving a standard ten-year-old of his rights. To illustrate, if it is wrong to kill a ten-year-old as a result of taking his kidneys and giving them to people the government thinks will benefit society (e.g., scientific geniuses on the verge of curing cancer or AIDS), it is wrong to kill a 20-week-old fetal-clone as a result of taking his kidneys and giving them to his genetic progenitor, a scientific genius, who needs them to survive so that he may continue his work on cures for cancer and AIDS.[36]

In what follows I first offer (5.2.A) a brief summary of the substance view and how I defend it, and then I present (5.2.B) Stretton's critique including an analysis of his arguments concerning (5.2.B.1) degreed natural capacities, (5.2.B.2) developed psychological capacities (DPCs), and (5.2.B.3) the moral permissibility of the intentional creation of mentally handicapped fetuses.

## 5.2.A. The Substance View

A substance is an individual being of a certain sort.[37] So, for example, the substance Jorge Mario Bergoglio (Pope Francis) is a human substance, a being with a particular nature that we call "human." The substance Lassie too is an individual being, but she is a canine substance, a being with a particular nature that we call "canine." W. Norris Clarke offers a four-part definition of what constitutes a human substance:

(1) it has the aptitude to exist *in itself* and not as a part of any other being; (2) it is the unifying center of all the various attributes and properties that belong to it at any one moment; (3) if the being persists as the same individual throughout a process of change, it is the substance which is the abiding, unifying center of the being across time; (4) it has an intrinsic dynamic orientation toward self-expressive action, toward self-communication with others, as the crown of its perfection, as its very *raison d'etre* ...[38]

Each kind of living organism or *substance*, including the human being, maintains identity through change as well as possessing a nature or essence that makes certain activities and functions possible. "A substance's inner nature," writes J. P. Moreland, "is its ordered structural unity of ultimate capacities.

---

[36] Beckwith, *Defending Life*, xii–xiii.
[37] Some portions of this section (5.2.A) are adapted from sections of chapter 6 of my *Defending Life*.
[38] W. Norris Clarke, S. J., *Explorations in Metaphysics* (Notre Dame, IN: University of Notre Dame, 1994), 105.

A substance cannot change in its ultimate capacities; that is, it cannot lose its ultimate nature and continue to exist."[39]

Another way to put it is to say that substances, including human beings, are ontologically prior to their parts,[40] which means that the organism as a whole maintains absolute identity through time while it grows, develops, and undergoes numerous changes, largely as a result of the organism's nature that directs and informs these changes and their limits. The organs and parts of the organism, and their role in actualizing the intrinsic, basic capacities of the whole,[41] acquire their purpose and function *because* of their roles in maintaining, sustaining, and perfecting the *being as a whole*. Organisms may lose and gain parts and yet remain identical to themselves over time. Consider the following illustration.

A domestic feline, because it has a particular nature, has the ultimate capacity to develop the ability to purr. It may die as a kitten and never exercise that ability. Regardless, it is *still* a feline as long as it exists, because it possesses a particular nature, even if it never acquires certain functions that by nature it has the ultimate capacity to develop. In contrast, a frog is not said to lack something if it cannot purr, for it is by nature not the sort of being that can have the ability to purr. A feline that lacks the ability to purr *is still a feline* because of its nature. A human being who lacks the ability to think rationally (either because she is too young or she suffers from a disability) *is still a human person* because of her nature. Consequently, this human being's lack makes sense *if and only if* she is a being of a certain sort, a rational moral animal.

Second, the feline remains the same particular feline over time from the moment it comes into existence. Suppose you buy this feline as a kitten and name him "Guido." When you first bring him home you notice that he is tiny in comparison to his parents and lacks their mental and physical abilities. But over time Guido develops these abilities, learns a number of things his parents never learned, sheds his hair, has his claws removed, becomes ten times larger than he was as a kitten, and undergoes significant development of his cellular structure, brain and cerebral cortex. Yet, this grown-up Guido is identical to the kitten Guido, even though he has gone through significant physical changes. Why? The reason is because living organisms, substances, maintain identity through change.

---

[39] J. P. Moreland, "Humanness, Personhood, and the Right to Die," *Faith and Philosophy* 12.1 (January 1995), 101.

[40] Moreland, 206.

[41] I am using the following terms interchangeably throughout this chapter: "ultimate capacities," "basic capacities," "intrinsic basic capacities," and "natural basic intrinsic capacities." This is what I mean by ultimate capacities: those capacities, given its nature, that the substance is ordered to actualize for the perfection of itself. For example, all human beings have the ultimate capacity for rational thought, even if it is never actualized due to illness, physical defect, or death.

According to the substance view, because a human organism can only develop certain functions she has the ultimate capacity to develop by nature because of the sort of being she *is*, a rational moral animal, at every stage of her development she is *never* a potential person. That is, she is *always* a person with potential, even if that potential is never actualized due to premature death or the result of the absence or deformity of a physical state necessary to actualize that potential. For example, a human being without vocal chords in a society in which there are no artificial or transplant vocal chords never ceases to be a "speaking being, because she never loses the ultimate capacity to speak, although she will in fact never speak because she lacks a physical state necessary to actualize that ultimate capacity.

The substance view is also *perfectionist*. That is, it sees the maturation of a human being's ultimate capacities as perfections of its nature. So, for example, the whole human being is harmed if his brain is not allowed to develop as a consequence of ailment or assault. Thus, if the embryo's brain development is intentionally obstructed so that it does not achieve higher brain function and thus cannot exercise his natural powers for rational thought and moral reflection, the human being has been morally harmed because a good to which he is entitled has been prevented from coming to fruition. Or, suppose a human being is brought up by his parents in such a way that they indoctrinate him to believe that he is property that is not qualitatively different than a commercial product such as a television or a microwave oven. This human being has suffered at least two harms: his parents have not fulfilled their proper roles as loving parents to which their child is entitled, and he has been taught false things about his nature that diminish in his own mind his real moral worth as a person.

In my defense of the substance view, I offer several illustrations. They are intended to show the inadequacy of alternative accounts of the human person that maintain that the prenatal human being does not become a moral subject (or "person") until she acquires one or more characteristics, such as organized cortical brain activity (OCBA),[42] self-conscious interest in her own existence,[43]

---

[42] David Boonin argues that the unborn human being does not become a moral subject until it acquires organized cortical brain activity (OCBA), which may occur as early as twenty-five weeks gestation or as late as thirty-two weeks. Writes Boonin: "[A]n individual cannot begin to acquire this special moral standing until it begins to have at least some actual desires.... A human fetus has no such desires prior to the point at which it has conscious experience, and it has no conscious experiences prior to the point at which it has organized electrical activity in its cerebral cortex. It therefore has no such desires prior to the point at which it has organized electrical activity in its cerebral cortex. One implication of this account of the wrongness of killing, then, is that the fetus does not acquire the moral standing that you and I have prior to the point at which it has such activity." (Boonin, *A Defense of Abortion*, 125–126).

[43] Tooley, *Abortion and Infanticide*.

interests that presuppose desires,[44] and/or rudimentary brain activity.[45] I argue that these characteristics, although perhaps sufficient conditions for person-hood, are not necessary, because we can easily conceive of cases in which human beings do not possess these characteristics while not ceasing to be per-sons. One illustration I use is the case of Uncle Jed.

Imagine that your Uncle Jed is in a car accident that results in him being in a coma for nine months. Suppose that at the beginning of the coma, his physician tells you this: "Your uncle Jed will come out of this coma in nine months. Initially, he will likely not remember anything, including the languages he knows as well as his ability to play the violin. But in time, roughly two years, he will likely regain all that he has lost." During the nine months in which Uncle Jed is in a coma he is in a state not unlike that of the standard prena-tal human being.[46] Nevertheless, it seems that the denier of fetal personhood would maintain that it would be morally *im*permissible to kill Uncle Jed while in this state, because Uncle Jed will eventually "return."

Now let's change the facts a bit. Suppose that same physician offers this prognosis: "Your uncle Jed (i.e., Uncle Jed$_2$) will come out of this coma in nine months. But when he does, he will have no memories and will have to relearn all his abilities, including his prolific violin playing. It will take him approximately three to five years to reacquire all his abilities, but his memories are gone forever. This means that he will have the opportunity to have new experiences and thus new memories. You should, of course, inform him and teach him about his family and friends. But it will be, in a sense, a new begin-ning for your Uncle Jed." Uncle Jed$_2$, like Uncle Jed, will be like a standard newborn child when he awakes. And like Uncle Jed, Uncle Jed$_2$, during the next nine months in the coma, will be like a standard prenatal human being. Yet, unlike in the case of Uncle Jed, it seems that the denier of fetal personhood would have to conclude that it is morally permissible to kill Uncle Jed$_2$ while in this state, because he would be, after all, in the same position as the standard prenatal human being without any prospect of the memories and abilities of

[44] Ronald Dworkin writes that it is "very hard to make sense of the idea that a fetus has rights from the moment of conception. Having rights seems to presuppose having interests, which in turn seems to presuppose having wants, hopes, fears, likes and dislikes. But an early fetus lacks the physical constitution required for such psychological states." (Ronald Dworkin, *Life's Dominion: An Argument About Abortion, Euthanasia, and Individual Freedom* [New York: Random House, 1993], 15).

[45] K. E. Himma, "A Dualist Analysis of Abortion: Personhood and the Concept of Self *qua* Experiential Subject," *Journal of Medical Ethics* 31 (2005): 48–55.

[46] Clearly, this is a reasonable way to think about these things, since even the abortion-choice advocate must claim to know something about what the typical prenatal human being can and cannot do in order to maintain that the prenatal human being is outside the scope of the moral community because it lacks certain presently exercisable abilities. In fact, knowledge of what constitutes the "standard prenatal human being" and its capacities, powers, and abilities dur-ing the entirety of its gestation is assumed in the cases made by Boonin, Tooley, Dworkin, and Himma (See footnotes 42–45).

the precoma mature Uncle Jed₂ making a return.[47] So, the difference between Uncle Jed and Uncle Jed₂ is this: the first will reacquire that to which he temporarily lost access while the latter will acquire something similar to what he had permanently lost. And it is on that basis alone that two similarly situated comatose patients may be morally distinguished as one not worthy of death and the other not worthy of life. This, frankly, seems like thin gruel on which to ground the difference between unjustified homicide and permissible killing.

## 5.2.B. Stretton's Critique

Stretton counters the substance view in several ways.[48] In this section, I will cover his arguments concerning (Section 5.2.B.1) degreed natural capacities, (Section 5.2.B.2) developed psychological capacities (DPCs), and (Section 5.2.B.3) the moral permissibility of the intentional creation of mentally handicapped fetuses.

### 5.2.B.1. The Argument from Degreed Natural Capacities

In *Defending Life* I make the argument (following Patrick Lee)[49] that because most abortion-choice[50] thinkers attempt to ground a human being's personhood in abilities that come in degrees – for example, rationality, self-awareness, ability to communicate, and so forth – that means that personhood is a degreed property and thus cannot be the ground for believing that all human persons

---

[47] Boonin, for example, writes:

> Of course, the critic might instead appeal to an imaginary case in which a temporarily comatose adult has had the entire contents in his brain destroyed so that there is no more information contained in his brain than is contained in that of the preconscious fetus. In this case, it seems right that my position does not imply that such an individual has the same right to life as you or I. But, as in the case of the adult who has never had conscious experiences, a critic of abortion cannot appeal to such a case as a means of rejecting my position because we cannot assume ahead of time that killing such individuals is seriously immoral. (Boonin, *A Defense of Abortion*, 78)

[48] One argument that Stretton offers in response to my Uncle Jed₂ illustration that I will not address in the text is this one: "This is unpersuasive, since many pro-choicers will simply deny that the foetal adult [Uncle Jed₂] has a right to life." (Stretton, "Critical Notice," 794). Finding an argument unpersuasive by denying the veracity of its conclusion is not the same as showing it to be unreasonable or flawed. What I am arguing is that the difference between Uncle Jed and Uncle Jed₂ is arbitrary and thus has no moral import in establishing that the killing of the latter is not homicide. What, then, are the premises that unseat this charge of arbitrariness? Stretton does not say. He just makes the observation that some people will remain unpersuaded by my argument because they will deny its conclusion. But turnabout is fair play. For I am certain that most of my prolife allies will not be persuaded that Stretton's observation is an adequate reason to abandon their belief that Uncle Jed₂ ought not to be killed.

[49] See Lee, *Abortion and Unborn Human Life*, 54–62; and Patrick Lee, "Substantial Identity and the Right to Life: A Rejoinder to Dean Stretton," *Bioethics* 21.2 (2007).

[50] As far as I know, it is Doris Gordon who coined the term "abortion-choice." See, for example, her introductory essay in *International Journal of Sociology and Social Policy* 19.3/4 (1999).

are equal in intrinsic moral worth.⁵¹ Stretton maintains that I am arguing that because natural capacities do not come in degrees while presently exercisable abilities do, and because the right to life cannot come in degrees (i.e., you either have it or you don't), therefore, a human being's right to life is grounded in his natural capacities and not in his presently exercisable abilities.⁵² Stretton responds by pointing out that natural capacities come in degrees as well, and thus the substance view is in the very same predicament as the views that ground the right to life in presently exercisable abilities.⁵³

Although Stretton is certainly correct that natural capacities come in degrees, being a human substance does not come in degrees. For it is in the latter, and not the former, that the defender of the substance view is locating a human person's moral worth. In fact, I cannot think of any defender of the substance view,⁵⁴ or any view similar to it,⁵⁵ who thinks otherwise. Take, for example, a portion of the two pages of my book to which Stretton refers but from which he does not quote. (The following includes changes from the original that I place in brackets, in order to be consistent with the use of language in this chapter):

[T]he AEA [the Anti-Equality Advocate, i.e., someone who believes that all human beings are not equal in dignity and intrinsic moral worth] cannot explain why fundamental

---

⁵¹ Beckwith, *Defending Life*, 138–139.

⁵² "Beckwith's second argument … is that since the right to life is not a matter of degree, but developed capacities are a matter of degree (for example, some are more rational and intelligent than others), the right to life cannot be grounded, as pro-choicers seek to do, in developed capacities, but rather must, as the substance view claims, be grounded in natural capacities …" (citations omitted) (Stretton, "Critical Notice," 794).

⁵³ "The obvious response … is that natural capacities also come in degrees, both within the human species (where some are naturally more rational and intelligent than others), and over the course of evolution (which we may assume involved imperceptibly gradual increases in natural capacities from our nonhuman ancestors to ourselves). Thus the substance view also grounds the right to life in degreed capacities or properties. Being human is of course not a degreed property – we are all equally human …; but on the substance view the reason humans are alleged to have a right to life is their natural capacity for rationality and communication (a degreed property) – and so the substance view must also explain why the right to life is not a matter of degree. I submit we are all committed to positing some kind of threshold within a continuous range of degreed properties or capacities" (citations omitted) (Stretton, "Critical Notice," 794).

⁵⁴ Patrick Lee writes: "However, Stretton has misconstrued my argument and the criterion I (along with many others) propose for the right to life. I argued that defenders of abortion have no good reason to base the right to life on developed capacities for conceptual thought and free choice rather than on basic, natural capacities for such acts – capacities which are possessed by unborn, as well as more mature, human beings. However, the conclusion of my argument was not that the criterion for the right to life is natural capacities, but that it is, being a certain type of substance. I then proposed that the genuine criterion for having a right to life is *being a person*, that is, a distinct substance of a rational nature (the classic Boethian or Thomistic definition of 'person')" (Lee, "Substantial Identity," 97) (note omitted).

⁵⁵ "A substance's capacities culminate in a set of its ultimate capacities that are possessed solely in virtue of the substance belonging to its natural kind: for example, Smith's ultimate capacities are his because he belongs to the *natural kind* 'being human'" (Moreland and Rae in *Body & Soul*, 73).

human rights [and moral worth] ought not to be distributed on the basis of native intellectual abilities and other value-giving properties, e.g., rationality, self-awareness. This is because capacities are stages along a continuum, with some basic capacities being exercisable only as a result of other capacities first being actualized (e.g., the proximate capacity to learn a language requires a certain level of brain development) and the present exercisability of those capacities differ in their degrees (e.g., people have a wide range of language skills). Some adult human beings are more or less rational and more or less self-aware in comparison to others, and some human beings, because they are damaged or immature, are in the process of developing, and have not yet achieved, certain second-order capacities (e.g., the requisite brain structure to develop the capacity to learn algebra) that make certain first-order capacities possible (e.g., the present capacity to do algebraic problems if you know algebra). But if that is the case, then some [intrinsically valuable human persons] are more or less "intrinsically valuable" than others. But morally intrinsic value [MIV] is not a degreed property; you either have it or you don't, and thus [MIV] cannot be conditioned upon the possession of a degreed property, for if you have more of it then you should have more moral worth. It would follow from this that the notion of the moral equality of human beings is not only illusory when applied to the [prenatal human being] (which the AEA already believes) but to all human beings as well. But the AEA does not want to deny human equality among [Intrinsically Valuable Persons, or IVPs]. Yet, the AEA can only reject this undesirable consequence if he embraces the notion that [all] human beings [are IVPs] because they are rational moral [animals] *by nature* from the moment they come into existence.[56]

I am arguing that the human being is a particular sort of substance – a rational moral animal – that by her nature has certain natural basic intrinsic capacities that may or may not mature into actual abilities that may be lost and regained during the human being's natural life. Unborn human beings, as do all human beings, are substances of this sort because of their nature. Clearly, this nature *entails* certain natural basic intrinsic capacities, including the capacity to develop the abilities to reason and to engage in moral choice. But that means it is the human being's nature that determines its natural basic intrinsic capacities, and it is that nature – rational moral animal – that grounds her moral worth as a person. Stretton, ironically, seems to see this as well: "Being human is of course not a degreed property – we are all equally human ...; but on the substance view the reason humans are alleged to have a right to life is their natural capacity for rationality and communication (a degreed property) – and so the substance view must also explain why the right to life is not a matter of degree."[57] Stretton is correct that all human beings are equally human. But for the supporter of the substance view, this means that all human beings share the nature of rational moral animal, which is not a degreed property. And it is because a human being has that nature that he or she has certain natural basic intrinsic capacities whose maturity and flourishing contribute to his or her

---

[56] Beckwith, 138–139, citing Moreland and Rae in *Body & Soul*, 202–204, in order to point the reader to a fuller explanation of the distinction between first-order and second-order capacities.
[57] Stretton, "Critical Notice," 794.

perfection (or proper end). But if the human being is immature or ill and his natural basic intrinsic capacities cannot develop as they are supposed to, that human being still possesses full moral worth and is thus equal in dignity to his fellow human beings precisely because he is a substance of a particular nature and that nature is not a degreed property. As Christopher Kaczor points out:

A mentally retarded human being and a normal hedgehog are equally incapable of exercising distinctly human reasoning and freedom, but the handicap of the human is tragic while the rational incapacity [of] a hedgehog is inconsequential. This difference rests on the fact that the human, but not the hedgehog cannot exercise his or her species-specific form of flourishing. Since even mentally handicapped human beings share in a species-specific form of flourishing ordered to the goods of rationality and freedom, they are human persons.[58]

In the cases of Uncle Jed and Uncle Jed₂, both lost their abilities to immediately exercise rational and moral choice, with the former, Uncle Jed, having the prospect of regaining his past achievements that resulted from the exercise of these abilities. But this does not change the fact that both Uncle Jed and Uncle Jed₂ are substances of a particular sort, rational moral animals. And it is because they share that nature – and not because of any abilities that they may regain or lose – that determines whether they are human persons. The purpose of the Uncle Jed stories is to illustrate why a human being's nature rather than her presently exercisable powers and abilities better grounds her personhood. Thus, Stretton is wrong in thinking that I am grounding personhood in natural basic intrinsic capacities. Rather, I am grounding natural basic intrinsic capacities in human nature, something equally shared by all human beings regardless of their size, level of development, environment, dependency, or health.

So, contra Stretton, the substance view is not in the same position as alternatives that attempt to ground personhood in degreed properties. But this, not surprisingly, leaves some proponents of the latter views not entirely comfortable with its nonegalitarian implications. For instance, Jeff McMahan, in his careful and thoughtful analysis of the difficulties of grounding human equality on degreed properties, laments that:

all this leaves me profoundly uncomfortable. It seems virtually unthinkable to abandon our egalitarian commitments.... Yet the challenges to the equal wrongness thesis, which is a central element of liberal egalitarian morality, support ... skepticism about the compatibility of our all-or-nothing egalitarian beliefs with the fact that the properties on which our moral status appears to supervene are all matters of degree. It is hard to avoid the sense that our egalitarian commitments rest on distressingly insecure foundations.[59]

---

[58] Kaczor, *The Ethics of Abortion*, 101.
[59] Jeff McMahan, "Challenges to Human Equality," *Journal of Ethics* 12.1 (2008): 104.

### 5.2.B.2. *Argument from Developed Psychological Capacities*

Stretton, relying on the work of McMahan, suggests that there could be other reasons as to why Uncle Jed$_2$ ought not to be killed: (1) the argument from respect and (2) the argument from DPCs. Because the second is the stronger of the two and relies on McMahan's more detailed work, I will briefly address the first before moving on to the second. Stretton writes, "[T]he adult's [Uncle Jed$_2$'s] past mental states may ground duties of respect *even though* they have been erased in roughly the way we may owe duties of respect to the dead even though *their* past mental states have been erased."[60] This is hardly to the point, because the question is whether Uncle Jed$_2$ while in the coma has a right not to be turned into a corpse. To suggest that we should respect him like we respect the dead is no real solution to the conundrum. After all, if the morgue were to discover a pulse emanating from what they presumed was the corpse of Uncle Jed$_2$ (with all the same prospects as in the story earlier) it seems incredible to suggest that the medical examiner would instruct his staff, "The only duties we owe him are those we owe a corpse."

Stretton's second, and more substantive, argument goes like this: "the continuation of DPCs – even primitive ones like the fetus has – may provide a sufficient psychological connection between the foetal adult and its future self to ground a right to life ..."[61] It is difficult to know what Stretton means by DPCs. However, because he refers the reader to McMahan's work,[62] that is the place to look. Because Stretton's "foetal adult" is undoubtedly like Uncle Jed$_2$, he is likely referring to McMahan's view that one's egoistic concern about the future grounds one's right to life. Writes McMahan:

I suggest that the basis for an individual's egoistic concern about the future – that which is both necessary and sufficient for rational egoistic concern – is the physical and functional continuity of enough of those areas of the individual's brain in which consciousness is realized to preserve the capacity to support consciousness or mental activity. Usually the functional continuity of these areas of the brain involves broad psychological continuity, but in the very earliest phases of an individual's life and in some instances near the end, the same mind or consciousness persists in the absence of any degree of psychological connectedness from day to day. And as we have seen, what matters may be present in these cases, at least to some minimal degree.[63]

Thus, what Stretton seems to be suggesting is that precoma Uncle Jed$_2$ in possession of DPCs has an egoistic concern about his future and thus an interest in "the physical and functional continuity of enough of those areas of ... [his]

[60] Stretton, "Critical Notice," 794 (emphasis in original), citing Jeff McMahan, *The Ethics of Killing: Problems at the Margins of Life* (New York: Oxford University Press, 2002), 497.

[61] Stretton, "Critical Notice," 794, citing McMahan, *The Ethics of Killing*, 73–75.

[62] McMahan, *The Ethics of Killing*, 73–75.

[63] Ibid., 66.

brain in which consciousness is realized to preserve the capacity to support consciousness or mental activity."[64] For this reason, comatose and postcoma Uncle Jed$_2$, also in possession of the same (or at least some of precoma Uncle Jed$_2$'s) DPCs, may have a right to life.

It's not clear, however, how this counts against the substance view, even if the DPC account does adequately account for the wrongness of killing Uncle Jed$_2$. For the defender of the substance view is not saying that there could not be other reasons aside from the substance view for believing a human being has a right to life. Rather, she is arguing that the substance view has, in comparison to other views, greater explanatory power in accounting for why we believe certain human beings are intrinsically valuable persons and why we should believe that of all other human beings as well. For example, if I say it is wrong to kill Jon because he is an innocent human person, but you say that it is wrong to kill Jon because he is handsome, the latter reason does not show the former to be inferior or false, even if it turns out that you restrain yourself from killing Jon because he is handsome. Moreover, Stretton's suggested alternative, the DPC account, ironically, may serve as a reason *not* to abandon the substance view, because the substance view does definitively ground the right to life of Uncle Jed$_2$ while Stretton admits that the DPC account only *may ground* his right to life.

Nevertheless, it seems to me that one can reject the DPC account on two grounds: (1) egoistic concern cannot ground moral worth, and (2) it relies on an artifactual account of cerebral architecture (CA) that can be plausibly challenged.

5.2.B.2.a. EGOISTIC CONCERN As I noted earlier, Stretton seems to be suggesting that precoma Uncle Jed$_2$ in possession of DPCs has an egoistic concern about his future and thus an interest in "the physical and functional continuity of enough of those areas of ... [his] brain in which consciousness is realized to preserve the capacity to support consciousness or mental activity."[65] But appealing to a human being's egoistic concern to resolve a moral question seems to get things backward. For objects of concern are either good or bad. That is, the morality of concerns, desires, projects, and interests are assessed by whether they are true goods for a being of this sort and not merely whether they are the being's own. Mob boss Tony Soprano, for example, may have an egoistic concern for his future because he desires to "rub out" Johnny Sacramoni a week from Monday. Or, Mr. Jones, after hearing of his wife's affair may lose any interest in life and seek to end his own as soon as possible. In neither case is one's egoistic concern remotely adequate to ground the person's moral worth, because it is the moral worth of human persons qua human persons that is in question, and the concerns of the individual ego, as in the cases of Tony and Mr. Jones, may be directed toward immoral ends inconsistent with a basic good for human beings as such. Thus, because one's egoistic concern about

64 Ibid.
65 Ibid.

one's future may not advance one's good or the good of other persons, and because moral worth is always good, therefore, egoistic concern about one's future cannot ground moral worth.

Nevertheless, it does seem to be the case that it is a good to be concerned about one's future, but only because of the role it plays in the actualization of the perfections to which a human being is ordered by virtue of his or her nature. According to the substance view, the goodness of one's concern for one's future means that life itself is a basic good and that being alive allows one to participate in a variety of other goods such as friendship, love of neighbor, the honing of talents and skills, engaging in acts of charity, serving the Lord, appreciating fine art and music, and so on. These goods contribute to the flourishing of the human person because he is an individual substance of the nature of rational moral animal ordered toward these goods. Thus, one's egoistic concern for the future is not what grounds one's moral worth. Rather, it is on the basis of one's moral worth by which one assesses the moral quality of one's egoistic concern for the future. That is, the question is whether or not one's egoistic concern aligns with the proper exercise of the powers of moral and rational choice for one's good appropriate for the sort of being one is. Therefore, the question of how we should treat Uncle Jed$_2$ while he is in the coma is not, "Did he have an egoistic concern for his future prior to entering the coma?" but, rather, "What sorts of actions toward Uncle Jed$_2$ would show proper respect for the good to which such a being is ordered by virtue of his nature?"

5.2.B.2.b. CEREBRAL ARCHITECTURE Although it seems that egoistic concern by itself cannot ground moral worth, McMahan's case is much richer than that. Recall, he argues that "*the basis for an individual's egoistic concern about the future ... is the physical and functional continuity of enough of those areas of the individual's brain in which consciousness is realized to preserve the capacity to support consciousness or mental activity.*"[66] So, it is by observing Uncle Jed$_2$'s CA that we are able to detect whether he has the DPCs that may ground his right to life. Consequently, by conscripting McMahan's argument, Stretton seems to be saying that Uncle Jed$_2$, while subsisting through precoma, comatose, and postcoma states, possessed DPCs because he had the CA of a mature rational moral animal. Nevertheless, Uncle Jed$_2$'s inability to employ his mature CA for the exercise of his moral and rational powers that he possesses as a consequence of being a rational moral animal by nature is a lack had by *both* the standard fetus (which like Uncle Jed$_2$, according to Stretton,[67] may have a right to life because it has primitive developed psychological capacities [pDPCs]) *as well as* the standard embryo that Stretton does

---

[66] McMahan, *The Ethics of Killing*, 66 (emphasis added).
[67] Recall his argument: "the continuation of developed psychological capacities – *even primitive ones like the fetus has* – may provide a sufficient psychological connection between the foetal adult and its future self to ground a right to life ..." (Stretton, "Critical Notice," 794) (emphasis added).

not think has a right to life because its psychological capacities are undeveloped (uDPCs).[68] Thus, if I am reading Stretton correctly (through McMahan), it is the temporal continuity of CA between precoma, comatose, and postcoma Uncle Jed$_2$ that *may ground* his right to life. I do not think this succeeds vis-à-vis the substance view.

When Stretton writes of "the continuation of developed psychological capacities."[69] what does he mean by "continuation"? He clearly does not mean that these capacities continue as a sort of independent cluster, an individual substance if you will, that subsists through time while losing and gaining parts and accidental properties. For these DPCs are themselves powers *had by* a being of a certain sort that may lose and gain DPCs while it subsists through time. After all, when these DPCs are functioning properly, they work in concert with properties and other abilities for the good of the whole being, or substance, that owns them. Thus, the only way that DPCs can continue through time is as powers had by a substance. So, if Stretton is correct that the temporal continuation of these DPCs is what gives (or may give) Uncle Jed$_2$ the right to life, this account requires that we think of both Uncle Jed$_2$ as a substance of a certain sort, a rational moral animal, for which the continuation of DPCs is a good that contributes to the being's perfection. In that case, it is the human being as a whole that is the proper subject of moral concern, because it is its good and proper end for which DPCs, as well as the being's other potencies, capacities and powers, acquire their meaning and purpose.

But in the case of Uncle Jed$_2$ the DPCs cannot be exercised because he is damaged in such a way that he lacks a necessary physical condition or state that the exercise of these capacities requires. For this reason, Uncle Jed$_2$ while in a comatose state is in the same position as the standard embryo, although, as Stretton implies, the standard embryo lacks DPCs. So, it is the embryo's lack of DPCs that morally permits one to kill him. But the embryo does possess from the moment he comes into being, and as he subsists through time, *un*developed psychological capacities (uDPCs). That is, from at least by the time the primitive streak arises about fourteen days after conception the human being subsists through time with the ultimate capacity to acquire DPCs because he is a being, with the nature of rational moral animal, intrinsically ordered to

---

[68] See Ibid., 794–795. See also Dean Stretton, "Kreeft Debunked: A Critique of Peter Kreeft's Essay 'Human Personhood Begins at Conception," available at http://eileen.250x.com/Main/KreeftBeckwith/KreeftBeckwith.html. Because I am not sure what Stretton means when he uses the term "fetus" – whether he is using it in the popular sense to mean an unborn human being during its entire gestation in the womb or in its more technical sense as an unborn human being in its ninth week after conception or later – I am assuming he means it in the latter sense. Prior to the ninth week, the appropriate technical term is "embryo." Thus, I am using "fetus" and "embryo" in the text with those technical definitions in mind. When I use the phrase "prenatal human being" I am referring to the being itself regardless of whether it is a fetus or an embryo.

[69] Stretton, "Critical Notice," 794.

do so.[70] Thus, for the embryo, the development of psychological capacities, like in the case of Uncle Jed$_2$'s developed, although impotent, psychological capacities, acquire their meaning and purpose because of the role they play in the good of the substance as a whole. So, both the embryo and Uncle Jed$_2$ are substances who possess the same ultimate capacities while they presently cannot exercise them, with the embryo requiring only further development and Uncle Jed$_2$ needing only to be healed. So, the only difference between the two is that one possesses the CA of a mature rational moral animal (DPCs) while the other does not (uDPCs). Thus, according to Stretton, a human being that subsists through time with DPCs may be a person who may not be killed without overwhelming reason while a human being that subsists through time with uDPCs is not a person and thus may be killed for a variety of lesser reasons. But the basis for this serious moral distinction – possessing a developed CA – seems arbitrary. For why should the possession or absence of *that* physical state make a moral difference if both beings share the same nature of rational moral animal and thus the same unexpressed intrinsic powers? Why precisely is the physical shape and maturity of a dormant organ system, by which a being's cognitive powers may be exercised, relevant to assessing a being's moral worth? Stretton does not say.

It seems to me that the confusion lurking behind Stretton's reliance on a mature CA is a crude physicalism that treats organisms as if they were artifacts rather than living substances. Consider this example. Imagine if two airline passengers were debating whether the object on the ground that they were viewing through their windows at ten thousand feet is a Catholic Cathedral or the Playboy Mansion. The building's external and internal architecture would be relevant to resolving this dispute. This is because the architecture of a building, whether a cathedral or a mansion, is not something intrinsically had by the building, as if the building were a unified substance over and above the sum total of its parts that acquire their meaning in relation to the whole and work in concert for the good of the whole. For the building is an artifact whose purpose is the result of an external mind imposing a pattern on bits of inert matter.

There is no "building substance" that subsists through time with its own intrinsic capacities and natural powers that may be actualized for the perfection of the building. For a building, or any artifact, its present architecture is everything, because there is no substance that subsists through time intrinsically ordered to a particular end. For a living organism, however, the development of its architecture, cerebral or otherwise, is suggestive of the sort of being it is. So, when it comes to a living substance, its nature is everything, for it

[70] I say "fourteen days," because there are a few prolifers, as I already noted in footnote 159 of Chapter 2, who argue that very early on in pregnancy (roughly during first the fourteen days after conception) the unborn is not yet an individual unified organism, because of the possibility of twinning, and thus is not a moral subject. See, e.g., Don Marquis, "The Moral-Principle Objection to Embryonic Stem-Cell Research," *Metaphilosophy* 38:2–3 (April 2007): 190–206.

reveals to us its intrinsically ordered ends, its architectonic hierarchy of powers, properties, and potencies.

This is why, as Aristotle points out, if you own a bed made out of wood and then plant a piece of the bed in the ground, "it would not be a bed that would come up, but wood."[71] This "shows that the arrangement in accordance with the rules of the art is merely an incidental attribute, whereas the real nature is the other, which, further, persists continuously through the process of making."[72] That is, the form and finality of the bed is imposed from without (an "arrangement in accordance with the rules of art") while the form and finality of the wood is intrinsic to the nature of the tree from which it was taken ("the real nature" that "persists continuously through the process of making").[73] As Etienne Gilson puts it: "The artist is external to his work; the work of art is consequently external to the art which produces it. The end of living nature is, on the contrary, consubstantial with it. The embryo *is* the law of its own development. It is already of its nature to be what will be later on an adult capable of reproducing itself."[74] Consequently, Stretton's appeal to CA as possibly dispositive to a being's right to life assumes a controversial understanding of living organisms that some, especially metaphysical realists, will find unconvincing.[75]

### 5.2.B.3. *The Argument from the Moral Permissibility of the Intentional Creation of Mentally Handicapped Fetuses*

In *Defending Life*,[76] as I do more briefly in Chapters 2 and 4 of this present volume, I argue that given the dominant understandings of personhood in the literature, understandings that connect a human being's moral worth to certain

---

[71] Aristotle, *Physics* (trans. R. P. Hardie and R. K. Gaye), bk. II, *available at* http://classics.mit.edu/Aristotle/ physics.2.ii.html.

[72] Ibid.

[73] For living beings (like human beings, trees, and squirrels) final causality is tightly tethered to formal causality. Thus, because a human being is a particular type of being, that is, he has a certain form or nature, specific ends or purposes are proper to that nature. So, for example, a human being's mental powers are ordered toward the acquisition of knowledge and wisdom, although they may not in fact achieve that end, as in the case of a child who dies in infancy or an adult who is impaired due to illness or accident. For this reason, we say that *technically* a being's final causality is "extrinsic," since it is aspirational, even if our judgment of its correctness is grounded in an intrinsic cause, its form or nature.

[74] Etienne Gilson, *From Aristotle to Darwin and Back Again: A Journey in Final Causality, Species and Evolution* (San Francisco: Ignatius Press, 2009; John Lyon trans., 1984; originally published in French in 1971), 148.

[75] Obviously, the view I am defending, the substance view, is no less controversial. But this means that how one views an organism's development will be shaped not only by the facts on the ground but how those facts cohere with one's metaphysics and the arguments one offers for it. My point is this: the force of Stretton's counterargument depends on his own prior metaphysical commitment to what appears to be an artifactual understanding of organisms. But if one has good reason to reject that metaphysics, then his counterargument loses much of its force.

[76] Beckwith, *Defending Life*, 139–140, 148–149, 158–159, 212.

presently exercisable mental abilities, it is difficult to account for the wrongness of intentionally creating mentally handicapped fetuses. For example, suppose that Mr. Jones clones himself.[77] That clone, X, is then implanted into a womb and it begins to develop normally. However, at a certain point in his gestation Mr. Jones orders that X's neural tube be stopped from developing so that X may not acquire the higher brain functions that are necessary for X to exercise his rational and moral powers. That is, a healthy embryo is manipulated so that he develops into something like an anencephalic child.[78] Mr. Jones issues that order because he wants to harvest X's body (which has Mr. Jones's genome) so that if and when any of Mr. Jones's organs become diseased or less functional, he can replace those organs with X's healthy ones.

But, as Dan W. Brock points out, as I noted in Chapter 4, "Most people would likely find this practice appalling and immoral, in part because here the cloned later twin's capacity for conscious life is destroyed *solely as a means* for the benefit of another."[79] What I suggest is that this intuition is best grounded in the substance view of persons. That is, only if the fetus is entitled to his higher brain functions does it make sense to say that the cloned twin has been wronged. Remember, the substance view is a perfectionist view, which means, as I noted earlier, it sees the maturation of a human being's intrinsic ends or purposes as perfections of its nature. So, for example, the whole human being is harmed if her brain is not allowed to develop as a consequence of ailment or assault. Thus, if the embryo's brain development is intentionally obstructed so that she does not achieve higher brain function and thus cannot exercise her natural powers for rational thought and moral reflection, the human being has been morally harmed because a good to which she is entitled has been prevented from coming to fruition. But if that's the case, then any act intended

---

[77] The following is similar to a scenario suggested in Carol Kahn, "Can We Achieve Immortality? The Ethics of Cloning and Other Life Extension Technologies," *Free Inquiry* (Spring 1989), 14–18. I offer a slightly different version of this scenario in Chapter 4 of this present volume.

[78] The National Institutes for Health provide this definition of anencephaly:

> Anencephaly is a defect in the closure of the neural tube during fetal development. The neural tube is a narrow channel that folds and closes between the 3rd and 4th weeks of pregnancy to form the brain and spinal cord of the embryo. Anencephaly occurs when the "cephalic" or head end of the neural tube fails to close, resulting in the absence of a major portion of the brain, skull, and scalp. Infants with this disorder are born without a forebrain (the front part of the brain) and a cerebrum (the thinking and coordinating part of the brain). The remaining brain tissue is often exposed – not covered by bone or skin. A baby born with anencephaly is usually blind, deaf, unconscious, and unable to feel pain. Although some individuals with anencephaly may be born with a rudimentary brain stem, the lack of a functioning cerebrum permanently rules out the possibility of ever gaining consciousness. Reflex actions such as breathing and responses to sound or touch may occur. (http://www.ninds.nih.gov/disorders/anencephaly/anencephaly.htm)

[79] Dan W. Brock, "Cloning Human Beings: An Assessment of the Ethical Issues Pro and Con," in National Bioethics Advisory Commission, *Cloning Human Beings*, vol. 2 (Rockville, MD: National Bioethics Advisory Commission, 1997), E8.

to disrupt or compromise the human being's proper end, including abortion, is prima facie immoral. After all, if it's wrong to prevent the embryo from acquiring her higher brain function by blocking her neural tube, it's wrong to do so by killing her via abortion.

In response to my argument, Stretton writes:

> To the contrary, this case seems to *refute* the substance view. To render a normal *adult* anencephalic would be tantamount to murder; surely then the same is true of *unborn* human beings, on the substance view? Yet our intuition is *not* that the creation of anencephalic clones is tantamount to murder. Our sense is rather that the deliberate creation of disabled beings is *prima facie* wrong (although well short of murder) even where those beings are not harmed by being created.... This intuition, however, provides no support for the substance view.[80]

Stretton, again, is misconstruing my argument. He reads into it something I do not defend. In no place in which I offer this argument do I suggest, imply, or claim that creating something like an anencephalic child is tantamount to murder. That belief plays no role in the argument's logic nor in the reason why I offered it. What then was I trying to accomplish with the argument?

Let us start with Stretton's moral claim "it is a *prima facie* wrong to intentionally create an anencephalic human being." For someone who holds the substance view this moral claim makes sense, for the human being whose brain is intentionally obstructed from normal development is being denied that which he is by nature entitled, because a functioning brain is a perfection of his nature. Stretton, however, concedes that intentionally creating an anencephalic-like human being is a *prima facie* wrong even if the intervention to alter the human being's brain development occurs before he acquires what Stretton and others consider the properties that impart personhood to the human being. So, what precisely are the grounds by which Stretton issues this judgment? He does not say. Is it because the fetus is entitled to his higher brain functions? If so, then abortion is unjustified, because it too robs the fetus of his higher brain functions (in addition to all of his bodily functions including the use of mature versions of his heart, lungs, legs, arms, ears, nose, eyes, etc.).

So, here's the problem: almost everyone agrees that it is a *prima facie* wrong to intentionally create an anencephalic human being. I, then, ask the question: what account of the human person best accounts for this intuition? It seems to me that the substance view has the best resources to do so, because views like those held by Stretton, McMahan, Boonin, and Dworkin affirm that it is morally permissible to destroy the fetus, including his developing brain, prior to his acquisition of certain value-making properties. So, if one

---

[80] Stretton, "Critical Notice," 794. I will not address Stretton's claim that rendering "a normal *adult* anencephalic would be tantamount to murder," since the truth or falsity of that claim is not relevant to my case.

can destroy the fetus for the apparent good of another (the pregnant woman) prior to him becoming a person, why cannot one use the fetus's body parts for the good of another (the cloned twin's progenitor) by making sure he does not become a person?

Although Stretton does suggest that such anencephalic-like "beings are not harmed by being created,"[81] that simply begs the question, for this thought-experiment is offered precisely to make the case that a being can be harmed even if it presently does not have the power to know or appreciate that it has been harmed. Nevertheless, let me offer another twist on this thought-experiment that will more clearly draw out how the substance view best accounts for the wrong in intentionally creating anencephalic-like children.

Suppose that the creating of anencephalic-like clones for organ harvesting becomes widespread. In response, millions of citizens rise up in protest, calling for the liberation of the clones. These citizens call their movement, clone-choice (CC), because they believe that it is morally wrong for the clones to have their moral and rational powers – that is, their choice – obstructed from maturing by cerebral mutilation. Those who support the practice respond, calling their movement, clone-life (CL), because they believe that it is morally wrong to interfere with a person's reproductive powers to create "nonperson" human beings (anencephalic-like clones) for the preservation of the lives of "real" persons. CL, with the assistance of the government, sets up thousands of "Life Centers" throughout North America in which cloning and harvesting procedures are offered to the public at a low cost. In these centers are millions of adult-looking human clones without higher brain functions resting in suspended animation. It turns out that some scientists working with CC have discovered a surgical procedure that will allow the adult clones to develop their higher brain functions. Suppose that some of these scientists break into several Life Centers, perform this surgery on about fifty of the adult clones, take these clones to safe houses where they are nourished, cared for, and sheltered, and over the course of nine months the clones do in fact develop higher brain functions. If you think what the scientists did was not only good but an act that justice requires, it seems that you must believe that the clones are beings of the nature of rational moral animal ordered toward certain perfections that when obstructed results in a wrong against these beings and thus harms them.

Consequently, contra Stretton, the strength of my argument does not depend on the claim, nor does it conclude, that the creation of anencephalic-like human beings is tantamount to murder. Rather, its strength depends on the inability of views contrary to the substance view – those embraced by Stretton and others – to account for the wrongness of an act for which the substance view can easily account.

---

[81] Ibid.

## 5.3. THE HOBBY LOBBY CASE, UNBORN HUMAN LIFE, AND RELIGIOUS LIBERTY

In 2014, the U.S. Supreme Court, in a 5–4 opinion, ruled in favor of two closely held, family-owned businesses, Hobby Lobby and Conestoga Wood Specialties, both of which objected to a regulation,[82] issued by the Secretary of HHS under powers given to her by the 2010 Affordable Care Act (ACA).[83] This regulation required for-profit companies to include in their employee health insurance plans birth control methods that the companies' owners believe may at times function to destroy human embryos soon after fertilization. The Hobby Lobby owners, members of the Green Family, are Evangelical Protestants, while the Hahns, owners of Conestoga, are Mennonite Christians. For this reason, the companies argued that because the HHS regulation requires that they directly pay-for, and thus cooperate with, the use of a product that violates what their respective theologies teach them about the sanctity of human life, the regulation is in violation of the 1993 Religious Freedom Restoration Act (RFRA).[84]

In order to grasp the significance of this case for religious liberty, imagine that publications supported by the research arm of the National Rifle Association (NRA), rather than those of Planned Parenthood,[85] were employed to help the Secretary of HHS in creating regulations for the ACA. Believing that self-defense saves lives,[86] and that an armed citizenry advances that good, the NRA data convinces the HHS secretary to require all employers to include in their employee health care plans two free firearms, including free bullets, depending on need. Quaker families that own for-profit businesses object on the grounds that it would involve them in directly providing instruments of war to their employees, in clear violation of their pacifist beliefs. The Quakers suggest that the government itself can give these weapons directly to the employees without involving the Quaker business owners in the activity. The government rejects this suggested accommodation and proceeds with the policy anyways. This is followed soon afterward with the Quaker businesses filing a lawsuit against the HHS Secretary.

---

[82] "The Guidelines provide that nonexempt employers are generally required to provide 'coverage, without cost-sharing' for [a]ll Food and Drug Administration [(FDA)] approved contraceptive methods, sterilization procedures, and patient education and counseling." (77 Fed. Reg. 8725, as quoted in Ibid., 8 [Alito, J., majority]).

[83] Patient Protection and Affordable Care Act (2010), Public Law, 111–148.

[84] Religious Freedom Restoration Act (1993), Public Law 103–141.

[85] See, e.g., *The Cost of Covering Contraceptives through Health Insurance* (ASPE Issue Brief) (February 2012), available at http://aspe.hhs.gov/health/reports/2012/contraceptives/ib.shtml. Among the brief's seventeen references, three are from The Guttmacher Institute, the research arm of the Planned Parenthood Federation of America.

[86] See, e.g., John R. Lott, Jr., *More Guns, Less Crime: Understanding Crime and Gun Control Laws*, 3rd ed. (Chicago: University of Chicago Press, 2010).

In the real-life Hobby Lobby case, the religious business owners were ultimately victorious. Writing for the majority, Justice Samuel Alito relies on RFRA, the federal law that passed in response to the 1990 case, *Employment Division v. Smith*.[87] In that case, the Supreme Court held, seemingly inconsistent with several prior holdings,[88] that a neutral and generally applicable law that happens to burden religious belief and practice, but was not intentionally written do so, is constitutional unless there is no rational basis for the law. So, the Oregon drug law that was the focus of this case is not unconstitutional, even though it burdened two practitioners of the Native American Church, who were denied unemployment benefits after being fired from their jobs as drug counselors because they had smoked sacramental peyote. Outraged by this decision, civil and religious liberty groups across the political spectrum joined forces to support what eventually became RFRA. Although the Supreme Court ruled it unconstitutional when applied to state laws,[89] RFRA may still be applied to federal laws, such as the regulations issued by the HHS secretary.

The relevant part of RFRA for this present case reads: "Government may substantially burden a person's exercise of religion only if it demonstrates that application of the burden to the person – (1) is in furtherance of a compelling governmental interest; and (2) is the least restrictive means of furthering that compelling governmental interest." According to Justice Alito, the HHS mandate at least violated (2),[90] because the government could have easily achieved in a variety of ways its goal of providing the birth control methods without burdening the businesses. Whether these businesses are legal persons under the meaning of RFRA, which was heavily debated in the media and on the internet before and after the Court's ruling, was carefully and artfully handled by Justice Alito.[91] On the matter of (1) – whether or not the HHS regulation furthered a compelling governmental interest – Justice Alito does not provide an answer, because, as he argues, even if the Court assumes that the government's interest is compelling, the regulation still violates RFRA based on the least restrictive means standard.[92]

For any advocate of taking rites seriously, there is much to commend Justice Alito's opinion. It presents the views of the business owners with respect, and it is highly critical of the government's attempt to make policy that seems to take

---

[87] Employment Div., Dept. of Human Resources of Ore. v. Smith 494 U.S. 872 (1990).

[88] See, e.g., Sherbert v. Verner 374 U.S. 398 (1963), and Wisconsin v. Yoder 406 U.S. 205 (1972).

[89] City of Boerne v. Flores 521 U.S. 507, 514 (1997).

[90] Burwell, 134 S. Ct. (2014), 2780-2783.

[91] Ibid., 16–25.

[92] "We find it unnecessary to adjudicate this issue. We will assume that the interest in guaranteeing cost-free access to the four challenged contraceptive methods is compelling within the meaning of RFRA, and we will proceed to consider the final prong of the RFRA test, *i.e.*, whether HHS has shown that the contraceptive mandate is 'the least restrictive means of furthering that compelling governmental interest'" (Ibid., 40) (citation omitted).

positions on controversial religious and philosophical questions.[93] Nevertheless, the way in which Justice Alito describes the business owners' objections is *consistent with* (although not necessarily supportive of) the court cases and legal scholarship we covered in Chapter 2, both of which treat religious beliefs as if they could never in-principle be deliverances of reason. Justice Alito writes that "the owners of the businesses have religious objections to abortion, and according to their religious beliefs the four contraceptive methods at issue are abortifacients.... [They] have a sincere religious belief that life begins at conception."[94] This is true enough, but it diminishes the intellectual credentials of the position held by the business owners, because, as we have already seen in the first two sections of this chapter, there is much more to the business owners' prolife position than mere religious belief. To better grasp this point, contrast Justice Alito's comments with those offered by Justice Ruth Bader Ginsburg in her dissent, in which she offers examples of other "mere religious beliefs" that sincerely devout business owners may hold:

Would the exemption the Court holds RFRA demands for employers with religiously grounded objections to the use of certain contraceptives extend to employers with religiously grounded objections to blood transfusions (Jehovah's Witnesses); antidepressants (Scientologists); medications derived from pigs, including anesthesia, intravenous fluids, and pills coated with gelatin (certain Muslims, Jews, and Hindus); and vaccinations (Christian Scientists, among others)? According to counsel for Hobby Lobby, "each one of these cases ... would have to be evaluated on its own ... apply[ing] the

---

[93] For example, Justice Alito writes:

> In taking the position that the HHS mandate does not impose a substantial burden on the exercise of religion, HHS's main argument (echoed by the principal dissent) is basically that the connection between what the objecting parties must do (provide health-insurance coverage for four methods of contraception that may operate after the fertilization of an egg) and the end that they find to be morally wrong (destruction of an embryo) is simply too attenuated ... HHS and the dissent note that providing the coverage would not itself result in the destruction of an embryo; that would occur only if an employee chose to take advantage of the coverage and to use one of the four methods at issue.
>
> This argument dodges the question that RFRA presents (whether the HHS mandate imposes a substantial burden on the ability of the objecting parties to conduct business in accordance with *their religious beliefs*) and instead addresses a very different question that the federal courts have no business addressing (whether the religious belief asserted in a RFRA case is reasonable). The Hahns and Greens believe that providing the coverage demanded by the HHS regulations is connected to the destruction of an embryo in a way that is sufficient to make it immoral for them to provide the coverage. This belief implicates a difficult and important question of religion and moral philosophy, namely, the circumstances under which it is wrong for a person to perform an act that is innocent in itself but that has the effect of enabling or facilitating the commission of an immoral act by another. Arrogating the authority to provide a binding national answer to this religious and philosophical question, HHS and the principal dissent in effect tell the plaintiffs that their beliefs are flawed. For good reason, we have repeatedly refused to take such a step ... (Ibid., 35–37) (citations and notes omitted).

[94] Burwell, 134 S. Ct. (2014), 2759, 2775.

compelling interest – least restrictive alternative test." ... Not much help there for the lower courts bound by today's decision.[95]

As should be evident, Justice Ginsburg raises these counterexamples precisely because they are based on beliefs that would seem to most people to be *prima facie* unreasonable. Although, as she notes, Hobby Lobby's counsel appealed to RFRA's compelling interest – least restrictive means test as the limiting principle that would allow future courts to thwart such counterexamples, she is not convinced of its judicial workability. For "there is an overriding interest ... in keeping the courts 'out of the business of evaluating the relative merits of differing religious claims' ... or the sincerity with which an asserted religious belief is held."[96] She also sees in this an Establishment Clause problem, because "approving some religious claims while deeming others unworthy of accommodation could be 'perceived as favoring one religion over another.' "[97]

But it's not clear how the judiciary can avoid "evaluating the merits of differing religious claims" and practices when dealing with claims and practices that dissent from dominant cultural understandings. Consider, for example, the cases involving Creation-Science and Intelligent Design,[98] ordinances that forbade Santeria animal sacrifice,[99] the Amish and compulsory education,[100] the Mormon practice of polygamy,[101] and nontheistic conscientious objection.[102] The point of bringing these cases to bear on my argument is not to suggest that they are analogous to the Hobby Lobby case. Rather, it is to show that the courts do in fact evaluate, in differing degrees, the reasonableness of the religious beliefs and practices in question to the extent to which those beliefs and practices impact a variety of legitimate state interests. In fact, none of these cases could have been resolved without judicial evaluation of the merits of religious claims and practices and their affect upon the common good. In, for example, the Santeria case, the Supreme Court held that a law that was not generally applicable or neutral that targeted religious practice was unconstitutional unless it survived strict scrutiny.[103] In order to engage in that assessment a court would have to figure out if the government's interest is compelling. But how can one do so without at some point evaluating the merits of the religious claims in question? After all, it makes a difference whether the law under scrutiny is criminalizing the use of communion wine or child sacrifice. In

---

[95] Burwell, 134 S. Ct. (2014), 2805 (Ginsburg, J., dissenting) (citation omitted).

[96] Ibid., 34 (citation omitted), quoting from United States v. Lee 455 U.S. 252, 263 n. 2 (1982) (Stevens, J., concurring).

[97] Ibid., 34 (citation omitted), quoting from *Lee*, 455 U.S., 263 n. 2 (1982) (Stevens, J., concurring).

[98] McLean v. Arkansas Board of Education 529 F. Supp. 1255 (1982); Edwards v. Aguillard 482 U.S. 578(1987); Kitzmiller v. Dover Area School District, 400 F. Supp. 2d, 722 (2005).

[99] Church of the Lukumi Babalu Aye, Inc. v. City of Hialeah 508 U.S. 520 (1993).

[100] Wisconsin v. Yoder 406 U.S. 205 (1972).

[101] Reynolds v. United States 98 U.S. (8 Otto.) 145 (1878).

[102] Welsh v. United States 398 U.S. 333 (1970); United States v. Seeger 380 U.S. 163 (1965).

[103] *Hialeah*, 508 U.S., 546 (1993).

other words, whether the government's interest is compelling depends on the prior background beliefs of reasonableness held by the judges and the justices.

In each of these cases, the courts (and the attorneys who argued the cases) employed *nonrevelatory beliefs* in order to determine (or defend or critique) the reasonableness of the religious claims and practices in question.[104] In the Creation-Science and Intelligent Design cases, involving the question of whether public school science curricula may include these views, it was the *nonscientific status of the theories* under scrutiny that ultimately did them in. In the Santeria case, it was the city council's *inconsistent application of the ordinance's principle purpose* that was essential to the church's victory: the council's announced purpose – health and safety and stopping animal cruelty – did not seem to be sincere, for the ordinance did not target, or announce any health concerns with, other forms of animal killing practiced by some nonSanteria entities and groups. The ordinances were crafted in such a way that they banned the Santeria practices but not other types of animal killing (e.g., kosher killing and butchers). The Amish were allowed to opt out of post-eighth-grade compulsory education because, among other things, they *"succeed in preparing their high school age children* to be productive members of the Amish community[, ...] *their system of learning* through doing the skills directly relevant to their adult roles in the Amish community ... [*is*] *'ideal,'* and *perhaps superior* to ordinary high school education. The *evidence* also showed that the Amish have an excellent record as law-abiding and generally self-sufficient members of society."[105] The federal prohibition of Mormon polygamy in the Territories, according to the Court, does not violate the Free Exercise Clause, because the Constitution allows Congress to criminalize actions, even if they arise from religious warrant, if those actions are "in violation of social duties or *subversive of good order.*"[106] In the nontheistic conscientious objection cases, the Supreme Court *justified* extending to nontheists the protections of a federal statute that textually limited objectors to theists *by arguing* that the atheist objector's "beliefs certainly occupy in the life of that individual 'a place parallel to that filled by ... God' in traditionally religious persons."[107]

Whether or not the court in each case vindicated the religious belief or practice in question (or an analogous belief or practice) was clearly guided by nonrevelatory standards of reasonableness. Appealing to *mere belief* was

---

[104] What I mean by "nonrevelatory beliefs" are those beliefs that are not derived exclusively from a religion's sacred scripture or magisterial authority. These nonrevelatory beliefs may very well serve to illuminate or clarify the deliverances of scripture or church dogma, as in the case of Aristotelian metaphysics applied to the Catholic doctrine of transubstantiation. In some traditions, such as Catholicism, nonrevelatory beliefs are central to the community's understanding of sacred doctrine. To put it another way, they are beliefs of natural reason, and include claims about philosophical theology, natural law, logic, or other forms of philosophical or scientific reasoning. Thus, they are the sorts of beliefs that people outside the religious tradition may grasp, find reasonable, or even believe, without actually converting to that faith.

[105] *Yoder*, 406 U.S., 212–13 (1972) (emphasis added).

[106] *Reynolds*, 98 U.S., 164 (1878).

[107] *Welsh*, 398 U.S., 340 (1970), quoting *Seeger*, 380 U.S., 176 (1965).

certainly not enough. Even though, as I argued in Chapter 2, there is a dominant stream in judicial thought that treats religious belief as not amendable to reason, courts nevertheless still have to determine the extent to which religious liberty or establishment ought to be tolerated under the First Amendment or RFRA *based on* standards of reasonableness that seem to be assumed rather than argued for. Thus, to treat all religious beliefs as *mere* religious beliefs (as Justice Alito seemingly does) or to maintain that courts ought not to evaluate the merits of competing religious claims (as Justice Ginsburg claims) is just not possible. Courts will, whether one likes or not, issue judgments about religious claims and practices that are guided by unchallenged assumptions of what counts as reasonable (including what counts as the public good).

This is why those who hold beliefs like those held by Hobby Lobby's owners cannot ignore the power of the received cultural understanding of reasonableness on the intellectual formation of judges. That understanding, as I have already argued in Section 5.1 of this chapter, assumes that the issue in dispute is really a matter of two allegedly incommensurable subjects – faith and reason – rather than a matter of two contrary answers to the same question: is the embryo one of us? This is why Justice Ginsburg and a generation of young lawyers (some of whom will someday sit on the federal bench) see Hobby Lobby's beliefs as outside rational discourse. If the friends of Hobby Lobby do not rebut this understanding – by making the argument in those venues outside the courtroom that really shape judicial reasoning, such as in the culture and in the law schools – a future court may conclude, as it would with a Christian Science business owner, that a sincere belief is not sufficient.

The fact that a particular law, such as the HHS mandate, burdens the religious liberty of a closely-held family-owned corporation, an individual citizen, or a nonprofit religious institution is a necessary condition for a plaintiff to charge the government with violating RFRA (or, in some cases, the First Amendment's Free Exercise Clause). But that is not enough. Even though in a RFRA case the legal burden is on the government, the cultural burden, whether one likes it or not, is on the plaintiff and his advocates. Thus, he has to not only show that his religious belief is substantially burdened (for legal purposes), he also must show (for cultural purposes) that his religious belief is reasonable (whether that means intrinsically reasonable or reasonable for the state to tolerate given its legitimate interests).[108]

## 5.4. CONCLUSION

Questions about the beginning of human life are at the heart of several controversial public issues over which citizens of good will are typically divided along religious lines. Not surprisingly, as I noted in Chapter 2, it has been pointed out

---

[108] I owe the articulation of this distinction – between intrinsically reasonable and reasonable for the state to tolerate – to Professor Richard Garnett (University of Notre Dame Law School) who suggested it to me in private email correspondence.

by no less a jurist than former U.S. Supreme Court Justice John Paul Stevens that the prolife view that the human being is a moral subject from conception is a "religious tenet of some, but by no means all, Christian faiths …"[109] That is, of course, true, with the Catholic Church asserting as much in the most recent edition of its catechism: "Human life must be respected and protected absolutely from the moment of conception. From the first moment of his existence, a human being must be recognized as having the rights of a person – among which is the inviolable right of every innocent being to life."[110]

Justice Stevens, nevertheless, concludes that such a belief cannot be reflected in our laws, because it "serves no identifiable secular purpose,"[111] and thus violates the U.S. Constitution's Establishment Clause. But, as we have seen in this chapter, to admit that such a belief is tightly tethered to a theological tradition (or is a "religious tenet," if we use Justice Stevens's language), actually tells us nothing about whether or not it is a belief that may be, or can be, defended by rational argument, or that it lacks a secular purpose.[112]

Calling a belief "religious" may be descriptively accurate, but we learn nothing of its plausibility or the sophistication of its case by merely attaching that adjective to it. Thus, labeling a belief "religious," and dismissing it on those grounds alone, does not serve the cause of justice, which I suspect that even Justice Stevens would agree has an identifiable secular purpose.

By contrast, as we saw in the case involving Hobby Lobby, in which the label "religious" was thought to advance the rights of the belief holder under RFRA, both the majority and the dissent side-stepped the role that culturally received understandings of reasonableness (including the public good) may very well undermine (or support) the religious liberty of the party who seeks the vindication of his rights. Consequently, in order to take rites seriously on the matter of the nature of prenatal life, *mere religion* is no safe haven for the advocates of religious liberty. They have to actually make the argument.[113]

---

[109] Webster v. Reproductive Health Services 492 U.S. 490, 566 (1989) (Stevens, J., dissenting) (notes and citations omitted).

[110] *Catechism of the Catholic Church: Revised in Accordance With the Official Latin Text Promulgated by Pope John Paul II*, 2nd ed. (Washington, DC: United States Conference of Catholic Bishops, 2000), 2270.

[111] *Webster*, 492 U.S. 566-47 (1989) (Stevens, J., dissenting).

[112] In Chapter 2 (Section 2.1.A), I point out that Justice Stevens begs the question in his argument for why the prolife view of prenatal life lacks a secular purpose.

[113] A special thanks to two of my former Baylor graduate assistants, Logan Gage (PhD 2014) and Ross Parker (PhD 2014), for proofreading an earlier version of Section 5.2 of this chapter as well as making some good suggestions. I would like to also thank an anonymous referee who really took me to task on an even earlier version of 5.2. He (or she) forced me to write with greater clarity, rigor, and precision, although any faults in this final version are entirely my own.

PART III

NATURE AND SEX

# 6

## How to Be an Anti–Intelligent Design Advocate: Science, Religion, and the Problem of Intelligent Design

> For when anyone in the endeavor to prove the faith brings forward reasons which are not cogent, he falls under the ridicule of the unbelievers: since they suppose that we stand upon such reasons, and that we believe on such grounds.
>
> St. Thomas Aquinas (1225–1274)[1]

> Here I would say what I heard from an ecclesiastical person in a very prominent position (Cardinal Baronio), namely that the intention of the Holy Spirit [in Scripture] is to teach us how one goes to heaven and not how heaven goes.
>
> Galileo Galilei (1564–1642)[2]

The debate in the United States over whether the teaching of Intelligent Design (ID) in public school science classes should be required, permitted, or prohibited has become a cantankerous affair. Like the issues we covered in Chapters 4 and 5, disputants fall along religious lines, with the more religiously conservative citizens generally advocating the teaching of ID in public school science classes, while secular and religiously liberal citizens generally arguing that ID is a religious position and thus teaching it in public school science classes would violate the Establishment Clause of the U.S. Constitution. Although as a matter of law I disagree with the latter's constitutional judgment,[3] I argue in this

---

[1] St. Thomas Aquinas, *Summa Theologica*, I, q. 32, art. 1, literally translated by Fathers of the English Dominican Province, 2nd and rev. ed. (1920), online edition (Copyright © 2008 by Kevin Knight), available at http://www.newadvent.org/summa/1032.htm.

[2] Galielo Galilei, "Galielo's Letter to the Grand Duchess Christina (1615)," in *The Galileo Affair: A Documentary History*, ed., trans. intro., notes Maurice A. Finnochiaro (Berkeley, CA: University of California Press, 1989).

[3] See, e.g., Francis J. Beckwith, "Science and Religion 20 Years After *McLean v. Arkansas*: Evolution, Public Education, and the Challenge of Intelligent Design," *Harvard Journal of Law and Public Policy* 26.2 (Spring 2003): 456–499; Francis J. Beckwith, *Law, Darwinism, and Public Education: The Establishment Clause and the Challenge of Intelligent Design* (Lanham, MD: Rowman & Littlefield, 2003); and Francis J. Beckwith, "Public Education, Religious

chapter that there are good reasons for religiously conservative citizens not to advance the cause of ID, and there are good reasons for secular and religiously liberal citizens not to equate the case for ID with the rational plausibility of theism (or even the case for design in nature). This chapter addresses both groups, and is critical of each.

In order to show how *both sides* of the ID dispute fail to "take rites seriously," I am going to address a question that, as far as I can tell, has been unanimously ignored in this debate, but should be of interest to anyone who may have a peculiar curiosity as to what "really" lurks behind, and may unconsciously form, the beliefs of those engaged in this cultural combat. That question is: what must one believe to be an *anti*–Intelligent Design advocate?

In order to answer this question, I consult several scholars (including ID critics) as well as Judge John E. Jones III's opinion in *Kitzmiller v. Dover*,[4] the well-known 2005 federal district court case that struck down a pro-ID school board policy. To set the stage, I explore two issues: (6.1) Distinguishing Creationism, Design, and Intelligent Design, and (6.2) Design Without Intelligent Design.

## 6.1. DISTINGUISHING CREATIONISM, DESIGN, AND INTELLIGENT DESIGN

The term "Intelligent Design" has become ubiquitous in American popular culture as the most recognizable alternative to Darwinian evolution since the ascendancy of "Creationism" (or "Creation Science").[5] Although "Creationism" and "Intelligent Design" are each offered by their respective proponents as alternative accounts of Darwinian evolution, they are not identical, even though some writers in fact claim that they are identical.[6] (One particularly annoying habit

Establishment, and the Challenge of Intelligent Design." *Notre Dame Journal of Law, Ethics, and Public Policy* 17.2 (2003): 461–519; Francis J. Beckwith, "Intelligent Design, Religious Motives, and the First Amendment," in *Intelligent Design: William A. Dembski and Michael Ruse in Dialogue*, ed. Robert B. Stewart (Minneapolis: Fortress Books, 2007). Even though I stand by the constitutional case I made in these works, I have since become quite critical of ID *as a view*, largely because I have come to better understand why many theistic philosophers (especially those in the Thomistic tradition) never warmed to ID. For an overview of my intellectual journey, see Francis J. Beckwith, "Or We Can Be Philosophers: A Response to Barbara Forrest," *Synthese*. Published Online First: 05 March 2011. doi 10.1007/s11229-011-9891-y.

[4] Kitzmiller v. Dover Area School District 400 F. Supp. 2d, 722 (2005).

[5] See Ronald H. Numbers, *The Creationists: From Scientific Creationism to Intelligent Design*, 2nd ed. (Cambridge, MA: Harvard University Press, 2005). See also, Francis J. Beckwith, review of *The Creationists*, 2nd ed., by Ronald H. Numbers, *Journal of Law and Religion* 23 (2007–2008): 735–738.

[6] See, e.g., the comments made by Judge Jones in *Kitzmiller*, 400 F. Supp. 2d, at 722 (citations omitted):

The weight of the evidence clearly demonstrates, as noted, that the systemic change from "creation" to "intelligent design" occurred sometime in 1987, *after* the Supreme Court's important Edwards [v. Aguillard] decision [482 U.S. 578 (1987)]. This compelling evidence strongly supports Plaintiffs' assertion that ID is creationism re-labeled. Importantly, the

on the part of these writers is to refer to "Intelligent Design" as "Intelligent Design Creationism" for the apparent purpose of instilling in their readers the practice of thinking that "guilt by association" is intellectually virtuous.)[7] It seems to me that their confusion (if it is truly a confusion) rests on two indisputable facts: (1) some ID advocates run in the same circles as some Creationists, and (2) some ID criticisms to Darwinian evolution resemble, and are in some cases identical to, Creationist criticisms of Darwinian evolution.[8] But that is a weak argument, for we can marshal just as bad a case against Darwinians who deny that their view supports atheism: (1) many politically passionate Darwinians run in the same circles as some atheists,[9] (2) most Darwinian critiques of Creationism and ID are practically indistinguishable from atheist

> objective observer, whether adult or child, would conclude from the fact that *Pandas [and People*, the ID text recommended to students according to the Dover policy,] posits a master intellect that the intelligent designer is God.

> Further evidence in support of the conclusion that a reasonable observer, adult or child, who is "aware of the history and context of the community and forum" is presumed to know that ID is a form of creationism concerns the fact that ID uses the same, or exceedingly similar arguments as were posited in support of creationism. One significant difference is that the words "God," "creationism," and "Genesis" have been systematically purged from ID explanations, and replaced by an unnamed "designer." Dr. [Barbara] Forrest testified and sponsored exhibits showing six arguments common to creationists. Demonstrative charts introduced through Dr. Forrest show parallel arguments relating to the rejection of naturalism, evolution's threat to culture and society, "abrupt appearance" implying divine creation, the exploitation of the same alleged gaps in the fossil record, the alleged inability of science to explain complex biological information like DNA, as well as the theme that proponents of each version of creationism merely aim to teach a scientific alternative to evolution to show its "strengths and weaknesses," and to alert students to a supposed "controversy" in the scientific community. In addition, creationists made the same argument that the complexity of the bacterial flagellum supported creationism as Professors Behe and Minnich now make for ID. The IDM [Intelligent Design Movement] openly welcomes adherents to creationism into its "Big Tent," urging them to postpone biblical disputes like the age of the earth. Moreover and as previously stated, there is hardly better evidence of ID's relationship with creationism than an explicit statement by defense expert Fuller that ID is a form of creationism.

[7] See, e.g., Robert T. Pennock, ed., *Intelligent Design Creationism and Its Critics: Philosophical, Theological, and Scientific Perspectives* (Cambridge, MA: M.I.T. Press, 2001).

[8] *See* Judge Jones's comments in note 6.

[9] See Jeffrey Koperski, "Two Bad Ways to Attack Intelligent Design and Two Good Ones," *Zygon* 43.2 (June 2008): 436. He comments on Dr. Barbara Carroll Forrest, the expert witness cited several times by Judge Jones in note 6:

> [She] is on the board of directors for the New Orleans Secular Humanist Association (*http:// nosha.secularhumanism.net*), a group that actively tries to prove that religious beliefs are based on ignorance and superstition. They strategically promote Secular Humanism; they hold conferences; they have their own newsletters and publications; they take donations. I submit that Forrest's academic publications are motivated by her antireligious views. That may be interesting in terms of biography, but friends and critics alike should agree that it is irrelevant when assessing her arguments.

criticisms of Creationism and ID,[10] and (3) most defenses of atheism maintain that Darwinian evolution is a defeater to theism.[11] These facts, like the ones about Creationism and ID, are indisputable. So, it seems that "guilt by association" is a game that each side can play.

In that case, why should one *not* think of Creationism and ID as identical? First, the cases offered for ID are much more like the argumentation one finds in philosophy or natural theology than they are like the biblicism on which Creationism relies. According to the ID advocate's account of the debate, Darwinian evolution claims to be an exhaustive account of the development of life on Earth. And because the Darwinian account is entirely a naturalist (and materialist) account requiring no mind behind it, as most of its supporters contend,[12] the burden of the ID advocate is to show *both* that Darwinism is an incomplete account of the development of life *and* that there is design in nature that requires a mind (or intelligence) to account for it. Because Creationists believe that God created the universe – and thus the universe is designed – it takes little imagination to see why Creationists and ID advocates would run in the same circles and find some of the same arguments congenial to their point of view. But that's where the similarities between the two views end. This is because for the Creationist a particular interpretation of the Bible's Book of Genesis is her starting point. Thus, it is in her interest to show that any account of the origin and nature of the universe, including Darwinian evolution, is inadequate in comparison to the biblical account. Although there are ID advocates who accept such a biblical account,[13] ID *as a point of view*

---

[10] Cf., e.g., Richard Dawkins's critique of ID in his brief for atheism (Richard Dawkins, *The God Delusion* [London: Bantam, 2007], 119–134) with Kenneth Miller's critique of ID in his case for the reality of both God and evolution (Kenneth R. Miller, *Finding Darwin's God: A Scientist's Search for Common Ground Between God and Evolution* [New York: Harper, 2000], 130–164). In fact, Dawkins relies on Miller's work in making his case against ID. I am, of course, not arguing that either writer is being duplicitous. What I am suggesting, by offering this comparison, is that "guilt by association" is a lousy way to argue on these matters.

[11] See, e.g., Dawkins, *The God Delusion*; and Richard Dawkins, *The Blind Watchmaker* (New York: W. W. Norton, 1986). In the latter, Dawkins writes (p. 6):

> An atheist before Darwin could have said, following Hume: "I have no explanation for complex biological design. All I know is that God isn't a good explanation, so we must wait and hope that somebody comes up with a better one." I can't help feeling that such a position, though logically sound, would have left one feeling pretty unsatisfied, and that although atheism might have been *logically* tenable before Darwin, Darwin made it possible to be an intellectually fulfilled atheist.

[12] "Darwin and his successors have shown how living creatures, with their spectacular statistical improbability and appearance of design, have evolved by slow, gradual degrees from simple beginnings. We can now safely say that the illusion of design in living creatures is just that – an illusion." (Dawkins, *The God Delusion*, 158).

[13] One such person is Paul Nelson, a fellow of the Discovery Institute. He is a young-earth creationist who earned his PhD in the philosophy of biology from the University of Chicago. Young-earth creationism (YEC) is "the point of view that holds that the first twelve chapters of

has no *necessary connection* to any biblical account. For, as I note later, the ID advocate is offering a case that depends exclusively on the plausibility of arguments whose premises consist of empirical, conceptual, mathematical, and/or philosophical claims. Of course, whether such arguments actually work (or are at least minimally plausible) is another question altogether, one that falls outside the narrow scope of this chapter. Nevertheless, the important point here is to understand that regardless of whether ID arguments work or not, ID is not Creationism, even though it shares some characteristics with it.[14]

Moreover, some design arguments embraced by ID advocates are also embraced by ID critics! For example, two strong critics of ID, former Human Genome Project director Francis Collins and Brown University biologist Ken Miller, both Christians, defend the plausibility of design arguments that support some form of theism. Miller, who testified as an expert witness for the plaintiffs in the *Kitzmiller* case,[15] maintains that the alignment of the cosmic constants soon after the Big Bang points toward an extra-natural mind as the Intelligent Cause of the universe.[16] Collins agrees,[17] but also offers an argument for the existence of God from the existence of the moral law, not unlike C. S. Lewis's argument in *Mere Christianity*.[18] The sorts of cosmic "fine-tuning" arguments presented by Collins and Miller are also defended by thinkers associated

Genesis are to be taken as scientifically accurate. This entails the special creation of all life forms including human beings, an earth no more than 10,000 years old, and a universal flood in which Noah's Ark safely floated." (Beckwith, review of *The Creationists*. 736). But, as I also point in that same review:

[F]or the ID advocate, the most important thing to do is to show the failure of philosophical materialism as a worldview. This may or may not involve a full-orbed critique of Darwinism. In fact, some ID advocates, including Lehigh University biochemist Michael Behe, believe in common descent, which is Creationist Kryptonite. On the other hand, Paul Nelson ... is a young-earth creationist (YEC). Yet, Nelsen makes a distinction between what he believes theologically and which of those theological beliefs he can legitimately defend scientifically and/or philosophically by means of natural reason. So, when Nelson is defending ID, he is not defending YEC. For Nelson, and others like him, ID is consistent with and lends support to YEC, but it does not rule out the falsity of YEC. For if it did, then Behe, a type of theistic evolutionist, and Nelson, a young-earth creationist, could not be "on the same ID team," so to speak. These subtle, though important, distinctions are sometimes lost on critics of ID, who often confuse an argument offered by an ID advocate with the ID advocate who offers the argument. (Ibid., 736–737)

[14] This point has been persuasively made by atheist philosopher Bradley Monton, *Seeking God in Science: An Atheist Defends Intelligent Design* (Calgary, AB: Broadview Press, 2009), especially Chapter 1.

[15] See, e.g., *Kitzmiller*, 400 F. Supp. 2d, 724.

[16] Miller, *Finding Darwin's God*, especially Chapter 8.

[17] Francis Collins, *The Language of God: A Scientist Presents Evidence for Belief* (New York: The Free Press, 2006), especially Chapter 3. Collins's criticisms of ID are in Chapter 6.

[18] C. S. Lewis, *Mere Christianity* (a revised and amplified edition, with a new introduction, of the three books, *Broadcast Talks, Christian Behaviour, and Beyond Personality*) (San Francisco: HarperCollins, 2001; originally published in 1952), Chapters 1–5.

with The Discovery Institute (DI),[19] the Seattle-based think-tank that is in the forefront in supporting ID research.

For these reasons, there is understandable confusion on what precisely constitutes ID. In my previous works I defined ID so broadly that it would include the arguments of thinkers like Miller and Collins who, although critical of ID in the life sciences, seem not to be troubled by the detection of design in cosmology. Here is how I defined ID in 2007:

Intelligent Design (or ID) is not one theory. It is a short-hand name for a cluster of arguments that offer a variety of cases that attempt to show, by reasoning unaccompanied by religious authority or sacred scripture, that intelligent agency rather than unguided matter better accounts for apparently natural phenomena and/or the universe as a whole. Some of these arguments challenge aspects of neo-Darwinism. Others make a case for a universe designed at its outset, and thus do not challenge any theory of biological evolution. Nevertheless, they all have in common the notion that the human intellect has the capacity to acquire knowledge of, or at least have rational warrant to believe in, an inference that mind, rather than non-mind, best accounts [for] some apparently natural phenomena or the universe as a whole.[20]

When I wrote this definition I was trying to explain to a wider audience that the best way to understand ID is to see it as a counter to the hegemony of philosophical materialism that some thinkers believe is entailed by both Darwinian evolution as well as a particular understanding of science. It is a view of science that maintains that the hard sciences are the best or only way of acquiring exhaustive knowledge of the natural world and its genesis, and that these sciences, in order to function properly, require methodological naturalism. According to ID advocate, William A. Dembski, *methodological naturalism* is "the view that science must be restricted solely to undirected natural processes."[21] Thus, it seemed to me that any view that challenged philosophical materialism, either by critiquing its methodological assumptions and/or its ontological commitments, could rightfully

---

[19] See, e.g., Stephen Meyer, "The Return to the God Hypothesis," *Journal of Interdisciplinary Studies* 11.1/2 (1999): 1–38; and Guillermo Gonzalez and Jay Wesley Richards, *The Privileged Planet: How Our Place in the Cosmos Is Designed for Discovery* (Washington, DC: Regnery Publishing, 2004).

[20] Beckwith, "Intelligent Design, Religious Motives, and the First Amendment," 93. The "for" in brackets is to replace "from," which was a typographical error in the original.

[21] William A. Dembski, *Intelligent Design: The Bridge Between Science and Theology* (Downers Grove, IL: InterVarsity Press, 1999), 119. According to another ID advocate, Phillip Johnson, "[a] methodological naturalist defines science as the search for the best naturalistic theories. A theory would not be naturalistic if it left something out (such as the existence of genetic information or consciousness) to be explained by a supernatural cause." Therefore, "all events in evolution (before the evolution of intelligence) are assumed attributable to unintelligent causes. The question is not *whether* life (genetic information) arose by some combination of chance and chemical laws, to pick one example, but merely *how* it did so." (Phillip E. Johnson, *Reason in the Balance: The Case Against Naturalism in Science, Law, and Education* [Downers Grove, IL: InterVarsity Press, 1996], 208).

be included under the big tent of ID.[22] I am now convinced that my definition – although an accurate description of what would constitute a central belief to a broad coalition of antinaturalists – does not truly capture the core arguments of what has come to be known as the Intelligent Design Movement (IDM).

Take, for example, Miller and Collins, who defend cosmological fine-tuning arguments (CFT)[23] for cosmic design, but who are at the same time critics of ID. Former DI vice president, Mark Ryland, points out that although ID advocates will, at times, incorporate CFT arguments into their works, CFT supporters, like Miller and Collins, do not reciprocate.[24] Ryland explains the reason for this:

CFT does not imply any intervention by God in the evolution of the cosmos. The laws and constants at issue are preordained, built into the very fabric of reality. IDT [Intelligent Design Theory], on the other hand, implies intervention, divine or otherwise, by arguing that an "intelligent cause" must have done something superadded to an "unguided natural process."[25]

Consequently, one ought not to confuse ID (or as Ryland calls it, "IDT")[26] with other views (such as CFT) that claim that the natural universe is designed and/or includes both formal and final causes. It seems to me, then, that Ryland is correct when he defines ID as a view that "purports to be a scientific theory about the development of life on earth.... [It] defines itself in part by arguing against the adequacy of standard neo-Darwinian evolutionary theory and in part by making allegedly scientific arguments in favor of *design* in biology."[27] Its three most important theorists are biochemist Michael Behe,[28] philosopher of science Stephen Meyer,[29] and mathematician and philosopher William A. Dembski.[30] Thus, when critics and defenders

---

[22] As I note in footnote 12 of Chapter 4, I have changed my mind about methodological naturalism (MN) in the sciences from the understanding I held in my 2003 book *Law, Darwinism, and Public Education*.

[23] I am borrowing the abbreviation CFT (for "cosmological fine-tuning") from Mark Ryland, "Intelligent Design Theory," *New Catholic Encyclopedia Supplement* 2009, 2 volumes, ed-in-chief, Robert L. Fastiggi (Detroit: Gale, 2009), 1: 473.

[24] Ibid.

[25] Ibid. As I point out in footnote 46, I am not sure that Ryland is entirely correct here, as the multiverse hypothesis defended by naturalists to thwart CFT arguments is intended to fill "the gap" that God fills in these arguments.

[26] Ibid., 470.

[27] Ibid.

[28] See, e.g., Michael Behe, *Darwin's Black Box: The Biochemical Challenge to Evolution* (New York: The Free Press, 1996); Michael Behe, *The Edge of Evolution: The Search for the Limits of Darwinism* (New York: The Free Press, 2008).

[29] See, e.g., Stephen C. Meyer, *Signature in the Cell: DNA and the Evidence for Intelligent Design* (New York: HarperOne, 2009); James Angus Campbell and Stephen C. Meyer, eds., *Darwinism, Design and Public Education* (Michigan State University Press, 2004).

[30] See, e.g., William A. Dembski, *The Design Inference* (New York: Cambridge University Press, 1998); William A. Dembski and Michael Ruse, eds., *Debating Design: From Darwin to DNA* (New York: Cambridge University Press, 2004).

write of the IDM, they are virtually always referring to the works of these and other thinkers associated with the DI. It was this view that was the focus of the 2005 *Kitzmiller* case.[31]

Nevertheless, both ID advocates and other believers in design (e.g., CFT supporters) hold at least one belief in common, namely, that the human mind has the capacity and power to detect and know that the universe and/or parts of it are designed and thus the product of mind rather than nonmind. ID advocates, however, typically argue for the application of certain design-detecting criteria to empirical observations *in* the natural world. Hence, according to Dembski, ID is "the study of patterns *in* nature that are best explained as the result of intelligence."[32] So, for example, Behe argues that because things that are *irreducibly complex* are the product of mind (e.g., a mousetrap), therefore some aspects of the natural world (e.g., the bacterial flagellum) are the product of mind because they too are irreducibly complex. Dembski offers a similar criterion based on a concept he calls *specified complexity*. He argues that because things that exhibit specified complexity are the product of mind (e.g., a lock's combination), therefore, aspects of the natural world (e.g., the bacterial flagellum) are products of mind because they too exhibit specified complexity.

Consequently, for both Behe and Dembski design is a property had by an entity that exhibits a certain type and level of complexity (or is irreducible). Both maintain that there is a threshold at which a living organism's irreducible complexity (in the case of Behe)[33] or specified complexity (in the case of Dembski)[34] becomes incapable of being accounted for by nonagent causes, such as natural selection, random mutation, and/or scientific laws. (Meyer offers a different criterion, "inference to the best explanation" [or IBE], although it, like

---

[31] *Kitzmiller*, 400 F. Supp. 2d.

[32] William A. Dembski, "Opening Statement," in William A. Dembski and Michael Ruse, "Intelligent Design: A Dialogue," in *Intelligent Design: William A. Dembski and Michael Ruse in Dialogue*, 20.

[33] Behe's project take its cue from Charles Darwin's (1809–1882) claim that "[i]f it could be demonstrated that any complex organ existed which could not possibly have been formed by numerous, successive, slight modifications, my theory would absolutely break down." (Charles Darwin, *The Origin of Species*, 6th ed. [6th ed. 1872], 154, as quoted in Michael Behe, "Intelligent Design as an Alternative Explanation for the Existence of Biomolecular Machines," *Rhetoric and Public Affairs* 1.4 [1998]: 566). Thus, reasons Behe, a system that is *irreducibly complex* (IC) is a serious challenge to the explanatory power of the Darwinian paradigm. Behe defines an IC system as "a single system of several well-matched, interacting parts that contribute to the basic function, wherein the removal of any one of the parts causes the system to effectively cease functioning." (Behe, *Darwin's Black Box*, 39).

[34] Writes Dembski:

> Intelligence leaves behind a characteristic trademark or signature – what I call "specified complexity." An event exhibits specified complexity if it is contingent and therefore not necessary; if it is complex and therefore not easily repeatable by chance; and if it is specified in the sense of exhibiting an independently given pattern. Note that complexity in the sense of improbability is not sufficient to eliminate chance: flip a coin long enough, and you'll witness a highly complex or improbable event. Even so, you'll have no reason not to attribute it to chance. (William A. Dembski, "Detecting Design in the Natural Sciences," *Natural History* 111.3 [April 2002]: 76)

Behe's and Dembski's, is a criterion by which one may detect intelligent, and exclude nonintelligent, causes for certain biological entities, including organs and systems, in nature)[35] For both Behe and Dembski it is the complex arrangement of an entity's parts and the end of that arrangement that requires an agent cause. However, short of achieving that threshold of irreducible or specified complexity, no design inference is warranted. And because ID offers an account of the natural world that is a rival to nondesign hypotheses, Behe and Dembski maintain that ID should be considered "science."[36]

Although this question – whether or not ID is science – turned out to be one of the central issues in the *Kitzmiller* opinion,[37] it seems to me that this question

[35] Meyer, *Signature in the Cell*, 154–228. In a 2000 essay in *First Things*, Meyer explains IBE as it applies to his argument from "DNA to design," which is defended with greater rigor in his massive 2009 monograph *Signature in the Cell*:

> The design argument from information content in DNA, therefore, does not depend upon analogical reasoning since it does not depend upon assessments of degree of similarity. The argument does not depend upon the similarity of DNA to a computer program or human language, but upon the presence of an identical feature ("information content" defined as "complexity and specification") in both DNA and all other designed systems, languages, or artifacts. While a computer program may be similar to DNA in many respects, and dissimilar in others, it exhibits a precise identity to DNA in its ability to store information content (as just defined).
>
> Thus, the "DNA to Design" argument does not represent an argument from analogy of the sort that Hume criticized, but an "inference to the best explanation." Such arguments turn, not on assessments of the degree of similarity between effects, but instead on an assessment of the adequacy of competing possible causes for the same effect. Because we know intelligent agents can (and do) produce complex and functionally specified sequences of symbols and arrangements of matter (i.e., information content), intelligent agency qualifies as a sufficient causal explanation for the origin of this effect. Since, in addition, naturalistic scenarios have proven universally inadequate for explaining the origin of information content, mind or creative intelligence now stands as the best and only entity with the causal power to produce this feature of living systems. (Stephen C. Meyer, "DNA and Other Designs," *First Things* 102 [April 2000]: 37–38.)

[36] Dembski writes: "The related concepts of irreducible complexity and specified complexity render intelligent causes empirically detectable and make intelligent design a full-fledged scientific theory, distinguishing it from the design arguments of philosophers and theologians, or what has traditionally been called *natural theology*." (William A. Dembski, *The Design Revolution: Answering the Toughest Questions About Intelligent Design* [Downers Grove, IL: InterVarsity Press, 2004], 37).

[37] Judge Jones writes:

> We find that ID fails on three different levels, any one of which is sufficient to preclude a determination that ID is science. They are: (1) ID violates the centuries-old ground rules of science by invoking and permitting supernatural causation; (2) the argument of irreducible complexity, central to ID, employs the same flawed and illogical contrived dualism that doomed creation science in the 1980's; and (3) ID's negative attacks on evolution have been refuted by the scientific community. As we will discuss in more detail below, it is additionally important to note that ID has failed to gain acceptance in the scientific community, it has not generated peer-reviewed publications, nor has it been the subject of testing and research. (*Kitzmiller*, 400 F. Supp. 2d, 735)

For a critique of Jones's criteria, see Bradley Monton, "Is Intelligent Design Science? Dissecting the *Dover* Decision," (2006), available at http://philsci-archive.pitt.edu/archive/00002592/.

is a red herring and serves to obscure the more important philosophical issues that percolate beneath the surface of this dispute. Both sides, however, have an interest in keeping this question alive. The ID advocates seem to believe that if they can prove that ID is indeed science, then it can get a fair hearing in the academy. The ID opponents seem to believe that if they can prove that ID is not science, then ID cannot be and ought not to be taken seriously by scientists. Nevertheless, it seems to me that the "science" question in this dispute is, in a sense, a sort of epistemological nuclear device that ensures total victory for the side that can successfully deliver it first. But the device is a philosophical dud, as I argued in my 2003 book on the subject:

[I]f ID arguments lack certain theoretical virtues that are considered earmarks of good theories or explanations – e.g., explanatory power, empirical adequacy, simplicity, pre-dictive and/or retrodictive success (as broadly construed in the historical sciences), testability, clarity of concepts – and/or exhibit the vices of bad theories – e.g., "God-of-the-gaps" strategy, heavy reliance on ad hoc hypotheses, lack of explanatory power – and if there are better alternatives, then perhaps one could reject ID as an explanation and/or theory for apparent design in nature. But one would be doing so, not because ID is unable to pass a metaphysical litmus test, but rather, because it fails as an hypoth-esis qua hypothesis. That is, whether ID fits some *a priori* definition of "science" or "pseudo-science" is a red herring, for such definitions tell us nothing about whether a theory and/or explanation, such as ID, provides us with real knowledge of the order and nature of things. In the words of [philosopher of science Larry] Laudan, who is not an ID supporter: "If we could stand up on the side of reason, we ought to drop terms like 'pseudo-science'.... They do only emotive work for us."[38]

In other words, the question of what is "science" and whether ID counts as science does not advance the conversation, because each side typically employs it as either a ticket to cultural acceptability (the ID advocates) or as an epis-temological exclusionary rule (the ID critics). Thus, it impermissibly shifts the discussion from the plausibility of ID arguments to the question of whether the whole idea of ID, regardless of the quality of the arguments for it, is capable of getting past a gauntlet of intellectual gatekeepers.

## 6.2. DESIGN WITHOUT INTELLIGENT DESIGN

We have seen that ID is not Creationism, that not all design arguments (e.g., CFT) are necessarily the spawn of the IDM, and that the question of whether or not ID is science is beside the point. Now I want to discuss another way of thinking about design in nature. It is a view defended by

---

[38] Francis J. Beckwith, *Law, Darwinism, and Public Education*, quoting Larry Laudan, "The Demise of the Demarcation Problem," in *But Is It Science?: The Philosophical Question In The Creation/Evolution Controversy*, ed. Michael Ruse (Buffalo, NY: Prometheus Books, 1988), 349.

Thomists,[39] followers of the philosopher and theologian St. Thomas Aquinas (1225–1274),[40] as well as others who embrace the classical theism taught and believed by Aquinas and virtually all serious Christians, Jews, and Muslims prior to the twentieth century.[41] It is a view that is both contrary to the dominant account of ID as well as those views of nature held by ID's materialist critics (although not all of its nonmaterialist critics). Calling this view Thomistic Design (TD), it maintains that the universe was brought into being by God *ex nihilo* and that this universe consists of a vast variety of inanimate and animate entities. Among the animate entities are human beings, whose mature and healthy members possess an active power for self-movement that allows them to engage in free acts initiated and/or accompanied by thought and reflection. The universe is not God's "artifact," because he did not change that which already existed,[42] as Aristotle (384–322 BCE) believed that his deity, "the Unmoved Mover," did to prime matter.[43] Rather, according to St. Thomas, the universe is radically contingent upon God for its genesis as well as its continued existence,

---

[39] See, e.g., Etienne Gilson, *From Aristotle to Darwin and Back Again: A Journey in Final Causality, Species and Evolution* (San Francisco: Ignatius Press, 2009; John Lyon trans., 1984; originally published in French in 1971); Edward Feser, *The Last Superstition* (South Bend, IN: St. Augustine's Press, 2008); Ric Machuga, *In Defense of the Soul: What it Means to be Human* (Grand Rapids, MI: Baker Book House, 2002), especially 161–166; and Thomas W. Tkacz, "Thomas Aquinas vs. the Intelligent Designers: What Is God's Finger Doing in My Pre-Biotic Soup?," in *Intelligent Design: Real Science or Religion in Disguise?*, ed. Robert Baird and Stuart Rosenbaum (Amherst, NY: Prometheus Books, 2007), 275–282.

[40] It is a common error to mistakenly link the arguments of contemporary ID advocates with St. Thomas Aquinas's argument from final causes in nature. See, for example, Martha Nussbaum's committing of this error in her for book *Liberty of Conscience: In Defense of America's Tradition of Religious Equality* (New York: Basic Books, 2008), 322. Although it is true that final causes imply design, the ID movement is a project in which the irreducible or degree of specified complexity of the parts in natural objects are offered as evidence that these entities are designed. But that is not the same as a final or formal cause (as we will see in what follows in the text in Section 6.2), which is something intrinsic to the entity and not detectable by *mere* empirical observation. For example, if I were to claim that the human intellect's final cause is to know because the human being's formal cause is his nature of "rational animal," I would not be making that claim based on the irreducible or degree of specified complexity of the brain's parts. Rather, I would be making a claim about the proper end of a power possessed by the human person. That end cannot be strictly observed, because in principle one can exhaustively describe the efficient and material causes of a person's brain-function without recourse to its proper end or purpose. Yet, the end or purpose of the human intellect seems in fact to be knowable. For more on St. Thomas and design, see Joseph A. Bujis, "On Misrepresenting the Thomistic Five Ways," *Sophia* 48 (2009): 15–34; Feser, *The Last Superstition*, 74–119; and Tkacz, "Thomas Aquinas vs. the Intelligent Designers."

[41] For a clear and compelling presentation of classical theism that interacts with contemporary thought, see David Bentley Hart, *The Experience of God: Being, Consciousness, Bliss* (New Haven, CT: Yale University Press, 2013).

[42] St. Thomas Aquinas, *Summa Theologica*, I, q. 45, art. 3, available at http://www.newadvent.org/summa/1045.htm.

[43] Aristotle, *The Metaphysics* (trans. W. D. Ross), bk. IX, *available at* http://classics.mit.edu/Aristotle/meta physics.9.ix.html.

including the development and order within it. This is why, in his famous Five Ways (or arguments) to show God's existence, St. Thomas includes as a fifth way an argument from the universe's design as a *whole*, appealing to the way in which natural bodies seem to act for an end. Writes St. Thomas:

The fifth way is taken from the governance of the world. We see that things which lack intelligence, such as natural bodies, act for an end, and this is evident from their acting always, or nearly always, in the same way, so as to obtain the best result. Hence it is plain that not fortuitously, but designedly, do they achieve their end. Now whatever lacks intelligence cannot move towards an end, unless it be directed by some being endowed with knowledge and intelligence; as the arrow is shot to its mark by the archer. Therefore some intelligent being exists by whom all natural things are directed to their end; and this being we call God.[44]

For St. Thomas, the design or purpose of nature refers to the interrelationship of "all things" in the universe, all inanimate and animate entities, which have their own natures that direct them to certain ends. And they are all kept in existence by God, who brought the universe into being *ex nihilo*. St. Thomas, although a believer in design, was no ID advocate. As the Eastern Orthodox theologian, David Bentley Hart, notes: "For St. Thomas Aquinas ... God creates the order of nature by infusing the things of the universe with the wonderful power of moving themselves toward determinate ends.... According to the classical arguments, universal rational order – not just this or that particular instance of complexity – is what speaks of the divine mind: harmony as resplendently evident in the simplicity of a raindrop as in the molecular labyrinths of a living cell."[45]

As I have already noted, the ID advocate tries to detect instances of design in nature by eliminating chance and necessity (or scientific law). This implies that one has no warrant to say that the latter two are the result of an intelligence that brought into being a whole universe whose parts, including its laws and those events that are apparently random, seem to work in concert to achieve a variety of ends. But this is precisely the position advanced by the Thomist. In response, someone could say that an ID advocate who accepts a CFT argument does in fact have warrant to believe that chance and necessity are the result of intelligence as well, because both function in the Creator's plan for the universe's fine-tuning.[46] But then, what happens to irreducible and specified

---

[44] St. Thomas Aquinas, *Summa Theologica*, I, q. 2, art. 3, available at http://www.newadvent.org/summa/1002.htm.

[45] Hart, *The Experience of God*, 38.

[46] I am not suggesting here that I agree with the CFT arguments offered by Miller and Collins, or anyone else for that matter. The point of bringing them up in this chapter is to show that not every argument for design in nature is a species of ID. However, insofar as the CFT arguments rely on the deliverances of contemporary science, they seem to have a "God of the gaps" quality to them that is not unlike what is found in the conventional ID arguments offered by Behe and Dembski. This is why the dominant response to CFT arguments – the multiverse hypothesis – is convincing to many philosophical naturalists. For it fills the same gap filled by God in the CFT arguments.

complexity as criteria by which to eliminate nonagent causes of apparently designed effects *in* nature? As Brad S. Gregory writes, this puts the ID advocates in the ironic position of sharing a philosophical assumption with the New Atheists,[47] the latest apologists for Darwinian evolution who claim that it entails unbelief:

> Advocates of intelligent design posit that ordinary biological processes of natural selection and genetic mutation can account for much but not everything in the evolution of species, the remainder requiring recourse to God's intervention. Insofar as proponents of intelligent design posit normally autonomous natural processes usually devoid of God's influence, they share important assumptions with the New Atheists.[48]

Gregory points out the fallacy in this understanding of God's relationship to nature: "[P]erhaps in the past Darwinism wasn't explanatorily powerful enough to drive God out, but recent, further scientific findings no longer leave room for God."[49] The result is a strange parallel of ferocious posturing between ID advocates and the New Atheists: "The intelligent design proponents scramble to find remaining places for supernatural intervention; the New Atheists claim there are none left. Both assume that God, conceived in spatial and quasi-spatial terms, needs 'room' to be God – which is precisely what traditional Christian theology says God does not need."[50]

TD also has something to say about the detection of purpose in the universe. For the Thomist, the human intellect has the power to "see" formal and final causes in both artifacts and in nature. Following Aristotle, St. Thomas maintained that there are four causes of change in the universe: efficient, material, formal, and final. In order to explain them, consider this example. Imagine a marble statute of Jesus made for the chapel of a large cathedral in order to facilitate worship. The marble is the material cause. Its maker, the artist, is the efficient cause. The reason for why it was made – to assist the chapel attendees in worship – is the final cause. And the formal cause is the pattern of the statute in the artist's mind that he imposes on the unformed marble. Consider now an

---

However, whether such a move succeeds for philosophical naturalists is another question altogether, one that falls outside the scope of this chapter.

[47] "The New Atheists" is a term that was coined to refer to several atheist thinkers and writers who have authored bestselling books during the middle of the first decade of the twenty-first century. This group usually includes Dawkins, Daniel Dennett, Sam Harris, and the late Christopher Hitchens.

[48] Brad S. Gregory, "Science v. Religion?: The Insights and Oversights of the 'New Atheists'," *Logos: A Journal of Catholic Thought and Culture* 12.4 (Fall 2009): 41. Perhaps this is why ID advocates are sometimes reluctant to say that the intelligent designer is "God." As three of them write: "Design theory, unlike neo-Darwinism, attributes this appearance to a designing intelligence, but it does not address the characteristics or identity of the designing intelligence." (David K. DeWolf, Stephen C. Meyer, and Mark Edward DeForrest, "Teaching the Origins Controversy: Science, or Religion, or Speech?," *Utah Law Review* [2000]: 85).

[49] Gregory, "Science v. Religion?," 41.

[50] Ibid.

organ system of a living organism, a human being's lungs. The organic material of which that system consists is its material cause. Its efficient cause is the biological parents of the human being in which the lungs reside. Its formal cause is the nature of the being in which the lungs function, for they are fully integrated parts that work in concert with the body's other parts to help sustain the whole being for its own flourishing (which depends on a "pattern," the sort of being it is). And the lungs' final cause is respiration. Their end is to exchange oxygen for the sake of the person who owns them.

For St. Thomas (again, following Aristotle), the formal and final causes of artifacts, like desks, computers, and iPads, are imposed from outside the collection of parts by an intelligent agent. By contrast, the formal and final causes of natural objects are intrinsic to those objects.[51] This is why, as Aristotle points out – and as I noted in Chapter 5 – if you own a bed made out of wood and then plant a piece of the bed in the ground, "it would not be a bed that would come up, but wood."[52] This "shows that the arrangement in accordance with the rules of the art is merely an incidental attribute, whereas the real nature is the other, which, further, persists continuously through the process of making."[53] In other words, the form and finality of the bed is imposed from without (an "arrangement in accordance with the rules of art") while the form and finality of the wood is intrinsic to the nature of the tree from which it was taken ("the real nature" that "persists continuously through the process of making"). In the words of Etienne Gilson:

> The artist is external to his work; the work of art is consequently external to the art which produces it. The end of living nature is, on the contrary, consubstantial with it. The embryo *is* the law of its own development. It is already of its nature to be what will be later on an adult capable of reproducing itself.[54]

Consequently, for example, a medical scientist may provide an exhaustive account of the mechanics of respiration without any reference to final and formal causes. But it does not follow that final and formal causes play no part in our rational

---

[51] Although "final causality" is technically extrinsic, there is a sense in which it is intrinsic when it comes to living beings. To repeat what I wrote in footnote 73 in Chapter 5: For living beings, like human beings, trees, and squirrels, final causality is tightly tethered to formal causality. Thus, because a human being is a particular type of being, that is, he has a certain form or nature, specific ends or purposes are proper to that nature. So, for example, a human being's mental powers are ordered toward the acquisition of knowledge and wisdom, though they may not in fact achieve that end, as in the case of a child who dies in infancy or an adult who is impaired due to illness or accident. For this reason, we say that *technically* a being's final causality is "extrinsic," because it is aspirational, even if our judgment of its correctness is grounded in an intrinsic cause, its form or nature.

[52] Aristotle, *Physics* (trans. Translated by R. P. Hardie and R. K. Gaye), bk. II, available at http://classics.mit.edu/Aristotle/physics.2.ii.html.

[53] Ibid.

[54] Gilson, *From Aristotle to Darwin*, 148.

deliberations about the world. In fact, as I show later in Section 6.3, some critics of ID simply cannot resist helping themselves to those causes in their assessments of ID and its advocates, even though many of these critics believe that Darwinian evolution (and the practice of modern science) has forever banished these causes from our study of nature. But there is a reason for this: formal and final causes are so much the woof and warp of our lives that we, like the water-skeptic fish submerged in H₂O, are blissfully unaware of the role they play in our ontological and normative pronouncements. As Stephen M. Barr, a physicist at the University of Delaware (and a critic of ID), puts it:

> Contrary to what is often claimed, even by some scientists, modern science has not eliminated final and formal causes. It uses them all the time, even if unaware that it is doing so. For example, a liver and a muscle are made up of the same material constituents – hydrogen, carbon, oxygen, and so on – acting on each other by the same basic forces. It is precisely their *forms*, their organic structures, that differ and enable them to play different roles in the body.
>
> The same is true in physics. The very same carbon atoms can form a diamond (transparent, hard, and electrically insulating) or a piece of graphite (opaque, soft, and electrically conducting). What explains their different properties is the difference in *form*, in intelligible structure. Indeed, as one goes deeper into fundamental physics, one finds that matter itself seems almost to dissolve into the pure forms of advanced mathematics.
>
> Some people think that the Darwinian mechanism eliminates final causes in biology. It doesn't; the finality comes in but in a different way. Why does natural selection favor this mutation but not that one? Because this one makes the eye see better in some way, which serves the *purpose* of helping the creature find food or mates or avoid predators, which in turn serves the *purpose* of helping the animal to live and reproduce. Why do species that take up residence in caves gradually lose the ability to see? Because seeing serves no *purpose* for them, and so mutations that harm the faculty of sight are not selected against. (Even a [Richard] Dawkins would not deny purpose in this sense; he would deny only that these purposes were in the mind of God.) Darwinian explanations can account for very little indeed without bringing intrinsic finality into the explanation.[55]

So, the problem with Darwinism in relation to belief in God is *not* that Darwinians claim that natural processes, including scientific laws, are sufficient to account for the variety of life forms that now populate the world. After all, for the Thomist, Darwinian mechanisms and algorithms, as well as scientific laws and other natural processes, no more count against the existence and necessity of God (or even final or formal causality) than does the exhaustive biological account of my conception by the natural processes of human reproduction count against the claim that God is Creator of the universe and thus

---

[55] Stephen Barr, "Correspondence about Avery Cardinal Dulles's 'God and Evolution'," *First Things* 179 (January 2008): 3–4. See also the work of Environmental Engineer at the University of St. Thomas (Houston), Sr. Damien Marie Savino, FSE, "Atheistic Science: The Only Option?," *Logos: A Journal of Catholic Thought and Culture* 12.4 (Fall 2009): 56–73.

my Creator as well.[56] Rather, the problem, in the words of Sr. Marie Damien Savino, FSE (an environmental engineer at the University of St. Thomas in Houston), "is when scientists presume that the material dimension is all there is, and then extend their scientific presumptions to a metaphysical stance, that is, atheism. Without an acknowledgement of formal and final causes, this is an easy leap to make."[57] This is because God is not in competition with nature. He is not a cause that is a rival to natural phenomena. For the Thomist, as well as for most theists, if the bacterial flagellum, for example, is not really irreducibly complex, it does not follow that it is not designed and that there is no room for a Designer (or God) to act.

Given their understanding of the inspiration of the Bible, it is surprising that conservative Evangelical Protestants tend to gravitate toward ID, a position that places God's action in competition with nature. For if I conceive of God's agency as I think of the agency of finite creatures in relation to the material and efficient causes in nature, that is, if I conceive of the agency of God and the activities of His creation *univocally*, then it would be correct to suggest that if the bacterial flagellum can be entirely accounted for by natural processes, then there is no room for a Designer (or God) to act. Just as it must be the case that either Robert Griffin III (RGIII) or someone else, but not both, threw a touchdown pass last Sunday, it must be the case that either God or natural processes, but not both, can account for the bacterial flagellum's irreducible complexity. That, however, is only true if God is an agent like RGIII or another quarterback. But that is an inadequate account of divine action, according to the dominant understanding of biblical inspiration embraced by Evangelical Protestants. For if it were adequate, then Evangelical Protestants could not say that God is the author of Scripture while each of its books has a human author as well. Under a univocal theory of divine action, the Evangelical Protestant would have to choose between a verbal dictation or a co-authorship theory,[58] neither of which would provide a satisfying account of Scripture as a book whose only author is God, although it is written by free human agents.

As I have already noted, for ID advocates Behe and Dembski no design inference about nature is warranted short of achieving that threshold of irreducible

---

[56] Writes St. Thomas:

> [T]he same effect is not attributed to a natural cause and to divine power in such a way that it is partly done by God, and partly by the natural agent; rather, it is wholly done by both, according to a different way, just as the same effect is wholly attributed to the instrument and also wholly to the principal agent. (*Summa contra Gentiles* III 70.8 [trans. Vernon J. Bourke], available at http://dhspriory.org/thomas/ContraGentiles3a.htm#70)

[57] Savino, "Atheistic Science," 60.

[58] Verbal dictation theory – which virtually no Evangelical Protestant holds to be true – maintains that the human authors of Scripture were either automaton conduits of God's agency or mere secretaries of God who dictated to them what he wanted in Scripture. A co-authorship view, which I have never known anyone to defend, would have to hold that God and the Bible's human authors composed Scripture like two human co-authors of an ordinary article or book.

or specified complexity. But that means that the person who believes he has good grounds for final and formal causes – while rejecting Behe's and Dembski's criteria – has no warrant to believe in the existence of final and formal causes he claims to "see" in living organisms. In other words, Behe and Dembski are implicitly accepting the assumption of the materialists – the opponents of final and formal causality – that God's role in nature may only be exhibited in properly arranged bits of matter so as to signify an agent cause of the arrangement.[59] But this means that design in nature is more like Aristotle's bed than the tree from which the bed was made.[60]

Suppose that in the next few years biologists discover another force (or process or law) in nature, similar to natural selection, that has the power to produce in living organisms organs and systems that *appear to be* irreducibly or specifically complex. According to the ID advocate, the rational person would have to abandon the idea that these organs and systems are intelligently designed, because his criterion would no longer detect "design" in those things he once had thought were irreducibly or specifically complex. Consequently, the rational person would have to conclude that these organs and systems are probably the product of necessity and/or chance (to employ Dembski's categories). TD, by

[59] In Dembski's narrative of the history of the design argument, he pretty much concedes this. He states that "with the rise of modern science in the seventeenth century, design arguments took a mechanical turn. The mechanical philosophy that was prevalent at the birth of modern science viewed the world as an assemblage of material particles interacting by mechanical forces. Within this view, design was construed as externally imposed on preexisting on inert matter." (Dembski, *The Design Revolution*, 66). He goes on to show how this view made possible the natural theology of William Paley (1743–1805), author of the famous Watchmaker Argument (Ibid., 67). However, writes Dembski, Darwin, with the publication of *Origin of Species*, "delivered the design argument its biggest blow" (Ibid., 68), though that did not spell the end of design arguments. Instead of "finding specific instances of design within the universe," design arguments focused "on determining whether and in what way the universe as a whole was designed." (Ibid., 69). But, fortunately, all was not lost. According to Dembski, "[d]esign theorists see advances in the biological and information sciences as *putting design back in the saddle* and enabling it to out-explain Darwinism, thus making design rather than natural selection currently the best explanation of biological complexity." (Ibid., 288).

[60] I am not suggesting that TD should, like ID, claim it is a "science." Rather, TD, like Dawkins' atheistic materialism, is a philosophical point of view. As Gilson states:

> [F]inalists [like TD advocates] ... are constrained by the evidence of facts which in the tradition and through the example of Aristotle they desire to make intelligible. As far as I know, they do not claim anymore that "scientific" evidence is on their side; the scientific description of ontogenesis and phylogenesis remains identically what it is without the need of going back to the first, transscientific principles of mechanism or finalism. Natural science neither destroys final causality nor establishes it. These two principles belong to the philosophy of the science of nature, to that which we have called its "wisdom." What scientists, as scientists, can do to help clarify the problem of natural teleology is not to busy themselves with it. They are the most qualified of all to keep philosophizing about it, if they so desire; but it is then necessary that they agree to philosophize.... Finalist philosophies [like TD] are responsible to themselves; they do not involve themselves with science at all, and science, as such, has no cause to concern itself with them. (Gilson, *From Aristotle to Darwin*, 20, 157).

contrast, is not threatened by such discoveries, because the TD advocate actually expects to find such forces, processes, and laws in nature, because she believes that God created *ex nihilo* a universe teeming with beings with ends or purposes that result in forces, processes, and laws, all of which cry out for a metaphysical explanation.[61] By rejecting the mechanistic assumptions of both the Darwinian materialists and the ID advocates,[62] TD does not have the burden of waiting with bated breath for the latest scientific argument or discovery in order to remain confident that the universe, or at least a small sliver of it, is designed. It has something better: rigorous philosophical arguments that challenge the assumptions of both the Darwinian materialists and the ID advocates who unconsciously (although sometimes purposely) offer their assumptions as undisputed premises under the guise of "science."[63] As Hart has noted:

On the one side, it has become perfectly respectable for a philosophically illiterate physicist to proclaim that "science knows that God does not exist".... On the other side, it has become respectable to argue that one can find evidence of an Intelligent Designer of the world by isolating instances of apparent causal discontinuity (or

---

[61] For a nice presentation of what I am suggesting here, see David S. Oderberg, *Real Essentialism* (New York: Routledge, 2007), 143–151.

[62] Although ID advocates sometimes claim their view is not mechanistic, their writings seem to say otherwise. In his book, *The Design Revolution*, Dembski writes: "According to the design critic [Fr.] Edward Oakes[, S.J.], intelligent design makes the task of theodicy impossible. Why is that? Because, he claims, intelligent design is wedded to a crude interventionist conception of divine action and to a mechanistic metaphysics of nature. Neither of these criticisms is accurate" (25). However, elsewhere in the same book, Dembski employs Aristotle's distinction between art and nature to argue that the design of life is like the design found in artifacts! (Ibid., 131–133). Dembski writes: "Aristotle claimed that art of shipbuilding is not in the wood that constitutes the ship. We've seen that the art of composing sonnets is not in the letters of the alphabet. Likewise, the art of making statues is not in the stone out of which statues are made. Each of these cases requires a designer. So too, the theory of intelligent design contends that the art of building life is not in the physical stuff that constitutes life but requires a designer" (Ibid., 133). (A thank you to Edward Feser for reminding me of these passages from *The Design Revolution*. See Feser's blog post on this topic, "Intelligent Design' theory and mechanism," *Edward Feser Blog* [10 April 2010], available at http://edwardfeser.blogspot.com/2010/04/intelligent-design-theory-and-mechanism.html).

[63] Because it falls outside the scope of this chapter, I cannot offer these philosophical arguments here. So, let me recommend the following works, some of which are more accessible to a general audience than others: William E. Carroll, "Creation, Evolution, and Thomas Aquinas," *Revue des Questions Scientifiques* 171 (2000): 319–347; William E. Carroll, "At the Mercy of Chance? Evolution and the Catholic Tradition," *Revue des Questions Scientifiques* 177 (2006): 179–204. Thomas Crean, O. P., *God is No Delusion: A Refutation of Richard Dawkins* (San Francisco: Ignatius Press, 2007); Edward Feser, *Aquinas: A Beginning's Guide* (Oxford, UK: Oneworld Publications, 2009); Edward Feser, *Scholastic Metaphysics: A Contemporary Introduction* (Neunkirchen-Seelscheid, Germany: Editiones Scholasticae, 2014); Feser, *The Last Superstition*; Marie I. George, "On Attempts to Salvage Paley's Argument from Design," in *Science, Philosophy, and Theology*, ed. John O'Callaghan (South Bend, IN: St. Augustine's Press, 2004). Gilson, *From Aristotle to Darwin and Back Again*; Machuga, *In Defense of the Soul*; y Hart, *The Experience of God*; Tkacz, "Thomas Aquinas vs. the Intelligent Designers"; and Oderberg, *Real Essentialism*.

ineptitude) in the fabric of nature, which require the postulate of an external guiding hand to explain away the gap in natural causality. In either case, "God" has become the name of some special physical force or causal principle located out there somewhere among all the forces and principles found in the universe; not the Logos filling and forming all things, not the infinity of being and consciousness in which all things necessarily subsist, but a thing among other things, an item among all the other items encompassed within nature.[64]

It would be one thing if the ID advocates were only offering their point of view as a mere hypothesis subjected to the usual give and take in scientific and philosophical discourse. (In fact, my earlier work on ID assumed as much.)[65] But that in fact is not the case. It has over the years morphed into a movement that treats the soundness of its arguments as virtually essential to sustaining the rationality of theism itself. Meyer, for example, suggests that before the 20th century's advances in biochemistry and microbiology, immaterialism and teleology were down for the count:

For two millennia, the design argument provided an intellectual foundation for much of Western thought. From classical antiquity through the rise of modern science, leading philosophers, theologians, and scientists – from Plato to Aquinas to Newton – maintained that nature manifests the design of a preexistent mind or intelligence. Moreover, for many Western thinkers, the idea that the physical universe reflected the purpose or design of a preexistent mind – a Creator – served to guarantee humanity's own sense of purpose and meaning. Yet today in nearly every academic discipline from law to literary theory, from behavioral science to biology, a thoroughly materialistic understanding of humanity and its place in the universe has come to dominate. Free will, meaning, purpose, and God have become pejorative terms in the academy. Matter has subsumed mind; cosmos replaced Creator.

The reasons for this intellectual shift are no doubt complex. Yet clearly the demise of the design argument itself has played an important role in the loss of this traditional Western belief. Beginning in the Enlightenment, philosophers such as David Hume raised seemingly powerful objections against the design argument. Hume claimed that classical design arguments depended on a weak and flawed analogy between biological organisms and human artifacts. Yet for most, it was not the arguments of the philosophers that disposed of design, but the theories of scientists, particularly that of Charles Darwin. If the origin of biological organisms could be explained naturalistically, as Darwin claimed, then explanations invoking an intelligent designer were unnecessary and even vacuous. Indeed, as Richard Dawkins has put it, it was "Darwin [who] made it possible to be an intellectually fulfilled atheist."[66]

But now ID stands ready, Meyer contends, to triumphantly procure its "advances" to help restore "some of the intellectual underpinning of traditional Western metaphysics and theistic belief."[67] Who knew?

---

[64] Hart, *The Experience of God*, 302–303.
[65] See footnote 3.
[66] Meyer, "DNA and Other Designs," 30. Dembski says something similar. See footnote 59.
[67] Ibid., 38.

This embellished sense of ID's importance in the march of history is not a virtue. It is an unattractive enthusiasm that clouds rather than showcases ID's important, although modest, publishing successes and the legitimate questions these writings bring to bear on many issues that overlap science, theology, and philosophy.[68] Combine this lack of academic modesty with the ubiquitous propagation of ID within Evangelical Protestantism and its churches, seminaries, and parachurch groups (and even among some Catholics) as a new and improved way to topple the materialist critics of theism,[69] and you have a recipe for widespread disappointment (and perhaps disillusionment with theism) if the ID ship takes on too much water in the sea of philosophical and scientific criticism. For this reason, other nonmaterialist theist academics, such

---

[68] Koperski makes a similar observation:

> What critics [of ID] rightly clamor for, however, is peer-reviewed research in which design has more than a mere heuristic role. To be fair, there are more published papers out there than most people realize. And, as ID proponents argue, there is a strong bias against design-motivated articles getting into academic journals.... Editors will not risk giving aid and comfort to the enemy. In my view, the ID community is itself partly to blame for this. Some think of ID primarily as a weapon in the culture wars. Anti-design bias in the academy is part of the backlash. Had ID consistently emphasized research over public exposure, the atmosphere of the debate would be different today. Instead, Phillip Johnson and others believed that the underlying ideas were so compelling that, once they were disseminated, ID thought would sweep across the landscape. A 2001 front-page story in *The New York Times* ... was cause for much celebration not because it was pro-ID but because it helped place the debate in the public eye. This is proving to be a failed strategy. (Koperski, "Two Bad Ways to Attack Intelligent Design and Two Good Ones," 442; notes omitted)

As for the peer-reviewed works mentioned by Koperski, he references a Discovery Institute list found online here: http://www.discovery.org/a/2640. So, Koperski is clearly right that these peer-reviewed works do exist.

[69] Take, for example, comments from a press release for an ID conference (30–31 October 2009) sponsored by Shepherd Project Ministries in Colorado:

> The conference will explore the cultural impact of Darwinism and the ground-breaking new evidence for Intelligent Design that is changing the shape of this crucial conversation today.

> With presentations by some of the world's foremost Intelligent Design experts, this conference will equip Christians to understand the key issues and be able to speak effectively into a culture that is foundering in the sea of meaninglessness that is Darwin's most lasting legacy. (http://www.shepherdproject.com/idconf/press/pressreleasechristian.pdf)

See also the descriptions of similar conferences held at Southwestern Baptist Theological Seminary, 23–24 October 2009 (http://www.discovery.org/e/901) and Westminster Theological Seminary in Philadelphia, 12–13 March 2010 (http://www.discovery.org/e/901). I am, of course, not suggesting that there is anything wrong with having conferences in which theology and science are integrated and their interaction critically assessed. And, to be sure, any such conference should give ID a fair hearing and explain how it interacts with theology and the life of the mind. However, what I am suggesting is that it is intellectually irresponsible to offer Christians, especially prospective clergy, ID as *the* only legitimate nonreligious alternative to Darwinian materialism that a Christian may authentically embrace, as these conferences seem to do.

as Thomists and some CFT supporters, who would ordinarily find ID's project intriguing and worth interacting with (as I do), are hesitant to cooperate with a movement that implies to churchgoers and popular audiences that the very foundations of theism and Western civilization rise or fall on the soundness of Behe's and Dembski's inferences.[70]

## 6.3. *KITZMILLER V. DOVER* AND THE UBIQUITY OF DESIGN

In November 2004 the board of the Dover Area School District of Pennsylvania formulated and promulgated a policy that required Dover High School ninth grade biology teachers to read in class a series of brief paragraphs:

The Pennsylvania Academic Standards require students to learn about Darwin's Theory of Evolution and eventually to take a standardized test of which evolution is a part.

Because Darwin's Theory is a theory, it continues to be tested as new evidence is discovered. The Theory is not a fact. Gaps in the Theory exist for which there is no evidence. A theory is defined as a well-tested explanation that unifies a broad range of observations.

Intelligent Design is an explanation of the origin of life that differs from Darwin's view. The reference book, *Of Pandas and People*, is available for students who might be interested in gaining an understanding of what Intelligent Design actually involves.

With respect to any theory, students are encouraged to keep an open mind. The school leaves the discussion of the Origins of Life to individual students and their families. As a Standards-driven district, class instruction focuses upon preparing students to achieve proficiency on Standards-based assessments.[71]

There are at least three reasons why I believe that this disclaimer is poorly worded and pedagogically weak. (The first two are nearly identical to the problems with the Cobb County, Georgia, disclaimer I raised in Chapter 3.) (1) It implies that Darwinism is a theory about "the origin of life." But that is at best misleading if it is referring to biological evolution, which concerns how living things that already exist change over time. (2) Its claim that

---

[70] After all, it is not as if ID is some kind of scientific and/or philosophical slam dunk about which no reasonable thinkers have not raised legitimate questions. In addition to the Thomist and CFT criticisms and critics already mentioned in the text and in the notes, there are scores of many other criticisms and critics. The latter include thinkers who exhibit virtually no visceral hostility to the ID Movement as well as those who are unsympathetic to the sort of Darwinian materialism defended by Dawkins and the other New Atheists. See, e.g., Stanley L. Jaki, *Intelligent Design?* (New Hope, KY: Real View Books, 2005); Leon R. Kass, "Teleology, Darwinism, and the Place of Man: Beyond Chance and Necessity," chapter 10 in *Toward a More Natural Science: Biology and Human Affairs* by Leon R. Kass (New York: The Free Press, 1985), 249–275; Leon R. Kass, "The Permanent Limitations of Biology." Chapter 10 in *Life, Liberty and the Defense of Dignity: The Challenge for Bioethics* by Leon R. Kass (San Francisco: Encounter Books, 2002), 277–298; Simon Conway Morris, *Life's Solution: Inevitable Humans in a Lonely University* (Cambridge, UK: Cambridge University Press, 2003).

[71] *Kitzmiller*, 400 F. Supp. 2d, at 709.

evolution is "not a fact" is inconsistent with the school board's call for it students to "keep an open mind." The board cannot say that evolution is not a fact and at the same time suggest to students that they should have an open mind on the subject, because having an open mind requires that they critically consider the possibility that evolution is a fact. (3) The board seems to believe that if scientists offer a "theory," they are offering something that they are unsure about, as if what they are proposing is a "hunch." Thus, the board seems to be saying that because scientists still call evolution "a theory," they don't consider it a fact. But the board is wrong. For the term "theory" is often applied in science and mathematics to what is solidly established, for example, "the theory of elasticity," "the BCS theory of superconductivity," "the theory of functions of a real variable," "the theory of relativity," and so on.[72]

However, the board's policy never took effect.[73] Several parents of Dover school children, assisted by attorneys from the American Civil Liberties Union (ACLU) of Pennsylvania, brought suit against the school district.[74] They argued that the policy violated the establishment clause of the United States Constitution's First Amendment.[75] Judge John E. Jones III agreed, and ruled in their favor.[76]

Judge Jones' opinion involves several lines of argument.[77] However, for the purposes of this chapter I will only focus on two. The first is his application of the endorsement test we covered in Chapter 3. As I noted there, it is a standard employed by the courts to determine whether a policy or law violates the First Amendment's Establishment Clause. The second line of argument concerns claims and assumptions of philosophical anthropology that Judge Jones asserts and implies in his assessment of the ID-policy, the motives and character of the citizens and school board members that supported it, and the end or purpose of science education.

---

[72] I owe this last observation to Stephen Barr, who provided me feedback after he read an earlier draft of this chapter.

[73] *Kitzmiller*, 400 F. Supp. 2d, at 709. (Plaintiffs sought injunctive and declaratory relief).

[74] Ibid., 708–710.

[75] Ibid., 709.

[76] Ibid.

[77] Judge Jones's opinion resulted in a number of works assessing it. See, for example, David K. DeWolf, John G. West, and Casey Luskin, "Intelligent Design Will Survive *Kitzmiller v. Dover*," *Montana Law Review* 68 (2007). For a rebuttal to this article and a defense of *Kitzmiller*, see Peter Irons, "Disaster in Dover: The Trials (and Tribulations) of Intelligent Design," *Montana Law Review* 68 (2007). For a reply to Irons, see David K. DeWolf, John G. West, and Casey Luskin, "Rebuttal to Irons," *Montana Law Review* 68 (2007). See also, Monton, "Is Intelligent Design Science?"; Koperski, "Two Bad Ways to Attack Intelligent Design and Two Good Ones," 434–440; and Jay D. Wexler, "Kitzmiller and the 'Is It Science?' Question," *First Amendment Law Review* 5 (2006).

## 6.3.A. The Endorsement Test, or the "God's Eye Point of View"

In his overturning of the Dover ID-policy, Judge Jones employs what has come to be known as the endorsement test. First suggested by Justice Sandra Day O'Connor in *Lynch v. Donnelly* (1984), the test stipulates that if a government action creates a *perception* that it is either endorsing or disfavoring a religion, the action is unconstitutional.[78] The concern of this test is whether the disputed activity suggests "a message to nonadherents that they are outsiders, not full members of the political community, and an accompanying message to adherents that they are insiders, favored members of the political community."[79] However, who counts as a "nonadherent" seems to have changed. In *Lynch* Justice O'Connor suggests that nonadherents are "ordinary citizens," actual flesh and blood human beings, who are the recipients of the government's message. In a subsequent school-prayer case, *Wallace v. Jaffree* (1985), which we discussed in Chapter 3, she proposes a type of "reasonable person standard" version of the endorsement test, suggesting that the nonadherent is an objective observer fully informed of all the facts: "[t]he relevant issue is whether an objective observer, acquainted with the text, legislative history, and implementation of the statute, would perceive it as a state endorsement of prayer in public schools."[80] Thus, a law may pass or fail the endorsement test depending on who (or what) counts as a nonadherent.

After offering a survey of the history of the endorsement test and how it developed over time, Judge Jones moves on to "ascertain whether the ID Policy 'in fact conveys a message of endorsement or disapproval' of religion, with the reasonable, objective observer being the hypothetical construct to consider this issue."[81] Accepting Justice O'Conner's more abstract definition of a reasonable, objective observer (or ROO) from her *Wallace* opinion,[82] Judge Jones defines the ROO for the purposes of the Dover policy as one "who knows the policy's language, origins, and legislative history, as well as the history of the community and the broader social and historical context in which the policy arose."[83] Judge Jones then offers an extensive presentation of what the ROO would

---

[78] Lynch v. Donnelly 465 U.S. 668, 687–694 (1984) (O'Connor, J., concurring suggesting an "endorsement test").

[79] *Lynch*, 465 U.S., 688 (O'Connor, J., concurring). O'Connor's endorsement test and versions of it defended by legal scholars have been criticized as well. See, for example, Steven D. Smith, "Symbols, Perceptions, and Doctrinal Illusions: Establishment Neutrality and the "No Endorsement" Test," *Michigan Law Review* 86 (November 1987); and Derek H. Davis, "Equal Treatment: A Christian Separationist Perspective," in *Equal Treatment in a Pluralistic Society*, ed. Stephen V. Monsma and J. Christopher Soper (Grand Rapids, MI: Eerdmans, 1998); 136–157.

[80] Wallace v. Jaffree 472 U.S. 38, 67, 76 (1985) (O' Connor, J., concurring).

[81] *Kitzmiller*, 400 F. Supp. 2d, 715, quoting *Lynch*, 465 U.S. at 690 (O'Connor, J., concurring).

[82] *Wallace*, 472 U.S., 76.

[83] *Kitzmiller*, 400 F. Supp. 2d, 715 (internal citations omitted).

have to know in order to conclude that the Dover policy violates the endorsement test.[84] Although such an exercise in juridical imagination may be worth
exploring, there is a deeper, more philosophical, question to be investigated
here: what precisely is a rational, objective observer, and why is it apparently
so useful to jurists?

The ROO is a sort of person who, if he really existed, would exhibit ideal
epistemological excellence. He would not be limited by biases, prejudices, or
ignorance. His reasoning powers would not only be functioning properly, but
the environment in which he would issue his judgment would contribute to,
rather than interfere with, this judgment. And it would be a judgment that
could never be wrong, for not only would he not have any internal or external
impediments or limitations, he would have inerrant knowledge of all the relevant facts – such as legislative history, the policy's cultural context – required
to make a just ruling. The ROO, of course, is a hypothetical construct and not
a real person. But its explanatory power depends on the judge taking the finite,
ordinary, and limited abilities, powers, and knowledge that human beings possess, and suggesting to his readers a hypothetical person who possesses perfect
versions of these attributes. These perfections, apparently, are not the deliverances of direct empirical observation, because there is no person on earth
who possesses or has possessed these attributes at their highest levels.[85] Oddly
enough, this exercise of predicating perfected attributes of the ROO is similar
to how St. Thomas suggests Christians ought to predicate the attributes of
God (although analogically).[86] And even more strangely, the ROO would seemingly possess what the philosopher Hilary Putnam calls a "God's Eye point of

[84] Ibid., 716–746.
[85] Of course, Christians believe that Jesus of Nazareth did in fact exemplify the perfection of
human attributes. So, if you, as I do, accept this view about Jesus, then simply include that
exception in your reading.
[86] St. Thomas writes:

> Since it is possible to find in God every perfection of creatures, but in another and more emi-
> nent way, whatever names unqualifiedly designate a perfection without defect are predicated
> of God and of other things: for example, goodness, wisdom, being, and the like. But when any
> name expresses such perfections along with a mode that is proper to a creature, it can be said
> of God only according to likeness and metaphor. According to metaphor, what belongs to one
> thing is transferred to another, as when we say that a man is a stone because of the hardness
> of his intellect. Such names are used to designate the species of a created thing, for example,
> man and stone, for to each species belongs its own mode of perfection and being. The same
> is true of whatever names designate the properties of things, which are caused by the proper
> principles of their species. Hence, they can be said of God only metaphorically. But the names
> that express such perfections along with the mode of supereminence with which they belong
> to God are said of God alone. Such names are the highest good, the first being, and the like.

(St. Thomas Aquinas, *Summa Contra Gentiles*, I 30.2 [trans. Anton C. Pegis], available at http://
dhspriory.org/thomas/ContraGentiles1.htm#30)

view."[87] Thus, in order to expunge the divine, or at least allusions to it, from the public schools, Judge Jones requires the divine's assistance, or at least the assistance of a hypothetical deity.

## 6.3.B. The Purpose or End of Education

A portion of Judge Jones' opinion concerns the purpose or end of education and how the Dover school board's policy is inconsistent with that end or purpose. But such a criticism – although certainly legitimate – seems to entail an understanding of the human person and mind that presupposes a robust view of the human person's intrinsic purpose that requires final and formal causality (i.e., TD). In order to better grasp how Judge Jones commits this philosophical faux pas, it is instructive to see how someone far more adept at critiquing ID, Dawkins, commits the same mistake.[88]

### *6.3.B.1. Richard Dawkins: Peeping Thomist?*
In his book *The God Delusion*, Dawkins laments the career path of Harvard-trained paleontologist Kurt Wise.[89] At the time Dawkins published his book, Wise was an associate professor of science at Bryan College, a small Protestant Evangelical school in Dayton, Tennessee.[90] After a brief stint at the Southern Baptist Theological Seminary in Louisville, Kentucky (2006–2009), Professor Wise took a position at Truett-McConnell College in Cleveland, Georgia, where he serves as professor of natural sciences and director of the college's Creation Research Center.[91]

---

[87] In his discussion on two philosophical perspectives on the question of what we can know about the world and of what that world actually consists, Philosopher Hilary Putnam writes:

> One of these perspectives is the perspective of metaphysical realism. On this perspective, the world consists of some fixed totality of mind-independent objects. There is exactly one true and complete description of "the way the world is." Truth involves some sort of correspondence relation between words or thought-signs and external things and sets of things. I shall call this perspective the *externalist* perspective, because its favorite point of view is a God's Eye point of view. (Hilary Putnam, *Reason, Truth, and History* [New York: Cambridge University Press, 1981], 49.)

[88] Portions of the following section (6.3.B.1) are adapted from portions of Francis J. Beckwith, "The Courts, Natural Rights, and Religious Claims as Knowledge." *Santa Clara Law Review* 49.2 (2009): 429–445. The term "Peeping Thomist" comes from the subtitle of a book by Ralph McInerny, *A First Glance at St. Thomas Aquinas: A Handbook for Peeping Thomists* (Notre Dame, IN: University of Notre Dame Press, 1990).

[89] Dawkins, *The God Delusion*, 284–286.

[90] Dawkins notes that, coincidentally, the school is named after William Jennings Bryan, three-time Democratic presidential candidate and prosecutor in the 1925 Scopes "Monkey Trial." (Ibid., 284).

[91] *See* "Creation Research Center Established at TMC," *available at* http://www.truett.edu/tmcnews/428-creation-research-center-established-at-tmc.html.

Dawkins writes that Wise was at one time a promising young scholar who had earned an undergraduate degree in geology from the University of Chicago as well as advanced degrees in geology and paleontology from Harvard University, where he studied under the highly acclaimed paleontologist Stephen Jay Gould.[92] Wise, surprisingly, is a Young Earth creationist, which means that he embraces a literal interpretation of the first chapters of Genesis, and maintains that the Earth is less than ten thousand years old. It is not a position I hold, and for that reason I am sympathetic to Dawkins's bewilderment of why Wise has embraced what appears to many Christians as a false choice between one controversial interpretation of Scripture (Young Earth creationism) and abandoning Christianity altogether.

In any event, at one point in his career Wise began to understand that his reading of Scripture was inconsistent with the dominant scientific understanding of the age of the Earth and the cosmos. Instead of abandoning what many of us believe is a false choice, he continued to embrace it and had a crisis of faith. Wise writes:

Either the Scripture was true and evolution was wrong or evolution was true and I must toss out the Bible.... It was there that night that I accepted the Word of God and rejected all that would ever counter it, including evolution. With that, in great sorrow, I tossed into the fire all my dreams and hopes in science.[93]

So, Wise abandoned the possibility of securing a professorship at a prestigious research university or institute.

Dawkins is disturbed by Wise's theological judgment and its consequence on his obvious promise as a scholar, researcher, and teacher. Writes Dawkins:

I find that terribly sad.... [T]he Kurt Wise story is just plain pathetic – pathetic and contemptible. The wound, to his career and his life's happiness, was self-inflicted, so unnecessary, so easy to escape.... I am hostile to religion because of what it did to Kurt Wise. And if it did that to a Harvard educated geologist, just think what it can do to others less gifted and less well armed.[94]

It goes without saying that some religious believers, including many devout Christians, may be just as troubled as Dawkins. Thus, one does not have to be an atheist to suggest that Professor Wise's faith may have been better served by embracing an alternative understanding of theology and science that did not require that he either reject the deliverances of modern science or the authority of Scripture.

However, given Dawkins's atheism, there is something odd about his lament, for it seems to require that Dawkins accept something about the

---

[92] Dawkins, *The God Delusion*, 284.

[93] Ibid., 285. According to Dawkins, this quotation from Wise is from an essay he contributed to the anthology, *In Six Days: Why 50 Believe in Creation*, ed. J. E. Ashton (Sydney: New Holland, 1999).

[94] Dawkins, *The God Delusion*, 285–286.

nature of human beings that his atheism seems to reject. Dawkins harshly criticizes Wise for embracing a religious belief that results in Wise not treating himself and his talents, intelligence, and abilities in a way appropriate for their full flourishing. That is, given the opportunity to hone and nurture certain gifts – for example, intellectual skill – no one, including Wise, should waste them as a result of accepting a false belief. The person who violates, or helps violate, this norm, according to Dawkins, should be condemned and we should all bemoan this tragic moral neglect on the part of our fellow(s). But the issuing of that judgment on Wise by Dawkins makes sense only in light of Wise's particular talents and the *sort of being* Wise is by nature, a being that Dawkins seems to believe possesses certain intrinsic capacities and purposes that if prematurely disrupted results in an injustice. So, the human being who wastes his talents is one who does not respect his natural gifts or the basic capacities whose maturation and proper employment make possible the flourishing of many goods. That is, the notion of "proper function,"[95] coupled with the observation that certain perfections grounded in basic capacities have been impermissibly obstructed from maturing, is assumed in the very judgment Dawkins makes about Wise and the way by which Wise should treat himself. That is, Dawkins's judgment of Wise depends on Dawkins knowing a human being's final and formal causes.

But Dawkins, in fact, does not actually believe that living beings, including human beings, have final and formal causes. Dawkins denies that human beings have intrinsic purposes or are designed so that one may conclude that violating one's proper function amounts to a violation of one's duty to oneself. Dawkins has maintained for decades that the natural world only *appears to be* designed: "Darwin and his successors have shown how living creatures, with their spectacular statistical improbability and appearance of design, have evolved by slow, gradual degrees from simple beginnings. We can now safely say that the illusion of design in living creatures is just that – an illusion."[96] He writes elsewhere: "[t]he universe we observe has precisely the properties we should expect if there is, at bottom, no design, no purpose, no evil, and no good, nothing but blind pitiless indifference."[97] Thus, if we are to take Dawkins seriously, his view of design means that his lament for Wise is misguided! For Dawkins is lamenting what only *appears* to be Wise's dereliction of his duty to nurture and employ his gifts in ways that result in his happiness and an acquisition of knowledge that contributes to his own good as well as the common good. Because there are no formal or final causes, and thus no intrinsic purposes, and thus no natural duties that we are obligated to obey, the intuitions that inform Dawkins' judgment of Wise are illusory because they depend on a type of design he explicitly rejects. But that is precisely one of the grounds

---

[95] See Alvin Plantinga, *Warrant and Proper Function* (New York: Oxford University Press, 1993).
[96] Dawkins, *The God Delusion*, 158.
[97] Richard Dawkins, *River Out of Eden: A Darwinian View of Life* (London: Phoenix, 1995), 133.

by which Dawkins suggests that theists are irrational and ought to abandon their belief in God.[98] So, if the theist is irrational for believing in God based on what turns out to be pseudo-design, Dawkins is irrational in his judgment of Wise and other creationists he targets for reprimand and correction. For Dawkins's judgment rests on a premise that he has uncompromisingly maintained throughout his career only *appears to be* true.

In an earlier work, *The Blind Watchmaker*, Dawkins claimed that Darwin had "made it possible to be an intellectually fulfilled atheist."[99] But given his embracing of pseudo-design as the ontological truth that accounts for what appears to be the human being's final and formal causes, that is, that there are no intrinsic ends or purposes in nature including the intellectual powers of human beings, why does Dawkins suppose that it is good for one to be "intellectually fulfilled"? If, of course, the mind has a proper function intrinsic to its nature, then one would be within one's intellectual rights in issuing a condemnation to anyone who violated that proper function. But this would also mean that a person has a responsibility to care for her mental life, and it would be a vice inconsistent with one's good to intentionally neglect such care. Thus, for Dawkins to assess the morality of his or another's acts, including acts that lead or do not lead to intellectual fulfillment, he must not only know how the parts of a human being function and for what end (for example, that the brain helps facilitate the acquisition of knowledge for the good of the whole person), he must also account for cases in which proper function is employed for the wrong end. So without final and formal causality, Dawkins has no rational basis by which to declare himself intellectually fulfilled or Dr. Wise intellectually impoverished. Thus, we may ask rhetorically a question once asked straightforwardly by Gilson: "[f]inal causes have disappeared from science but have they disappeared from the mind of scientists?"[100]

Notice that this analysis says nothing about contemporary science or anything critical about Darwinian evolution as a biological theory. What I have done here is simply to offer a philosophical analysis of Dawkins's judgment, showing that it requires a philosophical anthropology consistent with classical theism but inconsistent with the philosophical materialism that Dawkins mistakenly believes Darwinian evolution entails.

### 6.3.B.2. Education: What's the Point?

No one expects a federal district court judge to be conversant with the intricacies of issues that overlap a variety of subdisciplines in philosophy – including metaphysics and ethics. But no one expected, prior to its publication, that *Kitzmiller*'s Judge Jones would suggest that his opinion should be the final

---

[98]  See Dawkins, *The God Delusion*, chapter 3.

[99]  Dawkins, *The Blind Watchmaker*, 6.

[100]  Gilson, *From Aristotle to Darwin*, 150.

word on the contentious philosophical and scientific issues that came before his court.[101] Because it is rare that one finds such Olympian aspirations in the opinion of a federal district court judge (I will pass on saying anything about appellate judges), I want to focus on those issues that Judge Jones, like Dawkins, never seemed to entertain. Consider just these scathing comments about the Dover School Board:

> Although Defendants attempt to persuade this Court that each Board member who voted for the biology curriculum change did so for the secular purposed [*sic*] of improving science education and to exercise critical thinking skills, their contentions are simply irreconcilable with the record evidence. Their asserted purposes are a sham, and they are accordingly unavailing, for the reasons that follow.

> We initially note that the Supreme Court has instructed that while courts are "normally deferential to a State's articulation of a secular purpose, it is required that the statement of such purpose be sincere and not a sham." ... Although as noted Defendants have consistently asserted that the ID Policy was enacted for the secular purposes of improving science education and encouraging students to exercise critical thinking skills, the Board took none of the steps that school officials would take if these stated goals had truly been their objective. The Board consulted no scientific materials. The Board contacted no scientists or scientific organizations. The Board failed to consider the views of the District's science teachers. The Board relied solely on legal advice from two organizations with demonstrably religious, cultural, and legal missions, the Discovery Institute and the TMLC [Thomas More Legal Center]. Moreover, Defendants' asserted secular purpose of improving science education is belied by the fact that most if not all of the Board members who voted in favor of the biology curriculum change conceded that they still do not know, nor have they ever known, precisely what ID is. To assert a secular purpose against this backdrop is ludicrous.

> Finally, although Defendants have unceasingly attempted in vain to distance themselves from their own actions and statements, which culminated in repetitious, untruthful testimony, such a strategy constitutes additional strong evidence of improper purpose under the first prong of the *Lemon* test.[102]

---

[101] Judge Jones writes:

> [W]e find it incumbent upon the Court to further address an additional issue raised by Plaintiffs, which is whether ID is science. To be sure, our answer to this question can likely be predicted based upon the foregoing analysis. While answering this question compels us to revisit evidence that is entirely complex, if not obtuse, after a six week trial that spanned twenty-one days and included countless hours of detailed expert witness presentations, the Court is confident that no other tribunal in the United States is in a better position than are we to traipse into this controversial area. Finally, we will offer our conclusion on whether ID is science not just because it is essential to our holding that an Establishment Clause violation has occurred in this case, but also in the hope that it may prevent the obvious waste of judicial and other resources which would be occasioned by a subsequent trial involving the precise question which is before us. (*Kitzmiller*, 400 F. Supp. 2d, 734–735)

[102] *Kitzmiller*, 400 F. Supp. 2d, 762–763 (citations omitted).

There are at least two claims in these paragraphs that are worth assessing for the purposes of this chapter. First, Judge Jones correctly assumes that it would have been good if the school board had in fact passed a policy with "the secular purposes of improving science education and encouraging students to exercise critical thinking skills."[103] Setting aside the fact that the judge brings this to our attention because it involves the constitutional requirement that the policy have a "secular purpose,"[104] one may ask why improving science education and encouraging critical thinking are in fact good things for any society, including a secular one, to support as a matter of educational policy. Although virtually everyone believes these are noble ideals, the more interesting question is what sort of philosophical anthropology best grounds them. If, for example, one were to embrace Dawkins' point of view, that human beings have no final or formal causes, it would be difficult to know precisely what makes scientific knowledge and critical thinking skills goods that human beings ought to acquire.[105] By contrast, for the Thomist, scientific knowledge and critical thinking skills are goods because they contribute to a human being's flourishing. It is because human beings have a certain nature (i.e., rational animal) that entails certain normative ends (e.g., the purpose to acquire knowledge both for its own sake and for the sake of other goods) that a human being ought to, in the course of his intellectual formation, obtain certain types of knowledge including scientific knowledge and critical thinking skills. That is, without the resources of final and formal causality, Judge Jones, like Dawkins, cannot ground his correct observations about the scope and meaning of a human being's obligations to his own proper ends and why those proper ends should ground the policies of the secular state.

Second, Judge Jones is surely correct that it was wrong that most if not all of the school board members had voted on the ID policy without knowing ID's

---

[103] Ibid.

[104] Judge Jones refers to the famous "Lemon Test," a standard that the U.S. Supreme Court has employed in a variety of cases to assess the constitutionally of statutes that are claimed to be violations of the Establishment Clause:

> Every analysis in this area [church/state cases] must begin with consideration of the cumulative criteria developed by the Court over many years. Three such tests may be gleaned from our cases. First, the statute must have a secular legislative purpose; second, its principle or primary effect must be one that neither advances nor inhibits religion, Board of Education v. Allen 392 U.S. 236, 243 (1968); finally, the statute must not foster "an excessive government entanglement with religion." Walz [v. Tax Comm'n of New York City] 397 U.S. 664, 668 (1970). (Lemon v. Kurtzman 403 U.S. 602, 612–613 [1971])

[105] One may be tempted to offer the answer, "because we desire them" or "because they have survival value." But these are surely not adequate "reasons," because, concerning the former, there are some people who desire ignorance and we know that they ought not to desire it, and, concerning the latter, it requires that we believe that scientific knowledge and critical thinking are not goods to be pursued for their own sake, that they are purely instrumental goods. But we know that is not true.

true nature. Voting out of ignorance is indeed appalling. But why is ignorance not an appropriate ground for human action, unless knowledge is a necessary condition for human action? If so, then there is a normative end to a human being's active power for self-movement to engage in free acts initiated and/ or accompanied by thought and reflection. That is, a human being has the power to act consistently or inconsistently with her own good, a good that we can only know if we know the sort of being she is. So, again, final and formal causes come into play.

Moreover, for the materialist, such as Dawkins, there are only efficient and material causes in nature. But the justification of an act – that is, the *reason* why one may act – is not an efficient or material cause. If it were, then once a person became aware of the reason to act, she would automatically act, just as a billiard ball would automatically move once struck by another billiard ball moving at the correct velocity. As the comedian Steven Wright once joked: "I once got pulled over and the cop said, 'Why were you going so fast?' I said, 'Why? Because I had my foot to the floor. Sends more gas through the carburetor. Makes the engine go faster. The whole car just takes off like that.' "[106] This is funny because Wright mentions an efficient cause when we all know that the cop requested to know the purpose, the final cause, of his speeding.[107]

Consequently, reasons are not efficient or material causes, like the moving billiard ball or the heavy foot. Reasons are immaterial ideas that are believed and/or offered by agents in order to support a conclusion (and in this case, a conclusion that serves as a justification to act). They have a logical, not a material or spatial, relation to each other. Reasons are not *in* the billiard ball or *in* the foot, they are in the mind of the agent that acts, and they are employed to explain or justify one's act, as in one's moving of the billiard ball (e.g., "Fred is trying to defeat Minnesota Fats in a game of pool") or in one's pressing of the foot to the floor (e.g., "Steve is rushing his bleeding child to the hospital"). And these reasons are clearly not identical to anything material, such as the electrical impulses in the brain. For if they were, their relation to one another would be spatial, such as the spatial relationship between the wine glass on my desk that is to the left of my computer monitor. But the relationship between thoughts, such as reasons, is not at all spatial. For when I come to believe that my reasons for acting justify my acting, the relationship between the reasons and the conclusion is logical. As

---

[106] http://www.quotegeek.com/index.php?action=viewcategory&categoryid=9.

[107] The final cause in this scenario is like the one imposed on pieces of wood by the bed maker in Aristotle's example. It is not like the final cause of a living organism, something that arises from its formal cause, what is intrinsic to its being. For the driver, Wright, is imposing his end (whatever that may be) on the automobile so that he may achieve his end. The point of the illustration is not to defend final causes in nature, but to bring to the reader's attention that philosophical materialism has a difficult time accounting for something as ordinary and commonplace as offering reasons for one's actions.

J. P. Moreland puts it, "reasons are irreducibly teleological goals/ends for the sake of which agents act."[108]

Again, as in my analysis in Section 6.3.B.1, my analysis here says nothing about contemporary science or anything critical about Darwinian evolution as a biological theory. It is, like in the previous section, a philosophical assessment.

## 6.4. CONCLUSION

We have learned several things about Darwinism, Creationism, design, and the law. First, ID is not the same as Creationism, and not all forms of design are ID or products of the ID Movement. Second, the question of ID's status as "science" is a red herring. Third, some forms of design are consistent with Darwinian evolution, including fine-tuning (CFT) and TD (assuming that one does not abandon final and formal causes in one's philosophy of nature, even if one believes they should play no role in scientific theories). Fourth, and ironically, CFT tends to undermine the ID advocates' claim that necessity and chance are nondesign causal alternatives to a design inference, because the "laws and constants at issue [in CFT arguments] are preordained, built into the very fabric of reality."[109] Fifth, in some very important ways ID and Darwinian materialism share certain assumptions that the TD advocate maintains may be deleterious to the rationality of theism. Because both ID advocates and Darwinian materialists treat natural processes and divine action as rival accounts of natural phenomena, they unwittingly accept an understanding of design that assumes a view of God and nature that does not "take rites seriously." Sixth, if you are a Darwinian materialist critic of ID (like Dawkins), your project requires formal and final causality to establish your own fulfillment as well as to admonish those who have not achieved their potential. And, seventh, in order for a judge to declare a pro-ID school board policy unconstitutional, he must employ a "God's eye point of view," a hypothetical equivalent of the omniscient designer of the universe, as well as assume that public school pedagogy requires that we think of both students and public officials as beings who have final and formal causes.[110]

---

[108] J. P. Moreland, *The Recalcitrant* Imago Dei: *Human Persons and the Failure of Naturalism* (London: SCM Press, 2009), 65.

[109] Ryland, "Intelligent Design Theory," 1: 473.

[110] Although I have maintained and continue to maintain that ID may be taught in public schools without violating the Establishment Clause (see footnote 3), I sincerely hope that no public school teaches it. For I think that ID advances an inadequate philosophy of nature that suggests a philosophical theology that is inconsistent with classical theism. In other words, I reject Intelligent Design because I accept Thomistic Design. Nevertheless, a public school that privileges the Darwinism of the New Atheists should be resisted as well, because it pronounces on metaphysical matters that Darwinism, rightly understood, does not and cannot pronounce.

So, given these seven points, it's now time to answer the question this chapter is supposed to answer: "What must one believe to be an *anti*–Intelligent Design advocate?" It's simple: believe in design.[111]

---

[111] Those who are philosophically astute may think that the title of this chapter, "How to Be An Anti–Intelligent Design Advocate," is reminiscent of the title of a 1982 paper, "How to Be An Anti-Realist," authored by University of Notre Dame philosopher, Alvin Plantinga, (*Proceedings and Addresses of the American Philosophical Association*, 56.1. [September 1982]: 47–70). And they would be right.

# Same-Sex Marriage and Justificatory Liberalism: Religious Liberty, Comprehensive Doctrines, and Public Life

> Equal respect for persons requires equal conditions of liberty. But they do not require equal personal approval of all religious practices. Legality is not approval.
>
> Martha Nussbaum (1947–)[1]

> A tolerant secular community must therefore find its justification for religious freedom in a more basic principle of liberty that generates a more generous conception of the spheres of value in which people must be left free to choose for themselves. It must treat freedom of religion, that is, as one case of a more general right not simply of religious but of ethical freedom.
>
> Ronald M. Dworkin (1931–2013)[2]

> Now, I'm liberal, but to a degree
> I want ev'rybody to be free
> But if you think that I'll let Barry Goldwater
> Move in next door and marry my daughter
> You must think I'm crazy!
>
> Bob Dylan (1941–)[3]

Supporters of Justificatory Liberalism (JL) maintain that the state may not coerce its citizens on matters of constitutional essentials unless it can provide public justification that the coerced citizens would be unreasonable in rejecting.

---

[1] Quoted in Haroon Sidiquil, "Philosopher Martha Nussbaum takes aim at anti-Muslim intolerance," theStar.com (4 August 2012), available at http://www.thestar.com/opinion/editorialopinion/2012/08/04/philosopher_martha_nussbaum_takes_aim_at_antimuslim_intolerance.html.

[2] Ronald M. Dworkin, *Is Democracy Possible Here?: Principles for a New Political Debate* (Princeton, NJ: Princeton University Press, 2006), 61.

[3] Bob Dylan, "I'll Shall Be Free No. 10." Copyright © 1971 by Special Rider Music; renewed 1999 by Special Rider Music.

According to John Rawls, *constitutional essentials* include "basic rights and liberties," such as "[l]iberty of conscience and freedom of association, and the political rights of freedom of speech, voting, and running for office [,which] are characterized in more or less the same manner in all free regimes."[4] Moreover, because citizens, including religious citizens, have an *evidential set*[5] – sources of authority, background beliefs and reasons – not shared by their neighbors, they should restrain from employing those sources as the basis for the reasons why they enact laws that limit a constitutionally essential liberty of their fellow citizens who do not share those sources of authority. For this reason, Rawls writes that constitutional essentials are "the special subject of public reason."[6] As Gerald Gaus puts it: "Imposition on others requires justification; unjustified impositions are unjust.... The basic idea is that freedom to live one's own life as one chooses is the benchmark or presumption; departures from that condition – where you demand that another live her life according to your judgments – require additional justification. And if these demands cannot be justified, then we are committed to tolerating these other ways of living."[7]

Proponents of the legal recognition of same-sex marriage (SSM) usually offer some version of JL as the most fundamental reason why laws that limit marriage to one man and one woman are unjust.[8] The rationale goes something like this: because citizen opposition to the legal recognition of SSM is motivated and/or justified by religious and philosophical reasons that depend on contested comprehensive doctrines that other (mostly gay and lesbian) citizens may reasonably reject, and because the right to marry is a fundamental liberty

---

[4] John Rawls, *Political Liberalism*, 2nd ed. (New York: Columbia University Press, 1996), 228. For Rawls, there are two kinds of constitutional essentials. The second kind, which are relevant to this chapter, are the basic rights and liberties mentioned in the text. The first kind concerns the structure of government, for example, separation of powers, parliamentary system, etc. (Ibid).

[5] I am borrowing the phrase "evidential set" from Christopher Eberle, who defines it in this way:

> [A] citizen who conscientiously attempts to determine whether a given belief B merits his adherence must rely on a fund of beliefs and experiences he assumes to be true or reliable while evaluating B. Call that fund of beliefs and experiences his *evidential set*. Whether it's rational for a citizen to assent to B (or accept a given argument for B) depends, in addition to the manner in which he forms his beliefs [i.e., he is willing to subject his views to criticism, go where the evidence and arguments may lead, and is properly disposed to be intellectually virtuous], on the contents of his evidential set. (Christopher Eberle, *Religious Reasons in a Liberal Democracy* [New York: Cambridge University Press, 2002], 61–62.)

[6] Rawls, *Political Liberalism*, 214.

[7] Gerald F. Gaus, *Justificatory Liberalism: An Essay on Epistemology and Political Theory* (Oxford: Oxford University Press, 1996), 165.

[8] See, e.g., Elizabeth Brake, "Minimal Marriage: What Political Liberalism Implies for Gay Marriage," *Ethics* 120.2 (2010): 302–337; Linda C. McClain, "Deliberative Democracy, Overlapping Consensus, and Same-Sex Marriage," *Fordham Law Review* 66 (1997–98): 1241–1252; Frank I. Michelman, "Rawls on Constitutionalism and Constitutional Law," in *The Cambridge Companion to Rawls*, ed. Samuel Freeman. (New York: Cambridge University Press, 2003), 394–425; Martha Nussbaum, "A Right to Marry?: Same Sex Marriage and Constitutional Law," *Dissent* (Summer 2009): 43–55; Dworkin, *Is Democracy Possible Here?*, 1–24, 86–89.

(and thus a Constitutional essential), the state may not justly restrict marriage to one man and one woman. The U. S. Supreme Court in *Obergefell v. Hodges* (2015) seems to rely on similar reasoning as part of its 5-4 ruling that the U.S. Constitution requires that all 50 states and the District of Columbia legally recognize SSM. In his majority opinion, Justice Anthony Kennedy writes:

Many who deem same-sex marriage to be wrong reach that conclusion based on *decent and honorable religious or philosophical premises*, and neither they nor their beliefs are disparaged here. But when that sincere, personal opposition becomes enacted law and public policy, the necessary consequence is to put the imprimatur of the State itself on an exclusion that soon demeans or stigmatizes those whose own liberty is then denied.[9] (emphasis added)

In this chapter I argue that this application of JL seems to succeed handsomely, *until* one begins to take into consideration the legal and cultural consequences that will likely result when SSM is legally recognized. These consequences include government coercion, punishment, and marginalization of citizens who cannot in good conscience accept SSM as real marriage because their reasonable comprehensive doctrines require them to reject SSM. That is, these citizens' understanding of marriage is organically connected to their understanding of the good life including their familial roles as husband, wife, parent, child, aunt, uncle, and so on, their place in history in relation to patrimony and progeny, and their theological traditions and the metaphysical beliefs these traditions assume or entail. In that case, if SSM dissenters are coerced, punished, and marginalized by government because of their unwillingness to violate their consciences, this would be a clear violation of JL, if their resistance is based on their *reasonable comprehensive doctrines*.[10] I argue that is in fact the case, and for that reason, the JL case for SSM, given the internal structure of the legal systems and the nature of the judiciaries (and in some cases, Constitutional

---

[9] *Obergefell v. Hodges* Nos 14-556, 14-562, 14-571, 14-574, 2015 US LEXIS 4250, at *36 (26 June 2015).
[10] According to Rawls, *reasonable comprehensive doctrines* have three main features:

One is that a reasonable doctrine is an exercise of theoretical reason: it covers the major religious, philosophical, and moral aspects of human life in a more or less consistent and coherent manner. It organizes and characterizes recognized values so that they are compatible with one another and express an intelligible view of the world. Each doctrine will do this in ways that distinguish it from other doctrines, for example, by giving certain values a particular primacy and weight. In singling out which values to count as especially significant and how to balance them when they conflict, a reasonable comprehensive doctrine is also an exercise of practical reason. Both theoretical and practical reason (including as appropriate the rational) are used together in its formulation. Finally, a third feature is that while a reasonable comprehensive view is not necessarily fixed and unchanging, it normally belongs to, or draws upon, a tradition of thought and doctrine. Although stable over time, and not subject to sudden and unexplained changes, it tends to evolve slowly in the light of what, from its point of view, it sees as good and sufficient reasons. (Rawls, *Political Liberalism*, 59)

Law) in liberal democracies, cannot succeed as a just resolution to the SSM debate consistent with the liberal principles embraced by SSM advocates.

This chapter is divided into two main sections. (7.1) I offer a general account of JL, focusing on those aspects of it that I believe are central to understanding its application to the marriage debate. (7.2) I discuss Marriage and JL, in which I offer three sets of examples of the sorts of consequences that likely will result (and in some cases have already resulted) from the legal recognition of SSM and why those consequences may violate JL. I also answer three objections to my case.

I should note what I am not addressing in this chapter. First, I am not discussing the merits or demerits of the position of those who believe that the political defeat of the normativity of male-female marriage is a victory against "homophobia." After all, someone who embraces that position already believes that opposition to SSM is irrational and that the uncontroversial obligation of the government is to place in its laws the deliverances of one comprehensive doctrine on matters of human sexuality. That position – although held by some distinguished philosophers – is not part of the liberal tradition that I am engaging in this chapter, and nor is it part of Justice Kennedy's opinion in *Obergefell*, as the earlier quote from him clearly shows. It may, of course, be the correct position, and the most just. But whatever one may think of its moral status, merely asserting its correctness does not seriously engage, or show full appreciation for, the moral depth of the philosophical question that percolates beneath the SSM debate and how contrary reasonable comprehensive doctrines may answer it: What is the proper end of our sexual powers and their relationship to the nature of marriage? It is a question over which free and equal citizens in a liberal democracy are bound to offer different answers precisely because such regimes provide for their citizens the political freedom to exercise their rational powers consonant with their reasonable comprehensive doctrines. Thus, it seems wildly implausible to me that each and every citizen who opposes SSM suffers from a moral and rational dysfunction. (Just as it seems wildly implausible to suggest that each and every citizen who supports SSM has a visceral antipathy to religiously informed views of human sexuality that privilege heterosexual monogamy.[11]) From my own experience, it seems the reverse is true: very few who hold a strong position on this issue, whether

---

[11] Justice Kennedy, who wrote the majority opinion in *Obergefell*, exhibits great respect for those citizens that embrace religious traditions that reject SSM. He writes: "Many who deem same-sex marriage to be wrong reach that conclusion based on decent and honorable religious or philosophical premises, and neither they nor their beliefs are disparaged here.... [I]t must be emphasized that religions, and those who adhere to religious doctrines, may continue to advocate with utmost, sincere conviction that, by divine precepts, same-sex marriage should not be condoned. The First Amendment ensures that religious organizations and persons are given proper protection as they seek to teach the principles that are so fulfilling and so central to their lives and faiths, and to their own deep aspirations to continue the family structure they have long revered." (*Obergefell*, at *36, 48–49 (26 June 2015))

for or against SSM, are driven by irrational fear or animus. They seem to be driven by beliefs they hold to be properly basic in terms of justice, whether it is the rightly ordered ends of our sexual powers (including their relation to marriage's nature) or the rightly ordered ends of our public institutions. Both sides answer these concerns differently and thus come to contrary conclusions on whether the legal recognition of SSM is just.

Second, I am not going to address the question of whether civil marriage should be entirely abolished and replaced with some version of civil unions or other kinds of legally sanctioned relationships. Some thinkers in the liberal tradition have made suggestions of this sort as a possible resolution to the SSM debate.[12] They are surely worthy of serious consideration, and may very well resolve most or all of the problems to which I draw attention in this chapter. But I have chosen to focus on the application of JL to SSM by those thinkers who call for the grafting on of SSM to the laws, institutions, and practices that are currently in place.[13]

I should also note that the debate in the United States over SSM is not about either making SSM legal or banning it. It is about *legal recognition* of certain same-sex relationships as marriages. This is a subtle distinction, although an important one.

After the Supreme Court issued its opinions in the marriage cases in June 2013,[14] virtually all media outlets referred to the subject of one of those cases (*Hollingsworth v. Perry*), California's Proposition 8, as a constitutional amendment that "bans same-sex marriage."[15] This, however, is technically *not true*, because Prop 8 is exclusively concerned with the sorts of unions that the state of California may *legally recognize*: "Only marriage between a man and a woman is valid or recognized in California." Under such a government policy, no same-sex couple is banned from drawing up a private contract and participating in a ceremony officiated by a clergyman who has the ecclesial power to declare the couple "married." If their commitment is sincere, and if they and

---

[12] See, e.g., Blake, "Minimal Marriage"; and Andrew F. March, "Is There a Right to Polygamy?; Marriage, Equality and Subsidizing Families in Liberal Public Justification," *Journal of Moral Philosophy* 8.2 (2011): 246–272.

[13] See, e.g., Michelman, "Rawls on Constitutionalism and Constitutional Law"; Nussbaum, "A Right to Marry"; and Dworkin, *Is Democracy Possible Here?*, 1–24, 86–89; Richard D. Mohr, *The Long Arc of Justice: Lesbian and Gay Marriage, Equality, and Rights* (New York: Columbia University Press, 2005); Alex Rajczi, "A Populist Argument for Same-Sex Marriage," *The Monist* 91.3–4 (2008): 475–505; and Ralph Wedgwood, "The Fundamental Argument for Same-Sex Marriage," *The Journal of Political Philosophy* 7.3 (1999): 225–242.

[14] Hollingsworth v. Perry 133 S. Ct. 2652 (2013) and United States v. Windsor 133 S. Ct. 2675 (2013).

[15] "A federal appeals panel in San Francisco ruled Tuesday that California's Proposition 8, which bans same-sex marriage, is unconstitutional ..." (Robert Barnes, "California Proposition 8 same-sex-marriage ban ruled unconstitutional," *The Washington Post* [7 February 2012], available at http://www.washingtonpost.com/politics/calif-same-sex-marriage-ban-ruled-unconstitutional/2012/02/07/gIQAMNwkwQ_story.html.

the members of their community and family believe in the ceremony's authority, it would seem that the absence of the government's *imprimatur* should not diminish its authenticity for all the parties involved.

Nevertheless, there will be those who think the distinction I am making, between legal recognition and legal prohibition, is a little too cute by half. These critics will argue that denial of legal recognition of same-sex unions sends a clear message to the wider public that these bonds are not respected by the community and thus shows that the state, in the words of Justice Kennedy in *United States v. Windsor* (2013), is motivated by "animus," and that it intends to "impose inequality" and "stigma" on, as well as "demean," "disparage," and "injure," same-sex couples.[16]

Consequently, these critics will conclude that it is perfectly correct to say that jurisdictions that only recognize marriage as a union between one man and one woman do in fact "ban same-sex marriage." But under such an understanding of what constitutes a legal prohibition, other alleged matrimonial arrangements – not so obvious at first glance – must be described as "illegal" as well. For example, in all fifty U.S. states and the District of Columbia – which all now legally recognize SSM – no Catholic couple can obtain a legally recognized Catholic marriage.

According to the *Catechism*,[17] a Catholic marriage consists of five elements: consent, conjugality, indissolubility, exclusivity, and openness to children. There is no jurisdiction that confers legal recognition to a marriage in which these five elements are necessary conditions. (Louisiana does have a provision that allows couples to enter a "covenant marriage,"[18] but it is still not quite Catholic marriage.)

As is well-known, under "no fault divorce," which is the law in all U.S. jurisdictions, civil marriages are not only "dissoluble," as they were when specific grounds for dissolution were required, but may be legally ended without requiring any reason whatsoever. The Catholic Church, of course, allows, under certain conditions,[19] a marriage to be dissolved or declared invalid or null. (Hence, the term "annulment.") Also, under U.S. law, the Church's "openness to children" condition could not be honored, because it requires that the couple not use artificial contraception or procure an abortion, both of which are considered fundamental rights under U.S. Supreme Court jurisprudence.[20]

---

[16] *Windsor*, 133 S. Ct. 2693, 2695-2696 (2013), 20–21, 24–26 (Kennedy, J., majority).

[17] *Catechism of the Catholic Church: Revised in Accordance With the Official Latin Text Promulgated by Pope John Paul II*, 2nd ed. (Washington, DC: United States Conference of Catholic Bishops, 2000), 1601–1666.

[18] "Covenant Marriage," Department of Health and Hospitals, State of Louisiana, available at http://new.dhh.louisiana.gov/index.cfm/page/695.

[19] Fr. John T. Catoir, J.C.D., "Understanding Annulments," *St. Anthony Messenger* (September 1998), available at http://www.americancatholic.org/messenger/sep1998/feature1.asp.

[20] Griswold v. Connecticut 381 U.S., 479 (1965), and Roe v. Wade 410 U.S., 113 (1973).

Although two American Catholics may be legally married by a Catholic priest, no U.S. jurisdiction will legally recognize or enforce the contours and conditions of Catholic marriage as understood by the Church. Thus, there are no provisions in any state law that require family court judges to defer to the authority of ecclesial courts and canon law when confronted with a case involving two parties in a Catholic marriage. No American state court, for example, would ever issue an order requiring that the parties of a Catholic marriage (even if it includes a non-Catholic) agree to raise their children as Catholics, even though that is precisely what the Church teaches.[21] Consequently, given the fact that the government will not recognize Catholic marital unions in all their canonical fullness, is it fair to say that the government, by excluding them from such legal recognition, is denying them "equal dignity in the eyes of the law?"[22] Perhaps. But it is still not *banning* such unions.

So, if one insists on saying that SSM is (or was) illegal or banned in some jurisdictions, it stands to reason that Catholic marriage is illegal or banned in all fifty U.S. states and the District of Columbia. But such a conclusion is silly. This is why one should use, and why I use, the language of legal recognition rather than of legal prohibition when discussing the legal status of SSM.

## 7.1. JUSTIFICATORY LIBERALISM

Justificatory Liberalism is not a political theory concocted out of whole cloth. According to many of its advocates, it is what justice requires given the deep disagreements between citizens on the nature of the good life. As Rawls puts it: "[T]he problem of political liberalism is: How is it possible that there may exist over time a stable and just society of free and equal citizens profoundly divided by reasonable religious, philosophical, and moral doctrines?"[23] These disagreements, according to Rawls, arise precisely from the fact that citizens in liberal regimes live under conditions in which political, religious, and personal liberties are fully in place.[24]

Because JL comes in different versions, and space constraints prevent me from covering all of them, my focus will be on the two features that seem central

---

[21] "According to the law in force in the Latin Church, a mixed marriage needs for liceity the *express permission* of ecclesiastical authority. In case of disparity of cult an *express dispensation* from this impediment is required for the validity of the marriage. This permission or dispensation presupposes that both parties know and do not exclude the essential ends and properties of marriage; and furthermore that the Catholic party confirms the obligations, which have been made known to the non-Catholic party, of preserving his or her own faith and ensuring the baptism and education of the children in the Catholic Church" (*Catechism of the Catholic Church*, 1635) (notes omitted).

[22] *Obergefell*, at *51 (26 June 2015).

[23] Rawls, *Political Liberalism*, xv.

[24] "Under the political and social conditions secured by the basic rights and liberties of free institutions, a diversity of conflicting and irreconcilable – and what's more, reasonable – comprehensive doctrines will come out and persist if such diversity does not already obtain." (Ibid., 36).

to its most widely held understandings: (7.1.A) The Political Liberty Principle, and (7.1.B) The Public Justification Principle (PJP) and the Respect for Persons. There are, of course, different ways in which these features are understood among JL advocates. For this reason, I cast as wide a net as possible, offering definitions of these features that seem to be the most commonly held.

## 7.1.A. The Political Liberty Principle (PLP)

According to the JL advocate, a citizen does not have to justify her actions to the state. Rather, the state must justify itself to the citizen or citizens whose actions it intends to coerce. Gerald Gaus sees PLP as having two prongs:

(1) A citizen is under no standing obligation to justify her actions to the state.

(2) All use of force or coercion by the state against the persons of its citizens requires justification; in the absence of such justification, such force or coercion by the state is unjust.[25]

Because Gaus is a libertarian, his view of presumptive liberty is more expansive than what one finds in liberal authors like Rawls,[26] Ronald Dworkin,[27] and Martha Nussbaum,[28] who see a much more active role for government on matters such as economic justice, public education, and so forth. However, for these liberal philosophers, there are nevertheless certain fundamental rights – which Rawls includes in what he calls "constitutional essentials" – that have a strong presumption in their favor. As I noted in this chapter's introductory comments, they "concern basic rights and liberties and can be specified in but one way, modulo relatively small variations. Liberty of conscience and freedom of association, and the political rights of freedom of speech, voting, and running for office are characterized in more or less the

---

[25] Gerald F. Gaus, "Coercion, Ownership, and the Redistributive State: Justificatory Liberalism's Classical Tilt," *Social Philosophy and Policy* 27.1 (2010): 239.

[26] Rawls, *Political Liberalism*, 6.

[27] Ronald Dworkin, *Sovereign Virtue: The Theory and Practice of Equality* (Cambridge, MA: Harvard University Press, 2000).

[28] Martha Nussbaum, *Frontiers of Justice: Disability, Nationality, Species Membership* (Cambridge, MA: Harvard University Press, 2006). Nussbaum, it should be noted, has been highly critical of Rawls' social contract approach to justifying political liberalism. Nevertheless, she brings to the question of same-sex marriage what seems to be a Rawlsian approach. She writes: "[M]arriage is a fundamental liberty right of individuals, and because it is that, it also involves an equality dimension: *groups of people cannot be fenced out of that fundamental right without some overwhelming reason.* It's like voting: there isn't a constitutional right to vote, as such; some jobs can be filled by appointment. But the minute voting is offered, it is unconstitutional to fence out a group of people from the exercise of the right. At this point, then, the questions become, Who has this liberty/equality right to marry? And what reasons are strong enough to override it?" (emphasis added) (Nussubaum, "A Right to Marry?," 53).

same manner in all free regimes."[29] These constitutional essentials follow from the first of Rawls' two principles of justice: "Each person has an equal claim to a fully adequate scheme of equal basic rights and liberties, which scheme is compatible with the same scheme for all; and in this scheme the equal political liberties, and only those liberties, are to be guaranteed their fair value."[30] Dworkin argues that religious liberty, broadly construed, is a fundamental right that grounds a citizen's right to act consistently with her deeply held beliefs on matters that touch on the meaning and purpose of human life, including abortion,[31] euthanasia,[32] and marriage.[33] "[A] tolerant secular society," writes Dworkin, "could have no reason for embracing freedom of orthodox worship without also embracing freedom of choice in all ethical matters and therefore freedom of choice with respect to the ethical values that are plainly implicated in decisions about sexual conduct, marriage, and procreation."[34]

Consequently, whether one takes a liberal or a libertarian understanding of JL, it nevertheless affirms a strong presumption in favor of a citizen's liberty (whether of constitutional essentials or a broader array of rights). That is, because coercion of a citizen on a matter of fundamental liberty is presumptively unjust, the state must have a very good reason to engage in such coercion. (What sort of reason may trump that presumption will be discussed later.)

There are, of course, in any given liberal democracy a vast collection of laws, all of which to some extent or another place burdens on its citizens including limiting the ways in which they may lawfully act. Governments, for example, adopt laws requiring those driving automobiles to remain on a particular side of the road under a designated speed limit, as well as criminal statutes that prohibit citizens from engaging in a variety of acts including fraud, murder, burglary, and perjury. But in such cases the laws in question have in fact met the justification required by JL.

What sorts of cases would PLP provide a defeater to state coercion? Judith Jarvis Thomson provides an example: limitation on the abortion liberty. In a piece[35] recommended by Rawls as an example of his political liberalism applied to the abortion debate,[36] Thomson concedes that the antiabortion position on

---

[29] Rawls, *Political Liberalism*, 228.

[30] Ibid., 5. See Rawls's explication of these liberties in Ibid., 289–371.

[31] Ronald Dworkin, *Life's Dominion: An Argument About Abortion, Euthanasia, and Individual Freedom* (New York: Vintage, 1993), 30–178.

[32] Ibid., 179–241.

[33] Dworkin, *Is Democracy Possible Here?*. 1–24.

[34] Ibid., 62.

[35] Judith Jarvis Thomson, "Abortion: Whose Right?," *Boston Review* 20.3 (1995), *available at* http://bostonreview.mit.edu/BR20.3/thomson.html. (no pagination).

[36] Rawls, *Political Liberalism*, lvi note 31. Rawls, however, adds that he "would want to add several addenda" to the piece. Although Rawls recommends Thomson's essay, he seems more open than Thomson to the possibility that the antiabortion position may be reflected in our

the morally protected status of the fetus from conception is not unreasonable, but denies that reason requires that prochoice advocates embrace it. This is because the prochoice view, that the fetus lacks a right to life (at least during the earliest stages of pregnancy), is, according to Thomson, at least just as reasonable as the antiabortion point of view. Consequently, on the matter of the moral status of the fetus, no one side of the issue really wins the day.[37] Thomson, however, maintains that because of this impasse on the morally protected standing of the fetus, and because the freedom of certain citizens (i.e., pregnant women) hangs in the balance, we should err on the side of liberty. Writes Thomson:

One side says that the fetus has a right to life from the moment of conception, the other side denies this. Neither side is able to prove its case.... [W]hy should the deniers win? ... The answer is that the situation is not symmetrical. What is in question here is not which of two values we should promote, the deniers' or the supporters'. What the supporters want is a license to impose force; what the deniers want is a license to be free of it. It is the former that needs justification.[38]

Thomson is arguing that on the matter of the morally protected status of the fetus the government should err on the side of liberty, which means retaining or establishing the right to abortion. And the government should do so for four conjoined reasons: (1) the burden of proof is on the citizens who want to coerce their fellow citizens; (2) in order to meet the burden of proof, the coercers must show that the coerced are in fact unreasonable in rejecting the constraint on their freedom; (3) in order to constrain the liberty of pregnant women from having abortions, it must be the case that denying the fetus' morally protected status is in fact unreasonable; and (4) neither position on the

---

laws (Ibid., lvi–lvii including notes), a position he seems later to fully embrace. (John Rawls, *The Laws of Peoples; with "The Idea of Public Reason Revisited,"* [Cambridge, MA: Harvard University Press, 1999], 155–156). In this work, Rawls argues that even though the antiabortion position is consistent with Catholic moral theology, it still may be legitimately reflected in our laws if it is supported by public reason and is able to win a majority.

[37] In an earlier article (Judith Jarvis Thomson, "A Defense of Abortion," *Philosophy and Public Affairs* 1.1 [1971]), she concedes for the sake of argument that the fetus is a person, but then goes on to argue that the right to abortion is still justified. (For a response that claims that she is not really conceding the prolifer's view of fetal personhood, see Francis J. Beckwith, "Does Judith Jarvis Thomson Really Grant the Prolife View of Fetal Personhood in Her Defense of Abortion?: A Rawlsian Assessment," *International Philosophical Quarterly* 54.4 [December 2014].) However, in her 1995 article, Thomson sets aside that earlier argument and addresses the issue from a different angle, critiquing the papal encyclical, *Evangelium Vitae*, in which the late pontiff, John Paul II, affirms, "No circumstance, no purpose, no law whatsoever can ever make licit an act [like abortion] which is intrinsically illicit, since it is contrary to the Law of God which is written in every human heart, knowable by reason itself ..." (Pope John Paul II, *Evangelium Vitae* [25 March 1995], 62, available at http://www.vatican.va/holy_father/john_paul_ii/encyclicals/documents/hf_jp-ii_enc_25031995_evangelium-vitae_en.html).

[38] Thomson, "Abortion."

fetus's morally protected status is unreasonable.[39] Consequently, because the coercers do not meet their burden, therefore, abortion ought be permitted,[40] even though it is not unreasonable to believe as the prolife coercers do that fetuses have a morally protected status.[41]

What sorts of reasons, then, given PLP, would allow a citizen to pass laws that in fact coerce other citizens? To answer that question, the JL advocate offers the PJP, which is grounded in Respect for Persons.

### 7.1.B. The Public Justification Principle (PJP) and the Respect for Persons

"Liberals demand," writes Jeremy Waldron, "that the social order should in principle be capable of explaining itself at the tribunal of each person's understanding."[42] This demand is cashed out by most liberal theorists in the PJP. According to the JL advocate, if citizen X wants to procure the law to coerce other citizens, X must provide public justification. By public justification, the

---

[39] Thomson refers to abortion prohibition as a "severe constraint on liberty," and no doubt it is. (Thomson, "Abortion") But I am not arguing that all unjustified constraints on liberty have to be as severe as obstructing the abortion liberty in order to be violations of JL, and I cannot think of a Justificatory Liberal who does. After all, Thomson concedes that bans on interracial marriage do not count as severe constraints on liberty. (Judith Jarvis Thomson, "Judith Jarvis Thomson Replies," *Boston Review* 20.4 [1995], *available at* http://bostonreview.net/BR20.4/Thomson.html. [no pagination]). But it does not follow from this that such bans do not violate JL for other reasons, such as the denial of equality, as Thomson herself suggests (Ibid.).

[40] My own view is that Thomson's argument does not work, that in fact abortion may be justly prohibited in a liberal regime. (Francis J. Beckwith, "Thomson's 'Equal Reasonableness' Argument for Abortion Rights: A Critique," *American Journal of Jurisprudence* 49.1 [2004]). My reason for employing Thomson's argument is that it is such a clear example of the application of JL to a contested political question. For abortion, like SSM, touches on deep and important disagreements between citizens who embrace contrary, although reasonable, comprehensive doctrines.

[41] Thomson is not alone in arguing in this way. Like Thomson, Dworkin appeals to the same liberal principles, while applying them differently. Although he argues that the fetus, although intrinsically valuable, is not a person through most of its gestation (and thus is not a bearer of rights), he locates the disagreement over abortion on the matter of whether the state may use its power to restrict abortion when citizens widely disagree on whether, and on what grounds, it is morally permissible to destroy the fetus. Dworkin argues that prolifers do not *really* believe the fetus is a person. Because most prolifers maintain that abortion is permissible in some circumstances, for example, pregnancy due to rape or incest or when the life of the mother is in danger, Dworkin argues that prolife opposition is not *truly* grounded in the belief that the fetus is a rights bearer, but rather, on a more general respect for life ethic. Thus, Dworkin, like Thomson, locates the disagreement on broadly religious grounds, having to do with one's personal understanding of the meaning and purpose of life. But unlike Thomson, he denies that the question of the fetus' morally protected status, whether or not it is a rights bearer, is truly the issue in play. Thus, Dworkin argues that "[p]rocreative decisions are fundamental in a different way; the moral issues on which they hinge are religious in the broad sense I defined, touching the ultimate purpose and value of human life itself" (Dworkin, *Life's Dominion*, 158).

[42] Jeremy Waldron, "Theoretical Foundations of Liberalism," *Philosophical Quarterly* 37 (April 1987): 149.

JL advocate means a reason or reasons that all citizens from their particular perspectives (or "reasonable comprehensive doctrines") would or ought to find convincing. As Gaus writes, "Because only a morality that the reason of everyone endorses is consistent with our status as free and equal, we are lead to the public reason principle ... [or PJP]."[43]

Although Justificatory Liberals themselves cannot agree on what precisely counts as public justification,[44] to resolve this dispute, let alone catalog and explain the differing factions and nuanced distinctions between them, would require a book-length treatment. In this chapter, however, the focus is on the narrow question of whether those who are coerced due to the effects and consequences of the legal recognition of SSM are not unreasonable in rejecting the law and thus should not be subject to coercion, punishment or marginalization by the state. In order to answer that question we can limit our inquiry to two queries: (1) Is the citizen's SSM-dissent part of her reasonable comprehensive doctrine?, and (2) Will the legal recognition of SSM result in the government coercion, punishment, or marginalization of such a citizen, inconsistent with the constitutional essentials to which she is entitled? (I will address both queries in Section 7.2 of this chapter, although I will offer some support for the first query in this present section as well.) So, even without knowing exactly what counts as public justification, one can still assess the question of whether the effects and consequences of SSM legal recognition unjustly coerces, punishes, or marginalizes some citizens.

What I am suggesting, however, should not be confused with the constraints some (although not all) JL advocates believe PJP places on the legislator or citizen who wants to coerce other citizens based on his or her own nonpublic reasons. Robert B. Talisse, for example, maintains that because laws prohibiting homosexual acts cannot be justified apart from religious doctrine, then antisodomy laws fail to be justifiable.[45] Assuming that is true,[46] it does not

---

[43] Gerald F. Gaus, "On Two Critics of Justificatory Liberalism: A Response to Wall and Lister," *Politics, Philosophy and Economics* 9.2 (2010): 179.

[44] Eberle, *Religious Reasons*, 195–293.

[45] Robert B Talisse, "Religion in Politics," paper presented at the Social and Political Thought Workshop, Vanderbilt University (5 February 2010), available at SSRN: http://ssrn.com/abstract=1545563.

[46] This is a strong and controversial claim, one against which several philosophers have argued. However, my use of it, as part of Talisse's example, is merely to help illustrate the difference between PJP as applied to citizens who offer coercive legislation and PJP as applied to the plight of citizens who are coerced by legislation. Among the many works that contest Talisse's claim that there are no nonreligious arguments against homosexual conduct (as well as same-sex marriage) are David Bradshaw, "A Reply to Corvino," in *Same Sex: Debating the Ethics, Science, and Culture of Homosexuality*, ed. John Corvino (Lanham, MD: Rowman & Littlefield, 1997); Edward Feser, *The Last Superstition: A Refutation of the New Atheism* (South Bend, IN: St. Augustine Press, 2008), 132–153; John M. Finnis, "Law, Morality, and 'Sexual Orientation,'" *Notre Dame Law Review* 69 (1994); Mary Geach, "Lying With the Body," *The Monist* 91.3–4 (July–October); Robert P. George, "Nature, Morality, and Homosexuality," chapter 15 of *In Defense of Natural Law* by Robert P. George (Oxford: Clarendon, 1999); Robert P. George

follow that citizen Y is unreasonable because he morally objects to homosexual acts on the basis of religious doctrine. After all, it may be that Y has been intellectually, morally and spiritually formed by an evidential set that he has no reason to doubt, and has appropriately and conscientiously dealt with the most sophisticated objections to it and found all of them wanting. As Thomas Nagel puts it, one must distinguish "between what justifies individual belief [e.g., Y's religiously informed moral judgment] and what justifies appealing to that belief in support of the exercise of political power."[47] Consequently, the SSM dissenter who grounds his view in a reasonable comprehensive doctrine need not appeal to public reason or offer a public justification in order to have warrant in holding his belief when he argues that the state violates JL when it seeks to coerce, punish, or marginalize him for his belief, as in the cases I catalog in Section 7.2.A of this chapter. Rather, it is the state, the one that is wielding political power, which is required to provide justification to the SSM dissenter. This is why Rawls distinguishes between reasonable comprehensive doctrines, which include religious worldviews, and the grounds by which the government may be justified in coercing its citizens.[48]

To better understand this distinction, imagine that Y is a serious, thoughtful and observant Catholic fully committed to his church's catechism and all that it teaches about human sexuality and homosexual acts in particular.[49] (I could have easily chosen an Orthodox Jew, Presbyterian, or Religious Humanist to make my point as well.) In that case, Y would be, in Rawlsian terms, believing that which is integral to his reasonable comprehensive doctrine, an account of which Rawls says is "deliberately loose." "We avoid excluding doctrines as unreasonable," writes Rawls, "without strong grounds based on clear aspects of the reasonable itself. Otherwise our account runs the danger of being arbitrary and exclusive. *Political liberalism counts many familiar and traditional doctrines – religious, philosophical, and moral – as reasonable*, even though we could not seriously entertain them for ourselves ..."[50] (emphasis added)

and Gerard V. Bradley, "Marriage and the Liberal Imagination," *Georgetown Law Review* 84 (1995); Robert P. George and Jean Bethke Elshtain, eds., *The Meaning of Marriage: Family, State, Market, and Morals* (Dallas, TX: Spence Publishing, 2006); Sherif Girgis, Robert P. George and Ryan T. Anderson, *What is Marriage?: Man and Woman: A Defense* (New York: Encounter Books, 2012); Patrick Lee, "Marriage, Procreation, and Same-Sex Unions," *The Monist* 91.3–4 (July–October 2008); Patrick Lee and Robert P. George, *Conjugal Union: What Marriage Is and Why It Matters* (New York: Cambridge University Press, 2014); Alexander Pruss, *One Body: An Essay in Christian Sexual Ethics* (Notre Dame, IN: University of Notre Press, 2013).

[47] Thomas Nagel, "Moral Conflict and Political Legitimacy," *Philosophy and Public Affairs* 16 (1987): 229.

[48] "[S]ince the political conception is shared by everyone while the reasonable doctrines are not, we must distinguish between a public basis of justificaton generally acceptable to citizens on fundamental political questions and the many nonpublic bases of justification belonging to the many comprehensive doctrines and acceptable only to those who affirm them" (Rawls, *Political Liberalism*, xix).

[49] *Catechism of the Catholic Church*, 2357–2358.

[50] Rawls, Political Liberalism, 59–60.

Thus, if we employ Rawls' three main features of what constitutes a reasonable comprehensive doctrine (as quoted in footnote 10), the *Catechism of the Catholic Church* seems almost like a paradigm case. (1) It "covers the major religious, philosophical, and moral aspects of human life in a more or less consistent and coherent manner," organizing and recognizing "values so that they are compatible with one another and express an intelligible view of the world."[51] (2) It makes distinctions between its beliefs in such a way that it gives "certain primacy and weight" to different values in order to provide guidance "on how to balance them when they conflict," showing how "[b]oth theoretical and practical reason (including as appropriate the rational) are used together in its formulation."[52] And (3) it provides an account of how doctrine develops over time for what "it sees as good and sufficient reasons" while remaining stable within an identifiable "tradition of thought and doctrine."[53] Moreover, the *Catechism* offers an account of the common good and human rights[54] that contributes to the sort of overlapping consensus that Rawls suggests all reasonable comprehensive doctrines may be able to support from their distinctive points of view.[55]

Thus, given Rawls's understanding of a reasonable comprehensive doctrine, Y is within his epistemic rights in believing that homosexual acts, even between consenting adults, is immoral. Of course, given JL, Y cannot employ the power of government to ban consensual homosexual acts, even if his view is reasonable, because, according to the JL advocate, gay and lesbian citizens are not unreasonable in rejecting Y's moral judgment. But this constraint placed on Y's legislative agenda by JL *does not entail* that the government may now coerce Y

---

[51] Rawls, *Political Liberalism*, 59 cf. *Catechism of the Catholic Church*, 11, 18).
[52] Rawls, *Political Liberalism*, 59. Take, for example, the articulation of just war theory *Catechism of the Catholic Church*, 2309.
[53] Rawls, *Political Liberalism*, 59. Take, for example, this passage on the Church's social teachings from Ibid., 2421:

> The social doctrine of the Church developed in the nineteenth century when the Gospel encountered modern industrial society with its new structures for the production of consumer goods, its new concept of society, the state and authority, and its new forms of labor and ownership. The development of the doctrine of the Church on economic and social matters attests the permanent value of the Church's teaching at the same time as it attests the true meaning of her Tradition, always living and active.

On the issue of doctrinal development, see John Henry Cardinal Newman, *An Essay on the Development of Christian Doctrine*, 6th ed. (1878) (Notre Dame, IN: University of Notre Dame Press, 1989; reprint); John Rist, *What is Truth?: From the Academy to the Vatican* (New York: Cambridge University Press, 2008).

[54] *Catechism of the Catholic Church*, 1905–1912.
[55] Write Rawls, "[T]o see how a well-ordered society can be unified and stable, we introduce another basic idea of political liberalism to go with the idea of a political conception of justice, namely the idea of an overlapping consensus of reasonable comprehensive doctrines. In such a consensus, the reasonable doctrines [such as Catholicism] endorse the political conception each from its own point of view" (Rawls, *Political Liberalism*, 134).

to celebrate, support, morally approve, or bless consensual homosexual acts in ways that his church and its theological and moral traditions would judge as cooperating with evil. Although a religious doctrine (or any nonpublic reason), according to virtually every account of JL, may not serve as the basis of a law to restrict conduct on a constitutional essential in a liberal regime, religious doctrine (or any nonpublic reason) may indeed serve as the basis of a citizen's moral beliefs in such a state.[56] For this reason, writes Gaus, citizens like Y "have no reason to submit [to the state] their disputes about religion, ways of having sex, the good life, or good beers to adjudication: on these matters it is entirely reasonable to object that no public judgment is required, and so the use of state power – even in the service of reasonable views – is illegitimate."[57] For such a regime is committed to a principle of political liberty (PLP) that includes religious free exercise and thus a strong presumption against abdicating it. As Rawls puts it: "[I]f we argue that the religious liberty of some citizens is to be denied, we must give them reasons they can not only understand ... but reasons we might reasonably expect that they, as free and equal citizens, might reasonably also accept."[58]

Most liberal theorists maintain that the requirement of public justification (PJP) is grounded in the idea of *respect for persons*, "the clarion call of justificatory liberalism,"[59] as Eberle calls it. "[T]o respect another person as an end" in a liberal regime, writes Charles Laramore, "is to require that coercive or political principles be as justifiable to that person as they presumably are to us."[60]

Returning to Thomson's illustration, an antiabortion law would violate the principle of respect for persons because such a law would imply that the reasons, offered by a citizen to deny fetal personhood and to justify her abortion, are unreasonable, even though they are in fact *not* unreasonable. (To repeat what I stated in footnote 40, I actually don't think Thomson's argument works, that in fact abortion may be prohibited in a liberal regime.) Because citizens are free and equal in a liberal regime, it is inconsistent with the principle of respect for persons to employ state power to coerce citizens to act in accordance with

---

[56] As Rawls writes: "Certainly Catholics may, in line with public reason, continue to argue against the right to abortion. Reasoning is not closed once and for all in public reason any more than it is closed in any form of reasoning. Moreover, *that the Catholic Church's nonpublic reason requires its members to follow its doctrine is perfectly consistent with their honoring public reason.*" (emphasis added) (John Rawls, "The Idea of Public Reason Revisited," in *Political Liberalism* by John Rawls, expanded edition [New York: Columbia University Press, 2005], 480).

[57] Gerald F. Gaus, "Reasonable Pluralism in the Domain of the Political: How the Weaknesses of John Rawls' Political Liberalism Can Be Overcome by a Justificatory Liberalism.," *Inquiry* 42 (1999): 281.

[58] Rawls, *Political Liberalism*, 447.

[59] Eberle, *Religious Reasons*, 54.

[60] Charles Laramore, "The Moral Basis of Political Liberalism," *The Journal of Philosophy* 96.2 (1999): 608.

a policy or law grounded in a comprehensive doctrine that they are not unreasonable in rejecting. Although, as far as I can tell, Rawls does not employ the phrase "respect for persons," the idea seems to be what Rawls has in mind when he argues that the PJP ought to be guided by the *liberal principle of legitimacy*, the notion that "our exercise of political power is fully proper only when it is exercised in accordance with a constitution the essentials of which all citizens as free and equal may reasonably be expected to endorse in the light of principles and ideals acceptable to their common human reason."[61]

## 7.2. MARRIAGE AND JUSTIFICATORY LIBERALISM

Citizens who oppose the legal recognition of SSM typically do so because their understanding of the nature of the human person requires them to do so, and they realize that the effects and consequences of legalized SSM may oblige them to act inconsistently with what they believe morality demands.

SSM opponents see marriage, often significantly shaped and informed by their religious traditions, as a unique institution in which two members of the two halves of the human race – male and female – are united so that they may forge a permanent bond for the primary (although not exclusive) purpose of begetting and raising children. This bond is more than the sum total of its parts, because the permanent uniting of male and female in matrimony provides to the partners' progeny as well as the wider community a protected and honored place in which the different needs, desires, and complementary powers of each partner may flourish for the common good. That is, marriage is truly a merging – a wedding, if you will – of the only sorts of humans nature knows, male and female.[62]

J. Budziszewski offers a lengthy description of this understanding of marriage. Although he calls it "the traditional Christian understanding,"[63] the essence of it – that marriage is a conjugal, permanent, and exclusive union into which only one man and one woman may enter – is shared by observant

---

[61] Rawls, *Political Liberalism*, 137.

[62] One may bring up the phenomena of *intersex*. This is a term referring to a variety of conditions "where there is a discrepancy between the external genitals and the internal genitals (the testes and ovaries)." ("Intersex," Medline Plus: A service of the U.S. National Library of Medicine, National Institutes of Health, http://www.nlm.nih.gov/medlineplus/ency/article/001669.htm [accessed 15 March 2013]). Because these conditions are the result of a flaw in one's development – hence, they are called "disorders of sexual development" (see Allen L. "Disorders of sexual development," *Obstetrics Gynecology Clinics of North America* 36 [2009]: 25–45) – the defender of male-female marriage can argue that the existence of intersex individuals, however tragic, no more counts against the claim that human nature is divided into only two genders than the existence of children born without legs counts against the claim that human beings are by nature two-legged.

[63] J. Budziszewski, "The Illusion of Gay Marriage," *Philosophia Christi* 7.1 (2005).

Jews, Muslims, Hindus, Buddhists, and a wide variety of believers and unbelievers:[64]

The traditional Christian understanding of marriage is a mutual and binding promise between one man and one woman, before God, to enter into a procreative and unitive bond, with each other alone, for life. Every word in this definition is indispensable. The promise is mutual because the parties must both agree. It is binding because it creates inviolable duties. They promise because they commit their wills. A man and woman are required because that which marriage establishes cannot subsist between two persons of the same sex.... The promise is enacted before God because human marriage was His idea, a part of the plan of Creation; therefore the parties seek His blessing and are answerable to Him for unfaithfulness. We speak of the parties' entrance into marriage because they do not invent it around themselves; rather they choose to take upon themselves a preexisting possibility. We call marriage a procreative partnership because marriage is the unique source of families, the unique way in which we participate in the continuation of the species, the only thing we know that gives a child a fighting chance of being raised by a mom and a dad. Indeed that is why law protects it, for you will note that the law does not protect my relationship with my lunch partner, or define my duties toward my fishing buddy. We call marriage a unitive partnership because in joining, the man and woman become one flesh – there are still two bodies, but they function as the complementary parts of a single procreative organism. We say they have a bond because this union, this organism, is not merely sentimental, metaphorical, or euphemistic; rather it is the concrete reality in which the other dimensions of their intimacy are consummated. They enter marriage with each other alone because polygamy and unfaithfulness confuse and undermine not only their own relationship but their relationship with the resulting children. Finally, the marriage is for life because although many things may impair it, only death can truly sever it. The procreative partnership persists even after the children are grown, because then the spouses help their children establish their own new families, and when their powers at last fail, their children in turn take care of them.[65]

In the remaining sections of his article, Budziszewski makes a case for why the procreative and unitive dimensions of marriage – the lawful bridging of the genders and generations through time and space – make SSM a metaphysical impossibility. In this sense, Budziszewski, like most who share his perspective, is offering the sorts of public reasons (as Rawls and other political liberals would put it) that a liberal regime requires of its citizens who want to shape public policy, even though a citizen need not consciously embrace such public reasons to be rational in privately holding the belief that male-female marriage is the only possible form of marriage.

---

[64] See, e.g., Bradshaw, "A Reply to Corvino"; Finnis, "Law, Morality, and 'Sexual Orientation'"; Geach, "Lying With the Body"; George, "Nature, Morality, and Homosexuality"; George and Bradley, "Marriage and the Liberal Imagination"; George and Elshtain, *The Meaning of Marriage*; Girgis, George and Anderson, *What Is Marriage?*; Lee, "Marriage, Procreation, and Same-Sex Unions"; Lee and George, *Conjugal Union*; Pruss, *One Body*.

[65] Budziszewski, "The Illusion of Gay Marriage," 46.

Behind this understanding of marriage is a particular philosophical anthro-pology that maintains gender complementarity as essential to marriage. Consequently, on this view, sexual orientation is irrelevant to marriage. That is, gender is the only concrete and objective difference between human beings that bears on the nature of marriage. For that reason, as long as a marriage is consummated and it includes only one man and one woman, the sexual orientation of the partners is of no relevance to its licitness. This is based on the belief that marriage is a special sort of community whose qualities are part of the order and nature of things. And what is fundamental to the order and nature of the human species is gender, and it is only in marriage that the dis-cord of that fundamental difference may be truly unified for the common good, the good of its participants, and the children born of that union.

According to critics of SSM like Budziszewski, the consummation condi-tion, or what is sometimes called "conjugality," is a necessary condition that can only be actualized in real marriage (as they understand it) because of the nature of sexual intercourse: it is ordered toward bringing into existence off-spring of the union of the two parties. This is why handshakes, hugs, kisses, or other forms of bodily touching, penetration, or intimacy can never count as conjugality or consummation.

But this is also why, according to SSM critics, it is wrong to say that these other forms of bodily touching, penetration, and intimacy, often practiced by same-sex couples, are indistinguishable from conjugal acts that cannot bring forth offspring due to illness or age. For such conjugal acts, although sterile, do not cease to be conjugal acts, in the same way that a man in a coma does not cease to be a rational animal simply because he is not able to exercise his rational faculties. Just as the comatose man still possesses human dignity even though he is not able to exercise capacities that flow from his essential nature, the conjugal act between a husband and wife that cannot conceive, due to natural or artificial impairment, possesses no less dignity than if the impairment were absent. This is because the conjugal act, whether fertile or not, actualizes in every instance the same profound and mysterious union that is by nature ordered toward bringing into existence a unique and irreplaceable person that literally embodies that union. Thus, same-sex unions cannot prop-erly be described as "sterile," because sterility is a lack had only by acts that are by nature ordered toward their proper end, procreation. To put it another way: sterility is a privation of conjugality, whereas the absence of conjugality is the privation of nothing. In the same way, even though both the Pietà and Stevie Wonder cannot see, only Stevie is blind, because blindness is a lack had only by beings who by nature are ordered toward exercising the power of sight. I am not, of course, suggesting that the partners in a same-sex relationship can-not experience deep love for one another. It would be ludicrous for anyone to suggest such a thing. The point here is quite modest: to present the reasoning of the SSM-dissenters on the *nature of marriage*. The nature of love, whether same-sex or otherwise, is an important, although separate, topic.

For advocates of this view, what grounds the nature of marriage is similar to, and in some cases overlaps, what grounds a variety of other moral beliefs that ordinary people (and some philosophers) associate with the proper ends of human nature, such as the belief that human beings have intrinsic dignity, are not by nature property, ought not to kill each other without justification, and should eschew ignorance and seek knowledge and wisdom. Clearly, this philosophical anthropology is essentialist and teleological,[66] which means that it is out of step with the dominant understandings of the philosophy of nature in the academy.[67] Nevertheless, it is an integral aspect of many comprehensive doctrines, including the world's major religions[68] as well as several philosophical schools of thought.[69] And these are clearly *reasonable* comprehensive doctrines if we accept Rawls' understanding of the concept, which I have already quoted earlier: "*Political liberalism counts many familiar and traditional doctrines – religious, philosophical, and moral – as reasonable,* even though we could not seriously entertain them for ourselves...."[70] (emphasis added). Thus, it should not surprise us that some political and moral philosophers have gone so far as to suggest that the embracing of nominalism as the dominant metaphysical view in the West accounts for the decline in essentialist and teleological understandings of human nature, which, they argue, resulted

[66] That is, its advocates argue for the existence of final and/or formal causes in nature and the mind's ability to know them. However, it should be noted that opponents of SSM who embrace the New Natural Law Theory, e.g., Robert P. George, John Finnis, and Germain Grisez, are sometimes accused of offering a moral theory that ignores *nature* as such. For a defense of that charge, see F. Russell Hittinger, *A Critique of the New Natural Law Theory* (Notre Dame, IN: University of Notre Dame Press, 1987). For a reply, see Robert P. George, "Natural Law and Human Nature," chapter 3 of his *In Defense of Natural Law*.

[67] Nevertheless, there are sophisticated proponents of this perspective, e.g., Robert C. Koons, *Realism Regained An Exact Theory of Teleology, Causation, and the Mind* (New York: Oxford University Press, 2000); and David Oderberg, *Real Essentialism* (New York: Routledge, 2008). Even naturalist philosopher Thomas Nagel has suggested the possibility of a philosophically defensible natural teleology. See Thomas Nagel, "Secular Philosophy and the Religious Temperament," in *Secular Philosophy and the Religious Temperament: Essays 2002–2008* by Thomas Nagel (New York: Oxford University Press, 2009); and Thomas Nagel, *Mind and Cosmos: Why the Materialist Neo-Darwinian Conception of Nature is Almost Certainly False* (New York: Oxford University Press, 2012).

[68] We have already seen that the catechism of the largest body of Christians in the world, the Catholic Church, is a model of clarity on this matter, even if one winds up thinking that it is mistaken. For a gay Catholic critique of the Church's view, see Andrew Sullivan, *Virtually Normal: An Argument About Homosexuality* (New York: Alfred A. Knopf, 1995).

[69] See Aristotle, *Nicomachean Ethics* (350 B.C.), trans. W. D. Ross, bk. 8, ch. 12, available at http://www.constitution.org/ari/; Thomas Aquinas, *Summa Theologica* (1265–1274), Supplementum, 2nd and revised Edition, trans. Fathers of the English Dominican Province (1920), Suppl. Q 41, a 1, available at http://www.newadvent.org/summa/; John Locke, *Second Treatise on Government* (1689) (Indianapolis: Hackett Publishing, 1980). c. VII, s. 78; and Immanuel Kant, *The Science of Right* (1790), trans. W. Hastie (South Australia: eBooks@Adelaide, 2009), 24, available at http://ebooks.adelaide.edu.au/k/kant/immanuel/k16sr/.

[70] Rawls, *Political Liberalism*, 59–60.

in the ascendancy of liberationist views on human sexuality including the increasing tolerance to homosexual conduct and openness to SSM.[71] Although it is outside the scope of this chapter to assess the accuracy of this narrative, it is important to bring it to the reader's attention. For it shows that for some thinkers the issues that are driving the differing factions on the question of SSM are ultimately philosophical ones about the nature of the good life including the proper end of our sexual powers and their place in marriage. They are, in fact, just the sorts of beliefs that Rawls and others claim is an essential feature of a reasonable comprehensive doctrine embraced by some citizens in a liberal democracy that includes other citizens who hold contrary reasonable comprehensive doctrines.

Rawls, for example, writes: "[A] reasonable doctrine is an exercise of theoretical reason: it covers the major religious, philosophical, and moral aspects of human life in a more or less consistent and coherent manner. It organizes and characterizes recognized values so that they are compatible with one another and express an intelligible view of the world."[72] Citing the 2003 U.S. Supreme Court case, *Lawrence v. Texas*[73] – in which the Court held that Texas' criminal statute banning homosexual sodomy was unconstitutional – Dworkin writes that the Court "decided that sexual orientation and activity are also a matter of ethical value rather than some other form of value."[74] These are among "the convictions," writes Dworkin, "through which a person tries to identify the value and point of human life and the relationships, achievements, and experiences that would realize that value in his own life."[75] He then explains that "[o]rthodox religious convictions are plainly in that category, and so are people's convictions about the role and direction of love, intimacy, and sexuality in their lives."[76] Dworkin is in fact offering an account of a reasonable comprehensive doctrine, although, as he is apt to do, in a fashion more eloquent than Rawls. That is, one's ultimate beliefs and deepest convictions about the nature and purpose of the good life – one's comprehensive doctrine, if you will – inform,

[71] See, e.g., David A. J. Richards, *Toleration and the Constitution* (New York: Oxford University Press, 1989), 26, 67–102; Brad S. Gregory, *The Unintended Reformation: How a Religious Revolution Secularized Society* (Cambridge, MA: Harvard University Press, 2012), 48–73, 180–234; Francis A. Canavan, S. J., "From Ockham to Blackmun: The Philosophical Roots of Liberal Jurisprudence," *Courts and the Culture Wars*, ed. Bradley C. S. Watson (New York: Lexington Books, 2002), 15–25; Thomas Kupka, "Names and Designations in Law: Towards a Nominalist Approach to Constitutional Jurisprudence," *The Journal Jurisprudence* 6 (2010): 121–130; Peter Augustine Lawler, "Our Crisis of Self-Evidence," *Society* 45 (2008): 322–326; A. J. Conyers, *The Long Truce* (Waco, TX: Baylor University Press, 2001) 71–75; and Bradley C. S. Watson, *Living Constitution, Dying Faith: Progressivism and the New Science of Jurisprudence* (Wilmington, DE: ISI Books, 2009), 185–192.
[72] Rawls, *Political Liberalism*, 59.
[73] Lawrence v. Texas 539 U.S. 558 (2003).
[74] Dworkin, *Is Democracy Possible Here?*, 72.
[75] Ibid.
[76] Ibid.

shape, and direct one's understanding of the proper end of one's sexual powers and their place in marriage. "These beliefs and commitments," Dworkin explains, "fix the meaning and tone of the most important associations people form; they are drawn from and feed back into their more general philosophical beliefs about the character and value of human life."[77] It should not surprise us, then, that *Lawrence*, the Supreme Court opinion cited with approval by Dworkin, affirms the legitimacy of moral judgments critical of homosexual conduct, that they are integral to some reasonable comprehensive doctrines (to use Rawls' terminology), while at the same time declaring that such moral judgments may not be part of the criminal law: "The [moral] condemnation [of homosexual conduct] has been shaped by religious beliefs, conceptions of right and acceptable behavior, and respect for the traditional family. For many persons these are not trivial concerns but profound and deep convictions accepted as ethical and moral principles to which they aspire and which thus determine the course of their lives. These considerations do not answer the question before us, however."[78]

Consequently, even with these underlying philosophical and religious differences fully acknowledged, including the reasonableness of a citizen's rejection of SSM, this *by itself* would not make the *legal recognition* of SSM a violation of JL in relation to SSM dissenters. For there are many activities that one may be reasonable in thinking immoral and inconsistent with a person's proper end – for example, smoking cigarettes or viewing pornographic movies – whose legalization does not result in unjust coercion, punishment or marginalization of those who issue this judgment. Thus, it may be the case that while it is perfectly rational to think SSM immoral, as one would think cigarette smoking and consuming pornography immoral, it does not follow that the legal permission of these activities results in an injustice against those who believe these activities are immoral. And given the strictures of JL, it would follow that the SSM opponent could not forbid the legal recognition of SSM, even if her beliefs about the matter were perfectly rational to hold.

However, marriage – unlike cigarette smoking, consuming pornography, or even procuring an abortion – is an *institution*, that according to many reasonable comprehensive doctrines (as noted earlier) is integral to answering so many fundamental questions about the meaning and nature of life including the relationship between men and women and their children as well as the proper end of our sexual powers and their place in marriage. Marriage is so fundamental to our lives that virtually everyone connects his or her place in time and space to partner, paternity, maternity, patrimony, and progeny, whose commencements are often marked by solemn events such as weddings, baptisms, bar mitzvahs, and burials. For this reason, it would be as much of a mistake to think of marriage as just one institution among many as it would

---

[77] Ibid.
[78] *Lawrence,* 539 U.S., 539.

be to think oxygen were just one gas among many. For in the case of each, there is not much to life without it. This is why marriage is so fully integrated into so many complex and intersecting layers of our public and private lives – including family law, adoption, religion, education, property, civil rights, and employment.[79] In fact, traditional Christians – Catholics, Protestants, and Orthodox – liken Christ's relationship to His Church as a groom to his bride (Mt 9:15, Mk 2:19, Lk 5:34, Jn 3:29, 2 Cor 11:2, Eph 5:25, Eph 5:31–32, Rev 19:7, Rev 21:2, Rev 21:9, Rev 22:17). And in Catholic and Orthodox theology, marriage is one of the seven sacraments. In the words of the *Catechism of the Catholic Church*: "The marriage covenant, by which a man and a woman form with each other an intimate communion of life and love, has been founded and endowed with its own special laws by the Creator. By its very nature it is ordered to the good of the couple, as well as to the generation and education of children. Christ the Lord raised marriage between the baptized to the dignity of a sacrament."[80]

## 7.2.A. Effects and Consequences of Same-Sex Marriage

For these reasons, the legal recognition of SSM and the effects and consequences that will follow from it should not be taken lightly by those of us who take seriously JL as fundamental to the way we understand what it means for free and equal citizens to live in a liberal democracy. Given the nature of our laws, public institutions, and the scope of the welfare state as well as the role and purpose that marriage and family and our beliefs about them play in our public and private lives, our theological traditions, and the education and spiritual formation of our children, it seems undeniable that the legal recognition of SSM will result in the sorts of political conflicts that JL is supposed to resolve. Consider just these three sets of examples, although many more can be conscripted.[81]

---

[79] Charles J. Reid, Jr., "Marriage: Its Relationship to Religion, Law, and the State," *The Jurist* 68 (2008).

[80] *Catechism of the Catholic Church*, 1660.

[81] See, e.g., Douglas Laycock, Anthony Picarello, Jr., and Robin Fretwell, eds., *Same-Sex Marriage and Religious Liberty: Emerging Conflicts* (Lanham, MD: Rowman & Littlefield, 2008); Thomas C. Berg, "What Same-Sex-Marriage and Religious-Liberty Claims Have in Common," *Northwestern Journal of Law and Social Policy* 5.2 (Fall 2010): 206–235; Richard F. Duncan, "Who Wants to Stop the Church: Homosexual Rights Legislation, Public Policy, and Religious Freedom," *Notre Dame Law Review* 69.3 (1993–94): 393–445; Richard F. Duncan, "Homosexual Marriage and the Myth of Tolerance: Is Cardinal O'Connor a 'Homophobe'?" *Notre Dame Journal of Law, Ethics and Public Policy* 10 (1996): 587–608; Jonathan W. Heaton, "*Catholic League for Religious and Civil Rights v. City of San Francisco*: How the Ninth Circuit Abandoned Judicial Neutrality to Strike a Blow at Religion," *Brigham Young University Law Review* 101 (2010): 101–116; Roger Severino, "Or for Poorer? How Same-Sex Marriage Threatens Religious Liberty," *Harvard Journal of Law and Public Policy* 30 (2007): 941–992; and Eugene Volokh, "Same-Sex Marriage and Slippery Slopes," *Hofstra Law Review* 33 (2005): 1155–1201.

## 7.2.A.1. *Child Adoption Law*

In Massachusetts, soon after the state's Supreme Judicial Court required that the state issue marriage licenses to same-sex couples,[82] Catholic Charities, which was at the time in the child adoption business, was told by the state that it could no longer exclude same-sex couples as adoptive parents, even though the Catholic Church maintains that same-sex unions are deeply disordered and sinful.[83] Because it could not as a matter of conscience compromise its moral theology, Catholic Charities ceased putting children up for adoption.[84]

Because the Catholic citizen embraces a reasonable comprehensive doctrine, and because the issue in question touches on a matter of constitutional essentials and basic liberties (including religious liberty and freedom of conscience), and because the state has not provided her with reasons that are adequate for accepting state policies that she is not unreasonable in rejecting, the state's action, according to virtually every account of JL, is unjust. In the case of Catholic Charities, its requirement to find for each child an adequate replacement for her mother and father is grounded in the belief (which is hardly unreasonable) that a human child is the sort of being that has by nature a mother and a father, just as it is the sort of being that has the essential property to have the ultimate capacity to exercise rational thought (even if it never acquires the present capacity or the ability to exercise it). Thus, if we have an obligation not to interrupt a child's ability to exercise rational thought, we also have an obligation not to deny unjustly a child her mother and father or a

---

[82] Goodridge v. Dept. Pub. Health 798 N. E. 2d, 941 (Mass. 2003).

[83] The *Catholic Catechism* affirms:

> Homosexuality refers to relations between men or between women who experience an exclusive or predominant sexual attraction toward persons of the same sex. It has taken a great variety of forms through the centuries and in different cultures. Its psychological genesis remains largely unexplained. Basing itself on Sacred Scripture, which presents homosexual acts as acts of grave depravity, tradition has always declared that "homosexual acts are intrinsically disordered." They are contrary to the natural law. They close the sexual act to the gift of life. They do not proceed from a genuine affective and sexual complementarity. Under no circumstances can they be approved.

> The number of men and women who have deep-seated homosexual tendencies is not negligible. This inclination, which is objectively disordered, constitutes for most of them a trial. They must be accepted with respect, compassion, and sensitivity. Every sign of unjust discrimination in their regard should be avoided. These persons are called to fulfill God's will in their lives and, if they are Christians, to unite to the sacrifice of the Lord's Cross the difficulties they may encounter from their condition.

> Homosexual persons are called to chastity. By the virtues of self-mastery that teach them inner freedom, at times by the support of disinterested friendship, by prayer and sacramental grace, they can and should gradually and resolutely approach Christian perfection. (*Catechism of the Catholic Church*, 2357–2359) (citations omitted)

[84] Maggie Gallagher, "Banned in Boston: The coming conflict between same-sex marriage and religious liberty," *The Weekly Standard* 11.33 (May 15, 2006).

replacement for each in the case of a child put up for adoption.[85] Consequently, from the perspective of Catholic Charities, it is morally required to treat all children with equal dignity and respect, which means that no child should be denied a mother and a father or a replacement for each if it is in fact possible to do so. Including same-sex couples as adoptive parents, according to Catholic Charities, violates the equal dignity and respect of the children that have been placed in its care. Admittedly, this perspective is not shared by everyone. But it is certainly just the sort of reasonable perspective that JL's proponents claim it is supposed to protect in a free society of competing and contested comprehensive doctrines.

A 2010 foster care case in the United Kingdom reveals what may happen for potential adoptee parents in the United States who believe that homosexual conduct is morally wrong. The case concerned Eunice and Owen Johns, a Pentecostal Christian couple, who were rejected as foster parents by a panel of the Derby City Council. They were not rejected because they were child abusers, unstable, or lacked the requisite skills or background. In fact, according to one account, the couple had already been successful foster parents to twenty children.[86]

The Johns were denied foster children because they believe that human sexuality has a certain intrinsic purpose that may only be consummated by one man and one woman within the confines of matrimony, and that it is their responsibility to properly instruct the children in their care of this truth. According to Mrs. Johns's account, "The council said: 'Do you know, you would have to tell them that it's OK to be homosexual?' But I said I couldn't do that because my Christian beliefs won't let me. Morally, I couldn't do that. Spiritually I couldn't do that."[87] And for this reason, the council declared that the Johns were no longer fit to be foster parents. This is why in November 2010 they found themselves before the British High Court, which in 2011 ruled that no injustice was done to the Johns by denying them foster parenthood based on their moral beliefs about sexual conduct.[88]

Given the laws and cultural beliefs already in place in some jurisdictions, it is clearly not unthinkable to imagine that many married heterosexual couples

---

[85] I say "to deny *unjustly*," because there could be extreme situations, such as in the cases of abuse or a parent serving prison time for a crime, that the state may justly remove a child from her parent's custody. But what is doing the work here is the child's natural need for parental care and love, which in fact is essential to the position on adoption held by groups such as Catholic Charities.

[86] Sam Greenhill, "Christian Couple Barred From Fostering Children Because of Their Views on Homosexuality Go to Court," *The Daily Mail* (1 November 2010), available at http://www.dailymail.co.uk/news/-1325311/Gay-rights-laws-danger-freedoms-Bishops-speak-homosexuality.html#ixzz1S1LvMo6O.

[87] Ibid.

[88] Tim Ross, "Foster Parent Ban: 'No Place' in the Law for Christianity, High Court Rules," *The Telegraph* (2011 February 28), available at http://www.telegraph.co.uk/news/religion/8353496/Foster-parent-ban-no-place-in-the-law-for-Christianity-High-Court-rules.html.

in the United States (as well as in other countries like the United Kingdom) will be denied the opportunity to be adoptee and foster parents simply because they harbor beliefs about the immorality of homosexual conduct that are integral to their reasonable comprehensive doctrines, and that they intend to pass on those beliefs to their children or foster children.

### 7.2.A.2. *Businesses and Public Accommodations*

Wedding ceremonies typically require a host of businesses and services that the law marks off as public accommodations, such as photographers, caterers, wedding planners, facilities, etc.[89] And because they are public accommodations, the usual array of antidiscrimination laws would come into play in a SSM regime in which "marital status" and "sexual orientation" are protected categories. Thomas C. Berg cites the 2008 case of "an Albuquerque, New Mexico, photographer named Elaine Huguenin [who] had to pay more than $6,600 in legal fees for declining to photograph the same-sex commitment ceremony of Vanessa Willock and her partner."[90] The case eventually reached the New Mexico Supreme Court in 2013, where Ms. Huguenin and her husband lost their appeal.[91] Although this case did not involve SSM (because SSM was not legally recognized in New Mexico at the time), it is instructive, because it allows us a modest glimpse of what will likely happen to SSM dissenters when the state not only tolerates but blesses these unions as goods from which other citizens are not free to dissent in their public lives.

It is difficult to imagine the Huguenins being fined if they had declined to photograph the honeymoon rather than the commitment ceremony. Or suppose a brothel in Nye County, Nevada, where prostitution is legal, tried to hire the Huguenins to take a group photograph to be used for the business's Christmas card. Imagine the Huguenins refuse to provide the service on the grounds that they believe that Christmas is a Holy Day and that prostitution is deeply immoral. Should the Huguenins have a right to refuse? In both of these fictional cases, the reason for the refusals is clear: from the perspective of the Huguenins' reasonable comprehensive doctrine, they are being asked to cooperate with activities they believe are gravely immoral. And yet, they believe that the same-sex commitment ceremony that they declined to photograph is gravely immoral as well, for precisely the same sorts of reasons they would be justified in declining their participation in the other activities: each is a manifestation of what they believe is a gravely immoral understanding of the

---

[89] Berg, "What Same-Sex-Marriage and Religious-Liberty Claims Have in Common."

[90] Ibid., 206–207, citing Willock v. Elane Photography, LLC, Decision and Final Order, HRD No. 06-12-20-0685 (N.M. Hum. Rts. Comm. 9 April 2008), available at http://www.volokh .com/files/willockopinion.pdf, and Elane Photography, LLC v. Willock, No. CV-2008–06632 (N.M. Dist. Ct. 11 December 2009), available at http://oldsite.alliancedefensefund.org/userdocs/ ElanePhotoOrder.pdf.

[91] Elane Photography, LLC v. Willock 309 P.3d 53 (N.M. 2013).

nature of human sexuality including the proper end of our sexual powers and the nature of marriage.

Berg also tells of the case of "a Methodist meeting ground in Ocean Grove, New Jersey." It "opened its pavilion for weddings, but when it declined a same-sex commitment ceremony it lost a property tax exemption and received a bill for $20,000 in back taxes." Although "the main tax exemption there was for providing wide-open public access to beachfronts, ... the principle behind the withdrawal could easily extend to a host of religious nonprofits."[92] As in the New Mexico case, SSM was not legally recognized in New Jersey at the time. Nevertheless, given the laws that were already in place, the state withdrew a financial benefit from the Methodist meeting ground solely because it would not materially cooperate with a ceremony that its reasonable comprehensive doctrine says is deeply immoral.

Like in the case of the New Mexico photographer, we can think of counter-examples that would allow us to better understand why some citizens believe this state action to be an injustice. Imagine that the Methodists were approached by a man and three women wanting to procure the meeting ground for a polygamous commitment ceremony derived from their church's liturgical practices. Although this is, after all, their sexual orientation (and grounded in their religious beliefs), and thus apparently protectable under New Jersey's antidiscrimination statutes, the celebration of polygamy is no less inconsistent with the Methodists' understanding of human sexuality and the nature of marriage as is a same-sex commitment ceremony. Or imagine that the Methodists were contacted by a small remnant of Anton Szandor LaVey's Church of Satan that wanted to conduct a Black Mass on the site.[93] Or consider the possibility that a pornographic movie mogul requested to use the meeting ground to film scenes for his upcoming blockbuster, although only nonpornographic scenes would be filmed at the site. These three uses of the meeting ground, as in the case of the same-sex ceremony, would in fact put the Methodists in the position of materially cooperating with activities they believe are gravely immoral, a judgment that is integrally connected to their reasonable comprehensive doctrine.

It should be noted that in neither of the two actual cases were services denied because of anything about the religion, race, gender, nationality, or even sexual orientation of the prospective customers. Rather, the providers – the Huguenins and the Methodists – declined services because the prospective customer requested that they cooperate with what the providers believe is an

---

[92] Berg, "What Same-Sex-Marriage and Religious-Liberty Claims Have in Common," 210, citing Bill Bowman, "$20G Due in Tax on Boardwalk Pavilion: Exemption Lifted in Rights Dispute," *Asbury Park Press* (12 February 2008); and Jill P. Capuzzo, "Group Loses Tax Break Over Gay Union Issue," *New York Times* (18 September 2007).

[93] On the Black Mass, see Anton Szandor LaVey, *The Satanic Bible* (New York: Avon Books, 1969).

illegitimate presentation, and perhaps a mockery, of a liturgical event that has sacramental significance.

Maybe the prospective customers, like many Americans, do not see transcendent meaning in the ceremonial commencement of matrimony, because they associate a wedding as admittance to an institutional legal fiction that allows one access to nothing more than a cluster of political and social privileges not available to other friendships. So, given this understanding, it is not surprising that the customers see the provider's refusal as a negative judgment on the public legitimacy of their union. Thus, it's easy to see why the customers would be offended by the provider's refusal and subsequently seek legal redress.

But what the customers fail to see is that their demand that the courts force the providers to rescind their denial and be punished for it is really a demand that the state force the providers not to exercise their freedom of worship, the liberty not to participate in, or not provide assistance to, ceremonies that one believes have sacramental significance.

As I have already noted earlier in this chapter, the major religions, including Christianity, provide means by which their adherents solemnize certain moments in their lives, each often corresponding to a significant transition from one stage to another. For this reason, many of us mark these transitions with liturgical events such as baptisms, bar mitzvahs, weddings, and burials, and most of us refer to how these are conducted as rites. Thus, if the freedom of religion within the confines of JL *does not* include the right to abstain from, participate in, or provide assistance to these activities free of government coercion, religious liberty is a dead letter.

One response to these sorts of cases is to draw an analogy with race. Just as the state punishes businesses for discriminating on the basis of race even if their view of race is the result of religious sanction, the state may punish businesses that discriminate on the basis of sexual orientation even if their view of sexual orientation is based on religious beliefs. Although one can question, as I did earlier, whether these are actually cases of sexual orientation discrimination, we need not address it in order to challenge this analogy. For the problem with this analogy is that it begs the question. It assumes that SSM dissent is the same as racism. But there is also good reason to reject this claim: SSM dissent, given its integral connection to reasonable comprehensive doctrines, concerns the moral question of the proper exercise of our sexual powers and what that says about the nature of men and women, the begetting of children, and the institution of marriage. Dworkin, as I noted earlier, seems to concede this point by arguing that "sexual orientation and activity are ... a matter of ethical value rather than some other form of value" and that they are among "the convictions through which a person tries to identify the value and point of human life and the relationships, achievements, and experiences that would realize that value in his own life."

Consequently, "[o]rthodox religious convictions are plainly in that category, and so are people's convictions about the role and direction of love, intimacy, and sexuality in their lives."[94]

So, it seems, clearly mistaken to claim that one can analogize between the sorts of cases we covered in this section and cases involving businesses and public accommodations that engage in racial discrimination. For the former cases, as Dworkin notes, involve conflicting understandings of the good life, a phenomenon that we should expect from a free society for which contemporary liberal political theory, and JL in particular, was invented to not only account, but to provide a justification for its fundamental liberties that make such diversity possible. Racism, by contrast, concerns the equality of persons qua persons. So, the racism analogy fails.

For this reason, the SSM dissenter may view the issue in the form of a question: May the state coerce, punish, or marginalize its citizens who choose to live consistently with a reasonable comprehensive doctrine that entails that the nature of the good life depends on the intrinsic ends or purposes of our sexual powers and that marriage has sacramental significance? If that is the question that this dispute requires we answer, and it seems indeed to be, then the proper analogy is between the victim of racism and the SSM dissenter, for each is being coerced by laws that depend on understandings of the human person and the nature of religious conscience that one is not unreasonable in rejecting.

### 7.2.A.3. *Education*
There have arisen local disputes over the content of public school curricula that deal with human sexuality and the nature of marriage.[95] In these cases, parents have complained that the schools are instructing their children in ways that are inconsistent with the lessons they are given at home, church, synagogue, or mosque.[96] Instead of suggesting that citizens from different perspectives hold contrary, although reasonable, views on matters of sexual morality and family life, the public schools (at least, in these cases) are teaching that negative moral judgments of homosexual conduct or SSM constitute an irrational prejudice.[97] Thus, the schools are not portraying the parents' point of view as one entitled to respectful consideration and serious reflection, but rather, as an irrational view that no enlightened person would ever entertain.

---

[94] Dworkin, *Is Democracy Possible Here?*, 72.

[95] Charles S. Russo, "Same-Sex Marriage and Public School Curricula: Preserving Parental Rights to Direct the Education of Their Children," *University of Dayton Law Review* 32 (2007): 361–384.

[96] See, e.g., Jeff Vaznis, "Lawsuit Invokes Religious Freedom: Parents Say Beliefs Ignored by School," *Boston Globe* (4 May 2006), available at http://www.boston.com/news/local/articles/2006/05/04/in_lawsuit_parents_say_schools_ignore_their_beliefs/.

[97] Ethan Jacobs, "Show and Tell: Educators Say the Pre-School Set Needs Straight Talk on Gay Issues," *Bay Windows* (New England) (22 June 2006).

In such a school environment, orthodox religious students and their parents would be in precisely the same position as those who Dworkin and others claim are marginalized, or made to feel that they are outsiders, by mandatory public school prayer. Dworkin, for instance, asks us to first imagine that we are in a "tolerant religious state" in which public school prayer is allowed, and then asks us to contrast that with what would happen in a "tolerant secular state":

A tolerant religious state must take care not to coerce children into reciting even so ecumenical a prayer as ... [the Lord's Prayer], because it must leave them free to reject religion altogether. Perhaps simply allowing children who so choose to remain seated and silent would protect them from coercion. But perhaps not; it might be that children would be reluctant to identify themselves as outsiders in that way and would be pressured into reciting prayers in which they did not believe. Whether prayers would in the end be permitted in public schools in a tolerant religious society would depend on how that empirical psychological issue is resolved.

In a tolerant secular society, however, that empirical question would be irrelevant. It would be seen as wrong in principle to make any state institution such as a public school the venue of any exercise of any religion. Of course, a tolerant secular state would permit teaching about religion in public schools; no liberal education would be satisfactory without instruction in the doctrines of and differences between the main religious traditions, the history of religious divisions, and contemporary controversies about what role religion should play in public life. But a tolerant secular society would not allow its institutions to be used for practicing, as distinct from studying, religion.[98]

Recall what Dworkin says how a tolerant secular society should think of disagreements between citizens on matters of sexual morality. Such a society, writes Dworkin (as I have already quoted earlier), "could have no reason for embracing freedom of orthodox worship without also embracing *freedom of choice in all ethical matters and therefore freedom of choice with respect to the ethical values that are plainly implicated in decisions about sexual conduct, marriage, and procreation.*"[99] Thus, the same basic liberty that allows freedom of choice in religion and sexual matters, and requires that a tolerant secular state not allow student prayer-dissenters to feel that they are outsiders, would seem to require that a tolerant secular state make sure that its SSM-dissenters not feel that they are outsiders as well. Thus, such a state should require that its public schools instruct their students, both in word and by example, that one ought not to disrespect students, parents, fellow citizens or faculty colleagues who believe, for moral and theological reasons derived from their reasonable comprehensive doctrines, that nonmarital sexual acts, whether engaged in by heterosexual or homosexual citizens, are intrinsically wrong.

This means that such a state has to carefully distinguish between acts and persons, that one may disagree with one's fellow citizens on moral matters over which reasonable persons disagree, but it is wrong to disrespect one's fellow citizens as persons based on such disagreements. And clearly, it would be an injustice for the public school system to cooperate and nurture that disrespect. Hence, the use of terms like "homophobic," "bigot," and "hater" to describe SSM dissenters – which are often uttered carelessly by otherwise well-meaning activists – has no place in a liberal regime in which mutual respect between citizens from contested and contrary, although reasonable, moral traditions is fundamental to political justice. Because it is permissible for citizens in a free society committed to JL to embrace contrary reasonable comprehensive doctrines about the moral use of our sexual powers and their relation to the good life, the public schools have to balance competing and contrary moral traditions in a way that does not marginalize the practitioners of one at the expense of the practitioners of the other.

### 7.2.A.4. *Three Objections*
There are at least three objections to my use of the three sorts of cases I just surveyed : (1) They are not severe enough, (2) Using them commits the causal slippery slope fallacy, (3) They are not injustices, because dissenting from SSM legal recognition is like supporting antimiscegenation laws.

7.2.A.4.a. ARE THESE CASES SEVERE ENOUGH? Someone may raise the question as to whether the cases of coercion, punishment, and marginalization cataloged earlier are severe enough to count as violations as JL. If they aren't, then it's not clear what could possibly qualify as a violation short of the government requiring loyalty oaths, public renunciations of one's beliefs, a prohibition on religious worship, or other draconian measures. Compare, for example, the plight of the same-sex couple that cannot enter a legally recognized marriage (which is considered by JL advocates as a noncontroversial case of a violation of JL) with what happened to Catholic Charities in Massachusetts and the Johns in the United Kingdom.

Although the same-sex couple cannot enter a legally recognized marriage, they can live together, get married in a religious ceremony, draw up private agreements in order to share property and benefits, and in many jurisdictions they are protected under antidiscrimination laws, may enter a civil union, and may receive benefits from their employers that are no different than those given to married couples. Admittedly, this is not the optimal situation for the SSM advocate. But it seems remarkably liberal when compared to what happened to Catholic Charities and the Johns. In the first case, a Church that embraces a reasonable comprehensive doctrine is forced by the state to choose between abandoning an integral part of its charitable purpose on Earth – to care for widows and orphans[100] – and materially cooperating with what it believes is

---

[100] "Religion that is pure and undefiled before God, the Father, is this: to care for orphans and widows in their distress, and to keep oneself unstained by the world." (James 1:27 – NRSV)

evil. In the second, a married couple is publicly singled out by its government and declared unfit to be foster parents, simply because the couple desires to furnish its home with moral lessons tethered to its reasonable comprehensive doctrine's understanding of conjugal love. (Imagine, for example, Quaker foster parents forbidden by the state from telling their foster children of the virtues of pacifism, on the grounds that the government is required to provide for the "common defense" and that teaching pacifism undermines the goal of forming "a more perfect union."[101]) So, if the state not legally recognizing SSM violates JL, surely JL is violated in these other cases as well.

It seems, then, that we have to resist the temptation to interpret the seriousness of the constraint on another's liberty in light of our own comprehensive doctrine. For example, an atheist citizen subpoenaed to testify about what his friend had told him about a robbery the friend may have committed is not as serious a constraint on the atheist's liberty *in comparison to* the case of a Catholic priest subpoenaed to testify about what a penitent told him in the confessional about a robbery the penitent may have committed. For the atheist, revealing this secret, although perhaps emotionally painful, is not a mortal sin that he believes results in the loss of sanctifying grace and automatic excommunication from the Catholic Church. But it is for the Catholic priest.

Consider another example. For most sexual libertines, adultery, fornication, homosexual conduct, group sex, abortion, and all forms of birth control are not morally controversial. In fact, the libertine believes that if the government were to prohibit these activities and services it would be a serious constraint on his liberty. For this reason, he finds it difficult to imagine that it is a serious constraint on the liberty of certain institutions and individuals for the government to require that all employers – religious or otherwise – provide in their health insurance policies full contraception and abortion coverage free of charge. But it is nevertheless a serious constraint on liberty from the perspective of citizens who embrace certain reasonable comprehensive doctrines that teach that these services are gravely immoral and that materially cooperating with them is forbidden, even if the libertine cannot summon the imagination to grasp it.

7.2.A.4.b. CAUSAL SLIPPERY SLOPE FALLACY? Some may object that the case I am making commits a causal slippery slope fallacy, that I am arguing that the legal recognition of SSM will *cause* these undesirable consequences to result. If I were making such an argument, it would clearly be fallacious. For example, if one were to argue that the state ought to keep marijuana illegal because marijuana smoking will lead to the widespread ingestion of hard drugs such as cocaine and heroin, one would be making a causal slippery slope argument,

---

[101] "We the people of the United States, in order to form a more perfect union, establish justice, insure domestic tranquility, provide for the common defense, promote the general welfare, and secure the blessings of liberty to ourselves and our posterity, do ordain and establish this Constitution for the United States of America" (Preamble to the U.S. Constitution [1789]).

and that would be fallacious. For it does not follow that the legalization of marijuana by itself has the causal efficacy to increase the use of hard drugs that are not legal. By contrast, if one were to argue for the legal permissibility of marijuana-smoking based on a strong libertarian principle of self-ownership, it is not a causal slippery-slope fallacy to point out that the libertarian principle also requires the legal permissibility of hard drugs. A pro-marijuana advocate may claim that she is not arguing for the legal permissibility of hard drugs. But that's irrelevant. What is relevant is that she is basing her case on a principle that cannot in-principle exclude the legal permissibility of hard drugs.[102] (In fact, one could say that it practically entails it.)

The consequences and affects to which I have appealed in this chapter are not causal predictions. They are based on events that have actually happened, occurrences that *would not have happened if not* for the legal principles already in place. Thus, these consequences and effects will not be the result of the legal recognition of SSM *by itself*, but rather, they will be the result of the legal recognition of SSM within the confines of modern liberal societies with a complex array of intersecting and interdependent laws and institutions that have existed for quite some time. Because these laws and institutions have a logic of their own, this means that however the state presently protects rights and privileges and applies its antidiscrimination statutes to sexual orientation and marital status, the state would be unprincipled if it did not continue to apply these laws consistently when SSM becomes just another incidence of legally recognized marriage.

If, for example, the U.S. federal government were to treat sexual orientation like it treats race, then the sorts of principles that forced its Internal Revenue Service (IRS) to revoke the tax-exempt status of Bob Jones University because it forbade interracial dating[103] would *require* that the IRS act consistently with its principles and revoke the tax-exempt status of religious universities that prohibit their faculties and students from engaging in what they believe are nonmarital sexual relations including homosexual acts. In fact, during oral arguments for *Obergefell v. Hodges* (2015), Justice Samuel Alito, relying on the reasoning of the Bob Jones case, asked U.S. Solicitor General Donald B. Verrilli if private religious colleges would be subject to loss of tax-exempt status if SSM were to be legally recognized as a Constitutional right. General Verilli answered: "You know, I don't think I can answer that question without knowing more specifics, but it's certainly going to be an issue. I don't deny that. I don't deny that, Justice Alito. It is – it is going to be an issue."[104] If the IRS were to choose not to apply the reasoning of Bob Jones to tax-exempt religious

---

[102] See, e.g., Murray N. Rothbard, *For a New Liberty: The Libertarian Manifesto*, rev. ed. (San Francisco: Fox & Wilkes, 1978), 111–112.

[103] Bob Jones University v. United States 461 U.S. 574 (1983).

[104] Tr. of Oral Arg. on Question 1, at 36–38, in *Obergefell v. Hodges* Nos 14-556, 14-562, 14-571, 14-574, 2015 US LEXIS 4250.

institutions that dissent on SSM, it would not necessarily be because it could not in principle exercise that power. For this reason, a real threat to religious liberty would remain as long as the government has no principled reason not to exercise its power to violate that liberty. Nussbaum, in fact, has suggested that the reasoning of the Bob Jones case should apply to Catholic universities that require their presidents to be priests. She believes that because this requirement means that only men can hold these presidencies (because only men can become Catholic priests), this policy is discriminatory and the schools should lose their tax-exempt status.[105]

Unsurprisingly, in the academic literature, some advocates of SSM fully concede that that these sorts of consequences are plausible or likely,[106] or just and welcomed because they are principled entailments of current law.[107]

7.2.A.4.C. ANTIMISCEGENATION LAWS Many authors, including some judges, draw an analogy between bans on interracial marriage and any law that only recognizes marriage as a union between one man and one woman. Thus, those who dissent on SSM, and refuse to honor such unions in their public lives, are just like those citizens who resisted the overturning of laws that banned interracial marriage.

The court cases most often cited by these writers to support their case are *Loving v. Virginia* (1967),[108] the U.S. Supreme Court case that declared interracial marriage bans unconstitutional, and *Perez v. Sharp* (1948),[109] a California Supreme Court case that did the same in relation to its state constitution. Here's how Massachusetts' highest court in *Goodridge v. Department of Public Health* (2003) employs *Loving* and *Perez* in order to make the analogy between interracial marriage and SSM:

In this case [*Goodridge*], as in *Perez* and *Loving*, a statute deprives individuals of access to an institution of fundamental legal, personal, and social significance – the institution

---

[105] Nussbaum writes:

> Another government intervention that was right, in my view, was the judgment that Bob Jones University should lose its tax exemption for its ban on interracial dating ... Here the Supreme Court agreed that the ban was part of that sect's religion, and thus that the loss of tax-exempt status was a "substantial burden" on the exercise of that religion, but they said that society has a compelling interest in not cooperating with racism. Never has the government taken similar steps against the many Roman Catholic universities that restrict their presidencies to a priest, hence a male; but in my view they should all lose their tax exemptions for this reason. (Martha Nussbaum, "Beyond the Veil: A Response," *Opinionator: Exclusively Online Commentary from The Times* [*New York Times*] [15 July 2010], available http://opinionator.blogs.nytimes.com/2010/07/15/beyond-the-veil-a-response/).

[106] Volokh, "Same-Sex Marriage and Slippery Slopes."
[107] Chai R. Feldblum, "Moral Conflict and Conflicting Liberties," in *Same-Sex Marriage and Religious Liberty*, 123–156.
[108] Loving v. Virginia 388 U.S. 1 (1967).
[109] Perez v. Sharp 32 Cal. 2d, 711 (1948).

of marriage – because of a single trait: skin color in *Perez* and *Loving*, sexual orientation here. As it did in *Perez* and *Loving*, history must yield to a more fully developed understanding of the invidious quality of the discrimination.[110]

Despite the ubiquitous use of this analogy in the literature, it becomes clear that the analogy is not a very good one once one attends to the historical circumstances, and underlying assumptions about the nature of marriage, that gave rise to antimiscegenation laws in the first place.

Consider first that "at common law there was no ban on interracial marriage."[111] This means that antimiscegenation laws were *not part* of the jurisprudence that American law inherited from the English courts. Antimiscegenation laws were statutory in America (although never in England[112]), first appearing in Maryland in 1661 after the institution of the enslavement of Africans on American soil. This means that *interracial marriage was a common law liberty* that can only be superseded by legislation. The Maryland statute, for example, "prohibited the intermarriage of white women and negro slaves under the penalty of slavery to the white woman and all her issue,"[113] eventually expanding the penalties and including the prohibition of interracial cohabitation. Nevertheless, seven states (out of 13) at the time of the American Founding had such laws, although three repealed them long before the mid-20th century when *Perez* and *Loving* were decided: Massachusetts, 1843; Rhode Island, 1881; Pennsylvania, 1780. In fact, of the fifty current states, thirteen have never had antimiscegenation laws, and when *Loving* was decided in 1967, only sixteen of the fifty states still had such laws.[114]

It should also be noted that when antimiscegenation laws were on the books they were widely diverse in who they covered and what groups were forbidden from intermarrying. For example, Irving Tragen writes in his 1944 *California Law Review* article:

Although originally the statutes were directed wholly against Negro-Caucasian unions, the scope of the legislation now extends to interdictions against marriage between white men and Mongolians, Malayans, mulatto, or even American Indians. The ban on marriages between negroes and whites is still the most common one: the unions are banned

---

[110] *Goodridge*, 798 N. E. 2d, 958.

[111] Irving G. Tragen, "Statutory Prohibitions against Interracial Marriage," *California Law Review* 32.3 (September 1944): 269.

[112] "There was no rule at common law in England nor has any statute been passed in England banning interracial marriages." (Ibid., n. 2, citing Alexander Wood Renton and George Grenville Phillimore, *The Comparative Law of Marriage and Divorce* [London: Sweet & Maxwell, 1910], 142).

[113] Ibid., 270 n. 3, citing Edward Byron Reuter, *Race Mixture: Studies in Intermarriage and Miscegenation* (New York: Whittlesey House, 1931), 80.

[114] Brief *amici curiae* of African-American Pastors in California in Support of Respondents, *In Re: Marriage Cases*, California Supreme Court (2007), 13 available at http://www.courtinfo.ca.gov/courts/supreme/highprofile/documents/African-American_Pastors_in_CA_Amicus_Curiae_Brief.pdf.

throughout the South, the Southeast, and the West except for Washington and New Mexico; the interdictions are non-existent in New England, and the Middle Atlantic States outside of Delaware, and in the North Central States except Indiana; and, in the "great farm belt," typical is the situation of states like Nebraska and Iowa living side by side one with a miscegenation statute, and one without. Mongolian-Caucasian marriages are prohibited in fourteen states, mostly in the West but a few in the South. Some five western states prohibit Malay-white marriages. South Dakota especially names Koreans in its miscegenation statute. Five states, scattered throughout the South and West, place Indian-white marriages in their prohibited classes. In all the states which have miscegenation statutes, except California, these marriages are not only void but are subject to criminal penalties. The penalties fall upon all persons, white and "colored" alike, either for attempting such a marriage: or, as the attempted marriage is void, for engaging in illegal extramarital relations.[115]

The overwhelming consensus among scholars is that the reason for these laws was to enforce racial purity, an idea that begins its cultural ascendancy with the commencement of race-based slavery of Africans in mid-seventeenth-century America and eventually receives the imprimatur of "science," when the eugenics movement comes of age in the late nineteenth and early twentieth centuries.[116] In *Loving*, for example, the statue overturned, SB 219, The Racial Integrity Act of 1924 (for which the Virginia Legislature issued an official apology in 2001),[117] was the product of the eugenics movement.[118] On the same day that SB 219 was passed, 20 March 1924, Virginia also passed the Eugenical Sterilization Act (SB 281), a law the allowed the state to involuntarily sterilize, among others, the mentally unfit.[119] In the case of *Buck v. Bell* (1927),[120] the Supreme Court upheld the constitutionality of Virginia's forced sterilization of Carrie Buck under that statute. In some of the most memorable and chilling words ever penned by a Supreme Court justice, Oliver Wendell Holmes Jr. wrote, "It is better for all the world if, instead of waiting to execute degenerate offspring for crime or to let them starve for their imbecility, society can prevent those who are manifestly unfit from continuing their kind. The principle

---

[115] Tragen, "Statutory Prohibitions against Interracial Marriage," 270–271 (notes omitted).

[116] See Daniel J. Kevles, *In the Name of Eugenics* (Cambridge, MA: Harvard University, 1985); Paul A. Lombardo, "Miscegenation, Eugenics, and Racism: Historical Footnotes to *Loving v. Virginia*," *U.C. Davis Law Review* 21 (1987–1988): 421–452; Paul A. Lombardo, "Eugenics Laws Against Race Mixing," Image Archive of the American Eugenics Movement, available at http://www.eugenicsarchive.org/html/eugenics/essay7text.html; and Peggy Pascoe, "Miscegenation Law, Court Cases, and Ideologies of 'Race' in Twentieth-Century America," *Journal of American History* 83.1 (June 1996): 44–69.

[117] "Expressing the General Assembly's regret for Virginia's experience with eugenics," Virginia House Joint Resolution 607 (2001), available at https://leg1.state.va.us/cgi-bin/legp504.exe?011+ful+HJ607ER.

[118] Kevles, *In the Name of Eugenics*, 110.

[119] Paul A. Lombardo, "Three Generations, No Imbeciles: New Light on Buck v. Bell," *N.Y.U. Law Review* 60 (April 1985): 30–62.

[120] Buck v. Bell 274 U.S. 200 (1927).

that sustains compulsory vaccination is broad enough to cover cutting the Fallopian tubes.... Three generations of imbeciles are enough."[121] The Racial Integrity Act and The Eugenical Sterilization Act were of a piece, both legislative accomplishments of the eugenics movement and its goal of racial purity.[122]

Antimiscegenation laws, therefore, were attempts to eradicate the legal status of real marriages by injecting a condition – sameness of race – that had no precedent in common law. For in the common law, a necessary condition for a legitimate marriage was male-female complementarity, a condition on which race has no bearing.

It is clear then that the miscegenation/SSM analogy does not work. For if the purpose of antimiscegenation laws was racial purity, and there is no doubt that it was, such a purpose only makes sense if people of different races *have the ability by nature to marry* each other. And given the fact that such marriages were a common law liberty, the antimiscegenation laws *presuppose this truth*. But opponents of the legal recognition of SSM ground their viewpoint in precisely the opposite belief: people of the same gender *do not have the ability by nature to marry each other* because gender complementarity is a necessary condition for marriage. Supporters of antimiscegenation laws believed in their cause *precisely because* they understood that when male and female are joined in matrimony they may beget racially-mixed progeny, and these children, along with their parents, will participate in civil society and influence its cultural trajectory. In other words, the fact that a man and a woman from different races were biologically and metaphysically capable of marrying each other, building families, and living among the general population is precisely why the race purists wanted to forbid such unions by the force of law. And because this view of marriage and its gender-complementary nature was firmly in place, and the only understanding found in common law, the Supreme Court in *Loving* knew that racial identity was not relevant to what marriage requires of its two opposite-gender members. As the Court said in *Loving*, "Marriage is one of the 'basic civil rights of man,' fundamental to our very existence and survival."[123] In making this claim, the Court quoted from a passage in *Skinner v. Oklahoma* (1942), which says in its entirety: "We are dealing here with legislation which involves one of the basic civil rights of man. Marriage and procreation are fundamental to the very existence and survival of the race."[124] By injecting race into the equation, antimiscegenation supporters were, oddly,

---

[121] Ibid., 207 (note omitted).

[122] See footnote 116.

[123] *Loving*, 388 U.S., 13, quoting from Skinner v. Oklahoma 316 U.S. 535, 541 (1942)

[124] *Skinner*, 316 U.S., 541. The legislation in question was an Oklahoma statute that allowed criminal courts to order convicted habitual criminals to undergo vasectomies so that they would not able to pass on their "bad seed." The statute was declared unconstitutional on Equal Protection grounds because the law did not allow for the punishment of sterilization for higher classes of thieves (e.g. embezzlers), whose wayward practices could be just as habitual as those of Skinner and other small-time crooks.

not unlike contemporary proponents of the legal recognition of SSM. For in the case of each movement, male-female complementarity is diminished for the sake of establishing the goals of a utopian social cause: race purity or sexual egalitarianism.

Each movement, however, in order to achieve success, requires *contrary* projects. For the race purists, the goal was *not* to try to convince the government that the nature of marriage was not what everyone had always supposed it to be; it was to deny otherwise eligible couples from entering the institution, the nature of which was not in dispute. For the sexual egalitarians, by contrast, the goal is not to expand the pool of otherwise eligible couples who may enter the institution; *it is* to try to convince the government that the nature of marriage is *not* what everyone had always supposed it to be. Because the latter project's understanding of marriage's nature and its connection to the ends and moral limits of human sexuality is all that is in dispute – the sort of disagreement between free and equal citizens for which liberalism, and JL in particular, was invented to provide cultural and legal space – there is simply no analogy between SSM dissent and antimiscegenation advocacy.

## 7.3. CONCLUSION

The three sets of examples we covered – in child adoption, business accommodations, and education – are merely illustrative of the consequences and effects that will likely follow (and in some cases, have followed) wherever SSM achieves legal recognition. It does not take much of an imagination to think of the many other areas in which these sorts of conflicts will arise, especially given the increasing role that government plays in virtually every area of life. Consequently, if the examples catalogued earlier are prescient, it seems fair to say that everything from housing law, to employment law, to family law, to public education, to government funding, and to the tax-exempt status of religious academic institutions will fall within the orbit of the state's interest in making sure that SSM dissenters are coerced, punished, or marginalized if they refuse to treat SSM as licit as male-female marriage.

However, if, as Justificatory Liberals tell us, one cannot support a law that limits another's fundamental or basic liberty if one's reasons for the law are reasons that may be reasonably rejected by those who would be coerced, punished, or marginalized by the law, then the legal recognition of SSM would likely result in numerous injustices. On the other hand, according to the Justificatory Liberal, not legally recognizing SSM results in numerous injustices as well.[125] It is, of course, possible for legislators to craft statutes that would

---

[125] See, e.g., Angela Bolte, "Do Wedding Dresses Come in Lavender? The Prospects and Implications of Same-Sex Marriage," *Social Theory and Practice* 24.1 (Spring 1998); Brake, "Minimal Marriage"; McClain, "Deliberative Democracy, Overlapping Consensus, and Same-Sex Marriage"; Michelman, "Rawls on Constitutionalism and Constitutional Law"; Nussbaum, "A Right to Marry?"; and Dworkin, *Is Democracy Possible Here?*, 1–24, 86–89.

significantly mitigate most of the unjust consequences that would be borne by SSM dissenters. In fact, Dworkin thought this idea worth entertaining in some circumstances.[126] But this sort of compromise would likely be rejected by most SSM advocates who would see it as far less than full equality under the law.

So, given the internal structures of the legal systems and the nature of the judiciaries (and in some cases, Constitutional Law) in liberal democracies, grafting SSM on to their laws, institutions, and practices that are currently in place would most certainly legitimize violations of JL against SSM dissenters, even though, ironically, the advocates of SSM legal recognition almost always rely on Justificatory Liberalism in order to argue that it is illegitimate for any government not to legally recognize SSM.[127]

---

[126] Writes Dworkin: "[E]qual concern ... requires a legislature to notice whether any group regards the activity it proposes as a sacred duty. If any group does, then the legislature must consider whether equal concern for that group requires an exemption or other amelioration. If an exception can be managed with no significant damage to the policy in play, then it might be unreasonable not to grant that exception. Financing Catholic adoption agencies that do not accept same-sex couples as candidates, on the same terms as financing agencies that do, might be justified in that way, provided that enough of the latter are available so that neither babies nor same-sex couples seeking a baby are injured" (Ronald Dworkin, *Religion Without God* [Cambridge, MA: Harvard University Press, 2013], 136).

[127] I would like to thank two anonymous referees for some very helpful comments and suggestions on a much earlier draft of this chapter. They really forced me to think through some issues far more carefully than I would have without their assistance. I am especially grateful to one referee who took special care in assessing that draft *twice*. Nevertheless, all mistakes are strictly mine.

# 8

## Conclusion: Taking Rites Seriously

> There is, of course, a perfectly good and indispensible sense in which ... [the] language [of the separation of church and state] has application and should be zealously upheld. That is the sense of the First Amendment of the Constitution of the United States. But in general usage today, what it really means is that what religion teaches is not a matter of knowledge of reality. It is, rather, only a matter of what certain human groups have accepted as a part of their historical identity, and what (it is assumed) they are all too glad to force upon other groups and individuals as opportunity offers. If it were seriously imagined that the teachings of Christianity or other religions constituted a vital and irreplaceable knowledge of reality, there would be no more talk of the separation of church and state than there is of the separation of chemistry or economics and state.
>
> Dallas Willard (1935–2013)[1]

Imagine that you are watching on television a hearing of the U.S. Senate Judiciary Committee. Each of its members is asking questions of, and in some cases interrogating, the president's most recent nominee to the U.S. Supreme Court. She is an accomplished attorney with not only a law degree from an elite institution but holds a doctorate in biochemistry and had specialized in private practice on issues over which science and law overlap and intersect. For several years she had served on the federal bench on the DC circuit and had done so admirably, showing professional competence and jurisprudential insight that had become the envy of her peers, some of whom disagree with her conserva-tive judicial philosophy. Over the years she has published well-received articles in numerous law reviews and peer-reviewed science publications dealing with issues as wide ranging as the Daubert standard,[2] the reliability of DNA testing

---

[1] Dallas Willard, *Knowing Christ Today: Why We Can Trust Spiritual Knowledge* (New York: HarperCollins, 2009), 32.

[2] Daubert v. Merrell Dow Pharmaceuticals 509 U.S. 579 (1993).

in capital murder cases, and whether the Supreme Court's holdings in its reproductive rights cases provide support for a Constitutional right to clone oneself.

She is also a devout Catholic and has published several law review articles critical of the Supreme Court's reproductive rights jurisprudence, and in particular the Court's reluctance to make an argument on either the question of when human life begins or the moral status of that life when in fact it does begin. In one article in particular she offers her own argument by which she defends the Catholic view of the human person as a defeater to the right to abortion.

As the hearings proceed, the senators ask her a variety of questions about the most important court cases concerning equal protection, substantive due process, and criminal procedure. Several senators ask her questions about issues overlapping law and science and how some of them may play a part in future cases the Supreme Court may hear. She smartly and prudently declines to offer any answers about specific legal disputes, though in the process of her modest reluctance she reveals a deep and sophisticated understanding of the sciences in which she was trained and has done research. The senators are impressed.

They now move on to questions about her views on abortion and how they are informed by her religious beliefs. And then the senior senator from Massachusetts makes the query that everyone was expecting: "Are you going to allow your deeply held personal religious beliefs to influence your judgments on the bench"?[3] Such a question, of course, is not asked of the nominee's beliefs about biochemistry or the issues on which she has opined on matters over which law and science intersect, even though on those beliefs and issues, as in the question of abortion, there are a wide variety of informed and thoughtful perspectives. And yet none of these beliefs and issues are described as "deeply held personal beliefs," as if they were irreducibly subjective opinions about which rational deliberation is not possible. It seems safe to say that it would

---

[3] Columnist Charles Krauthammer provides an example from a real life U. S. Senate Judiciary Committee hearing:

> [William] Pryor has more recently been attacked from a different quarter. Senate Democrats have blocked his nomination to the 11th U.S. Circuit Court of Appeals on the grounds of his personal beliefs. "His beliefs are so well known, so deeply held," charged his chief antagonist, Sen. Charles Schumer [D-NY], "that it's very hard to believe – very hard to believe – that they're not going to deeply influence the way he comes about saying, 'I will follow the law.'"

> An amazing litmus test: Deeply held beliefs are a disqualification for high judicial office. Only people of shallow beliefs (like Schumer?) need apply.

> Of course, Schumer's real concern is with the *content* of Pryor's beliefs. Schumer says that he would object to "anybody who had very, very deeply held views." Anybody? If someone had deeply held views in *favor* of abortion rights, you can be sure that Schumer would not be blocking his nomination. Pryor is being pilloried because he openly states (1) that Roe v. Wade was a constitutional abomination, and (2) that abortion itself is a moral abomination. (Charles Krauthammer, "A Judge Prejudged," *Washington Post* [29 August 2003], A23 [emphasis added]).

never cross any senator's mind to ask the question of whether the nominee's background in any of the hard sciences would influence her judicial opinions on the Supreme Court. It would, of course, not really matter if she had instead possessed identical expertise in "softer" disciplines, such as history, political science, sociology, psychiatry, or American Studies. For a sitting senator would be thought foolish to imply that there was something amiss with a judge who brought to bear the resources of her education, training, and knowledge to her opinions in appropriate cases.

Take, for example, that famous exchange between two justices with contrary opinions in the case of *Rosenberger v. Virginia* (1995).[4] Justice Clarence Thomas[5] and Justice David Souter[6] sparred over differing interpretations and applications of James Madison's *Memorial and Remonstrance Against Religious Assessments* (1785).[7] Each offered what he believed was the correct historical understanding of the meaning of Madison's famous essay. We think this perfectly appropriate even if it turns out that one of the justices is mistaken. Other illustrations from science, mathematics, economics, professional ethics, and personal lived experience are easy to come-by as well. Consider just the following two examples.

In a well-known article on the use and misuse of probability theory by advocates and courts,[8] Harvard law professor Laurence Tribe cites a California Supreme Court case in which "the court ruled improper a prosecutor's misconceived attempt to link an accused interracial couple with a robbery by using probability theory."[9] However, as Tribe notes, the court "discerned 'no inherent and intend[ed] no general disapproval ... of the latter [i.e., probability theory] as an auxiliary in the fact-finding processes of the former [i.e., the prosecutor].' "[10] When President Barack Obama in 2009 appointed Federal Appeals Court judge, Sonia Sotomayor, to the U.S. Supreme Court (to which she was eventually confirmed), the media reported that the future justice had said in a 2001 speech, "I would hope that a wise Latina woman with the richness of her experiences would more often than not reach a better conclusion than a white male who hasn't lived that life."[11] Although conservatives were quick to criticize these comments, one wonders if they would have been as eager to do

[4] 515 U.S. 819 (1995).

[5] Ibid., 852–863 (Thomas, J., concurring).

[6] Ibid., 863–899 (Souter, J., dissenting).

[7] James Madison, *Memorial and Remonstrance against Religious Assessments* (20 June 1785), available at http://press-pubs.uchicago.edu/founders/documents/amendI_religions43.html.

[8] Laurence H. Tribe, "Trial by Mathematics: Precision and Ritual in the Legal Process," *Harvard Law Review* 84 (1971): 1329.

[9] Ibid.,1334. The case Tribe is writing about is People v. Collins 68 Cal. 2d, 319, 438 P. 2d, 33, 66 Cal. Rpt. 497 (1978). As Tribe points out, the California Supreme Court, in overturning the conviction, corrected the prosecutor's use of probability theory by employing mathematics and other extra-legal conceptual notions. (Tribe, "Trial By Mathematics," 1334–1338).

[10] Ibid.,1337, quoting *People*, 68 Cal. 2d, at 320, 438 P. 2d, at 33, 66 Cal. Rptr. at 497.

[11] Carolina A. Miranda, "Just What is a 'Wise Latina' Anyway?" *Time Magazine* (14 July 2009), http://content.time.com/time/politics/article/0,8599,1910403,00.html.

so if a similar appeal to lived experience within a cultural tradition had come from the lips of a Russian dissident out of his first-person familiarity of Soviet life and government confinement in a Gulag.[12]

We do not consider these examples troubling because we have come to correctly believe that certain disciplines and areas of study – such as history and mathematics – are knowledge-traditions, and that personal lived experience within a cultural tradition may provide us with real insights that may be useful to a court in a particular case or to a legislator or citizen when he or she advances a specific policy. We, of course, do not believe that there cannot be legitimate disagreement between experts in these areas, as the dispute between justices Thomas and Souter clearly shows, or that the cultural tradition in which one was formed may not be the object of critical reflection or even reformation. However, religious beliefs and their attendant notions are for the most part categorized differently.

For, as we have seen in this book, they are presented as rationally suspect (Chapter 2), illicit motives that may be cited by courts in order to limit a citizen or legislator's political powers (Chapter 3), inconsequential to grounding human dignity (Chapter 4), inconsistent with "secular reason" on the matter of the beginning of human personhood (Chapter 5), refuted by the hard sciences' alleged entailment that the universe exhibits no design (Chapter 6), and ignored or diminished on the issue of marriage by a liberalism that claims to be neutral between reasonable, though contested and contrary, comprehensive doctrines (Chapter 7). But, as I have carefully argued in this book, none of these postures is justified. Nevertheless, this is the dominant, and unquestioned, approach to religion in our law and in our politics. Consequently, our story of the fictionalized Supreme Court nominee seems not only not far-fetched, but exactly how we would expect it to be played out in reality.

Is it any wonder then that in court cases that concern more explicitly religious activities – such as prayer at government meetings, reciting the pledge of allegiance in public schools – in comparison to the issues that we have covered in this book – such as abortion, intelligent design, SSM – judges seem to make no effort to see the deeper, and perhaps legitimate, philosophical issues that gave rise to these activities in the first place? As if they were amateur anthropologists investigating a primitive culture, jurists often portray such activities as no more significant than interesting sociological facts that may have pernicious consequences if taken too far – like a college fraternity's initiation rituals or its secret hand shakes. In line with that account, Justice William Brennan writes that "such practices as the designation of 'In God We Trust' as our national motto, or the references to God contained in the Pledge of Allegiance to the flag can best be understood, in Dean Rostow's apt phrase, as a form a 'ceremonial

---

[12] Here I am thinking of Alexander Solzhenitsyn's 1978 Harvard University Commencement Address: "A World Split Apart" (8 June 1978), available at http://www.americanrhetoric.com/speeches/alexandersolzhenitsynharvard.htm.

deism,' protected from Establishment Clause scrutiny chiefly because they have lost through rote repetition any significant religious content."[13] In other words, explicit references or appeals to the divine – either by public officials at government events or ceremonies, in public displays on government property, or recited by students in public school classrooms- – do not violate the Establishment Clause if they are devoid of theological substance.

To show why this understanding of "ceremonial deism" does not "take rites seriously," consider just the 2002 Ninth Circuit Court of Appeals case, *Newdow v. Elk Grove School District*.[14] The court held that a California public school district's requirement of teacher-led recitation of the Pledge violated the Establishment Clause, even though students could opt-out.[15] For, according to the court:

> the phrase "one nation under God" in the context of the Pledge is normative. To recite the Pledge is not to describe the United States; instead, it is to swear allegiance to the values for which the flag stands: unity, indivisibility, liberty, justice, and – since 1954 – monotheism. The text of the official Pledge, codified in federal law, impermissibly takes a position with respect to the *purely religious question* of the existence and identity of God.[16]

Two years later the U.S. Supreme Court overturned the Ninth Circuit's decision,[17] but only on a technicality: Michael Newdow, the parent who had brought the suit on behalf of his public school student daughter, did not have standing to file the suit because he did not have legal custody of his daughter. Although three justices had argued that the recitation of the Pledge with the words "under God" did not run afoul of the Constitution, the Court's holding did not address that question.

What stands out about the controlling opinions of both courts is how little care their authors take in understanding the primary reason why the 1954 Congress amended the Pledge. Here's what the 1954 *Congressional Record* states (as quoted in the Ninth Circuit's opinion):

> At this moment of our history the principles underlying our American Government and the American way of life are under attack by a system whose philosophy is at direct odds with our own. Our American Government is founded on the concept of the individuality and the dignity of the human being. Underlying this concept is the belief that

---

[13] Lynch v. Donnelly 465 U. S. 688, 716 (1984) (Brennan, J., dissenting).

[14] Newdow v. Elk Grove Sch. Dist., 292 F. 3d 597 (2002), rev'd by Elk Grove Sch. Dist. v. Newdow 542 U.S. 1 (2004).

[15] "Newdow does not allege that his daughter's teacher or school district requires his daughter to participate in reciting the Pledge. Rather, he claims that his daughter is injured when she is compelled to 'watch and listen as her state-employed teacher in her state-run school leads her classmates in a ritual proclaiming that there is a God, and that our's [sic] is "one nation under God"'" (*Newdow*, 292 F. 3d, 601) (citation omitted).

[16] Ibid., 607 (emphasis added).

[17] *Elk Grove*, 542 U.S. 1 (2004).

the human person is important because he was created by God and endowed by Him with certain inalienable rights which no civil authority may usurp. The inclusion of God in our pledge therefore would further acknowledge the dependence of our people and our Government upon the moral directions of the Creator. At the same time it would serve to deny the atheistic and materialistic concepts of communism with its attendant subservience of the individual.[18]

The Ninth Circuit, though it acknowledged this reasoning, did not take it very seriously. It promptly dismissed the appeal to God as the source of human rights and dignity as merely an answer to a "purely religious question," even though, as we shall see, it is in fact a philosophical question that may or may not have God as its answer.

Justice John Paul Stevens, who wrote the Supreme Court's controlling opinion, does not even quote from the passage, but from another portion of the 1954 *Congressional Record* that suggests that "under God" in the Pledge is more about the country's long tradition of believing in God rather than the reality of God as the guarantor of our natural rights: "[f]rom the time of our earliest history our peoples and our institutions have reflected the traditional concept that our Nation was founded on a fundamental belief in God."[19]

But the whole point of inserting "under God" in the Pledge was neither "purely religious" nor an appeal to "tradition." It was to address the philosophical claim that our natural rights, grounded in the natural moral law, are imparted to us by an Eternal Lawgiver, and how that claim differs from an alternative philosophical understanding of rights embraced by a government, the Soviet Union, committed to atheistic materialism. Thus, the question that the 1954 Congress was answering was no more a "religious question" or a matter of historical observation than was the grounding of the Thirteenth Amendment's prohibition on involuntary servitude purely the result of a change in national labor policy.

For the 1954 Congress, as for most ordinary Americans, whether one's natural rights issue from an Eternal Lawgiver or from a state with no higher authority than itself and its will, makes all the difference between a limited government constrained by moral principles it did not invent and a government based on nothing more than its own power to stipulate whatever ends it desires. It is the difference between liberty and tyranny.

Granted, there are sophisticated detractors from this position, including the late Ronald Dworkin,[20] who maintain that our belief in fundamental rights may be rationally justified even if these rights are not grounded in either government fiat or a natural moral law that requires a self-existent transcendent

---

[18] *Newdow*, 292 F. 3d, 610, quoting H.R. Rep. No. 83-1693, 1-2 (1954), reprinted in 1954 U.S.C.C.A.N. 2339, 2340).

[19] *Elk Grove*, 542 U.S., 7 (2004), quoting H. R. Rep. No. 1693, 83d Cong., 2d, Sess., 2 (1954).

[20] Ronald Dworkin, *Religion Without God* (Cambridge, MA: Harvard University Press, 2013), 21–29.

source that is identical with the Good (i.e., God). Although one may challenge such an alternative account of our fundamental rights, the point here is that philosophers like Dworkin admit that the question at issue is philosophical in nature, and that "God," the Ground of Being offered to account for our fundamental rights, is believed by some to be a conclusion of an argument rather than a mere dogma issued by a magisterial authority.

Thus, it should not surprise those acquainted with the discipline of philosophy that the understanding of the 1954 Congress, that human rights have their source in God, has been a conclusion drawn in the arguments of many philosophers and legal scholars over the past several decades.[21] Of course, this does not mean that a rational person, like a Dworkin, may not reject these arguments. But it does mean that a claim of theology, what the Ninth Circuit dubbed a "merely religious question," can be the subject of rational assessment, and may even convince many that it is in fact a deliverance of reason, as philosophically well-supported as John Rawls's theory of justice,[22] Ludwig Wittgenstein's philosophy of language,[23] or even H. L. A. Hart's legal positivism.[24] All of these views have been contested and challenged by philosophers and legal scholars no less rational and no less equipped with sophisticated arguments than were Rawls, Wittgenstein, or Hart. And yet, no one would say that the contested nature of these debated questions means that some or all of the disputants are irrational for embracing the views they hold.

---

[21] *See e.g.* Jerome J. Shestack, "The Jurisprudence of Human Rights," in *Human Rights in International Law: Legal and Policy Issues*, vol. 1, ed. Theodore Meron (Oxford: Clarendon, 1984), 69–113; Louis P. Pojman, "A Critique of Contemporary Egalitarianism: A Christian Perspective," *Faith and Philosophy* 8 (October 1991): 481–506; Richard Swinburne, "What Difference Does God Make to Morality?," in *Is Goodness Without God Good Enough?: A Debate on Faith, Secularism, and Ethics*, ed. Robert K. Garcia and Nathan L. King (Lanham, MD: Rowman & Littlefield, 2009), 151–166; Nicholas Wolterstorff, *Justice: Rights and Wrongs* (Princeton, NJ: Princeton University Press 2008), 342–361; John Finnis, *Natural Law and Natural Rights* (Oxford: Clarendon, 1980), chapter XIII; J. Budziszewski, "Accept No Imitations: The Rivalry of Naturalism and Natural Law," in *Uncommon Dissent: Intellectuals Who Find Darwinism Unconvincing*, ed. William A. Dembski (Wilmington, DE: ISI Books 2004), 99–114; Samuel W. Calhoun, "Grounding Normative Assertions: Arthur Leff's Still Irrefutable, but Incomplete, 'Sez Who?' Critique," *Journal of Law and Religion* 20 (2004–05): 31–96; Arthur A. Leff, "Unspeakable Ethics, Unnatural Law," *Duke Law Journal* 6 (1979): 1229–1249; J.P. Moreland, "Ethics Depend on God," in *Does God Exist?: The Debate Between Theists and Atheists*, ed. J.P. Moreland and Kai Nielsen (Amherst, NY: Prometheus Books 1993), 111–126; Paul Copan, "The Moral Argument," in *The Rationality of Theism*, ed. Paul Copan and Paul K. Moser (New York: Routledge 2003), 149–174; John E. Hare, "Naturalism and Morality," in *Naturalism: A Critical Analysis*, ed. William L. Craig and J. P. Moreland (New York: Routledge 2000), 189–212; John M. Rist, *On Inoculating Moral Philosophy Against God* (Milwaukee: Marquette University Press, 1999).

[22] John Rawls, *A Theory of Justice* (Cambridge, MA: Harvard University Press, 1971).

[23] Ludwig Wittgenstein, *Philosophical Investigations*, trans. G.E.M. Anscombe (Oxford: Basil Blackwell, 1968).

[24] H. L. A. Hart, *The Concept of Law* (Oxford: Clarendon Press, 1961).

Nevertheless, the Ninth Circuit focused on Congress' apparent religious purpose for the insertion of "under God" in the Pledge, concluding that it was inconsistent with contemporary Establishment Clause jurisprudence, and for that reason, was unconstitutional: "This language reveals that the purpose of the 1954 Act was to take a position on the question of theism, namely, to support the existence and moral authority of God, while 'deny[ing] ... atheistic and materialistic concepts.' ... Such a purpose runs counter to the Establishment Clause, which prohibits the government's endorsement or advancement not only of one particular religion at the expense of other religions, but also of religion at the expense of atheism."[25]

But because, as should be obvious by now, the question at issue – the philosophical grounding of our rights – is not merely a religious question, the government taking a position on it (while not coercing its citizens to believe or affirm it) no more violates the Establishment Clause than when the government takes a position on a variety of other questions that puts it at odds with, and may offend, the religious beliefs and sensibilities of many of its citizens. The Health Human Services (HHS) mandate, as I noted in Chapter 5, not only takes a position on philosophical anthropology that is inconsistent with the moral theology of the owners of Hobby Lobby and other businesses, it coerces them to materially cooperate with acts inconsistent with their beliefs. In Chapter 6, in our assessment of the Intelligent Design controversy, we saw that the federal judge who struck down the Dover policy clearly implied that the government *should endorse and advance* in its public schools views on evolution that are the most scientifically defensible, even if they are intrinsically hostile to the religious perspectives that motived some of the school board's members to support the discredited policy. As we saw in Chapter 7, on the question of the nature of marriage, there are those who believe it is an obligation of justice for the state to punish, marginalize, and coerce citizens who, for reasons of religious conscience, cannot cooperate in their business enterprises in celebrating same-sex unions. It does not take much of an imagination for one to think of numerous other examples in which the government takes a position that endorses or advances a view or policy that implies a negative judgment of some or many religious beliefs and/or practices. I am, of course, not implying that there could not be good reasons to resist these positions. Rather, what I am suggesting, by employing these examples, is that when the government endorses or advances a position hostile to a religious belief or practice, that in and of itself does not tell us whether the government's action is or is not justified.

Why such counterexamples are entirely absent from cases like *Newdow* is the consequence of a cluster of uncritically assimilated prejudices about the nature of both religious beliefs as well as those beliefs tightly tethered to them. These prejudices are widely held in the rarefied corridors of both the academy and our legal institutions, and considered by their most passionate advocates

[25] *Newdow*, 292 F. 3d, 610.

to be the indubitable deliverances of dispassionate reason. They can, however, be effectively challenged, as I think I have shown in this book. So, until those who champion these prejudices are willing, as a matter of simple justice, to critically examine their own conceptual reflexes, we can say with confidence that, inconsistent with their own commitment to a society that treats all citizens with equal dignity and respect, they do not truly take rites seriously.

# Index